Microsoft®
PowerPoint® 2013

ILLUSTRATED

Brief Introductory

Microsoft®
PowerPoint® 2013
ILLUSTRATED   Brief   Introductory

David W. Beskeen

CENGAGE
Learning·

Australia · Brazil · Japan · Korea · Mexico · Singapore · Spain · United Kingdom · United States

Microsoft® PowerPoint® 2013—Illustrated Introductory
David W. Beskeen

Executive Editor: Marjorie Hunt

Associate Acquisitions Editor: Amanda Lyons

Senior Product Manager: Christina Kling-Garrett

Product Manager: Kim Klasner

Editorial Assistant: Brandelynn Perry

Brand Manager: Elinor Gregory

Developmental Editor: Rachel Biheller Bunin

Full-Service Project Management: GEX Publishing
Services

Copyeditor: Mark Goodin

Proofreader: Brandy Lilly

Indexer: Alexandra Nickerson

QA Manuscript Reviewers: John Freitas, Danielle
Shaw, Susan Whalen, Jeff Schwartz

Cover Designer: GEX Publishing Services

Cover Artist: GEX Publishing Services

Composition: GEX Publishing Services

For product information and technology assistance, contact us at
Cengage Learning Customer & Sales Support, 1-800-354-9706

For permission to use material from this text or product, submit all
requests online at **www.cengage.com/permissions**
Further permissions questions can be emailed to
permissionrequest@cengage.com

Library of Congress Control Number: 2013937997
ISBN-13: 978-1-285-08259-2
ISBN-10: 1-285-08259-1

Cengage Learning
200 First Stamford Place, 4th Floor
Stamford, CT 06902
USA

Cengage Learning is a leading provider of customized learning solutions
with office locations around the globe, including Singapore, the United
Kingdom, Australia, Mexico, Brazil, and Japan. Locate your local office at:
www.cengage.com/global

Cengage Learning products are represented in Canada by
Nelson Education, Ltd.

For your course and learning solutions, visit **www.cengage.com**

Purchase any of our products at your local college store or at our
preferred online store **www.cengagebrain.com**

Printed in the United States of America
1 2 3 4 5 6 7 19 18 17 16 15 14 13

Brief Contents

Preface x

Office 2013

Unit A: Getting Started with Microsoft Office 2013 .... Office 1

PowerPoint 2013

Unit A: Creating a Presentation in PowerPoint 2013.......................................PowerPoint 1

Unit B: Modifying a Presentation...PowerPoint 25

Unit C: Inserting Objects into a Presentation ....PowerPoint 49

Unit D: Finishing a Presentation..PowerPoint 73

Unit E: Working with Advanced Tools and Masters ....PowerPoint 97

Unit F: Enhancing Charts...PowerPoint 121

Unit G: Inserting Graphics, Media, and Objects...PowerPoint 145

Unit H: Using Advanced Features ....PowerPoint 169

Cloud

Appendix: Working in the Cloud .... Cloud 1

Glossary ....Glossary 1

Index...Index 5

Contents

Preface x

Office 2013

Unit A: Getting Started with Microsoft Office 2013 .... **Office 1**

    Understand the Office 2013 Suite...Office 2
        What is Office 365?
    Start an Office App...Office 4
        Starting an app using Windows 7
        Using shortcut keys to move between Office programs
        Using the Office Clipboard
    Identify Office 2013 Screen Elements...Office 6
        Using Backstage view
    Create and Save a File...Office 8
        Saving files to SkyDrive
    Open a File and Save It with a New Name ....Office 10
        Exploring File Open options
        Working in Compatibility Mode
    View and Print Your Work...Office 12
        Customizing the Quick Access toolbar
        Creating a screen capture
    Get Help, Close a File, and Exit an App...Office 14
        Enabling touch mode
        Recovering a document
    Practice ....Office 16

PowerPoint 2013

Unit A: Creating a Presentation in PowerPoint 2013 .... **PowerPoint 1**

    Define Presentation Software.. PowerPoint 2
        Using PowerPoint on a touch screen
    Plan an Effective Presentation .... PowerPoint 4
        Understanding copyright
    Examine the PowerPoint Window... PowerPoint 6
        Viewing your presentation in gray scale or black and white
    Enter Slide Text... PowerPoint 8
        Saving fonts with your presentation
    Add a New Slide .... PowerPoint 10
        Entering and printing notes
    Apply a Design Theme... PowerPoint 12
        Customizing themes
    Compare Presentation Views .... PowerPoint 14
    Print a PowerPoint Presentation .... PowerPoint 16
        Microsoft Office Web Apps
    Practice .... PowerPoint 18

Unit B: Modifying a Presentation .... **PowerPoint 25**

Enter Text in Outline View .... PowerPoint 26
Using proofing tools for other languages

Format Text .... PowerPoint 28
Replacing text and fonts

Convert Text to SmartArt .... PowerPoint 30
Choosing SmartArt graphics

Insert and Modify Shapes .... PowerPoint 32
Use the Eyedropper to match colors

Rearrange and Merge Shapes .... PowerPoint 34
Changing the size and position of shapes

Edit and Duplicate Shapes .... PowerPoint 36
Editing points of a shape

Align and Group Objects .... PowerPoint 38
Distributing objects

Add Slide Footers .... PowerPoint 40
Creating superscript and subscript text

Practice .... PowerPoint 42

Unit C: Inserting Objects into a Presentation .... **PowerPoint 49**

Insert Text from Microsoft Word .... PowerPoint 50
Sending a presentation using email

Insert and Style a Picture .... PowerPoint 52
Saving slides as graphics

Insert a Text Box .... PowerPoint 54
Changing text box defaults

Insert a Chart .... PowerPoint 56

Enter and Edit Chart Data .... PowerPoint 58
Adding a hyperlink to a chart

Insert Slides from Other Presentations .... PowerPoint 60
Working with multiple windows

Insert a Table .... PowerPoint 62
Drawing tables

Insert and Format WordArt .... PowerPoint 64
Saving a presentation as a video

Practice .... PowerPoint 66

Unit D: Finishing a Presentation .... **PowerPoint 73**

Modify Masters .... PowerPoint 74
Create custom slide layouts

Customize the Background and Theme .... PowerPoint 76

Use Slide Show Commands .... PowerPoint 78

Set Slide Transitions and Timings .... PowerPoint 80
Rehearsing slide show timings

Animate Objects .... PowerPoint 82
Attaching a sound to an animation

Use Proofing and Language Tools .... PowerPoint 84
Checking spelling as you type

Inspect a Presentation..PowerPoint 86
    Digitally sign a presentation

Evaluate a Presentation..PowerPoint 88
    Setting permissions

Practice ....PowerPoint 90

Unit E: Working with Advanced Tools and Masters.......................**PowerPoint 97**

Draw and Format Connectors...PowerPoint 98
    Changing page setup and slide orientation

Use Advanced Formatting Tools ....PowerPoint 100
    Creating columns in a text box

Customize Animation Effects ....PowerPoint 102
    Understanding animation timings

Create Custom Slide Layouts ....PowerPoint 104
    Restoring the slide master layout

Format Master Text ....PowerPoint 106
    Understanding exceptions to the slide master

Change Master Text Indents ....PowerPoint 108

Adjust Text Objects ....PowerPoint 110
    Changing text direction

Use Templates and Add Comments...PowerPoint 112
    Understanding PowerPoint templates and themes

Practice ....PowerPoint 114

Unit F: Enhancing Charts ....**PowerPoint 121**

Work with Charts in PowerPoint..PowerPoint 122
    Using Paste Special

Change Chart Design and Style..PowerPoint 124
    Using AutoFit Options to divide and fit body text

Customize a Chart ....PowerPoint 126
    Using the Research task pane

Format Chart Elements..PowerPoint 128
    Changing PowerPoint options

Animate a Chart...PowerPoint 130
    Insert a picture as a slide background

Embed an Excel Chart..PowerPoint 132
    Embedding a worksheet

Link an Excel Worksheet..PowerPoint 134

Update a Linked Excel Worksheet ....PowerPoint 136
    Editing links

Practice ....PowerPoint 138

Unit G: Inserting Graphics, Media, and Objects ....**PowerPoint 145**

Create a Custom Table ....PowerPoint 146

Design a SmartArt Graphic ....PowerPoint 148
    Creating mathematical equations

Enhance a SmartArt Graphic .... PowerPoint 150
    Saving a presentation in PDF, XPS, or other fixed file formats

Insert and Edit Digital Video .... PowerPoint 152
    Trimming a video

Insert and Trim Audio .... PowerPoint 154
    Recording a narration on a slide

Edit and Adjust a Picture .... PowerPoint 156
    Things to know about picture compression

Add Action Buttons .... PowerPoint 158
    Change the transparency of a picture

Insert Hyperlinks .... PowerPoint 160
    Inserting a screenshot

Practice .... PowerPoint 162

Unit H: Using Advanced Features .... **PowerPoint 169**

Customize Handout and Notes Masters .... PowerPoint 170
    Creating handouts in Microsoft Word

Send a Presentation for Review .... PowerPoint 172
    Packaging a presentation

Combine Reviewed Presentations .... PowerPoint 174
    Coauthoring a presentation

Set Up a Slide Show .... PowerPoint 176
    Apps for Office

Create a Custom Show .... PowerPoint 178
    Link to a custom slide show

Prepare a Presentation for Distribution .... PowerPoint 180
    Recording a slide show

Create a Photo Album .... PowerPoint 182
    Publish slides to a Slide Library

Deliver a Presentation Online .... PowerPoint 184
    Supported PowerPoint features and online presentations

Practice .... PowerPoint 186

Cloud

Appendix: Working in the Cloud .... **Cloud 1**

Understand Office 2013 in the Cloud .... Cloud 2

Work Online .... Cloud 4
    Getting a Microsoft account

Explore SkyDrive .... Cloud 6
    How to disable default saving to Skydrive

Manage Files on SkyDrive .... Cloud 8

Share Files .... Cloud 10
    Co-authoring documents

Explore Office Web Apps .... Cloud 12
    Exploring other Office Web Apps

Team Project .... Cloud 14

Glossary .... **Glossary 1**
Index .... **Index 5**

Preface

Welcome to *Microsoft PowerPoint 2013—Illustrated Introductory*. This book has a unique design: each skill is presented on two facing pages, with steps on the left and screens on the right. The layout makes it easy to learn a skill without having to read a lot of text and flip pages to see an illustration.

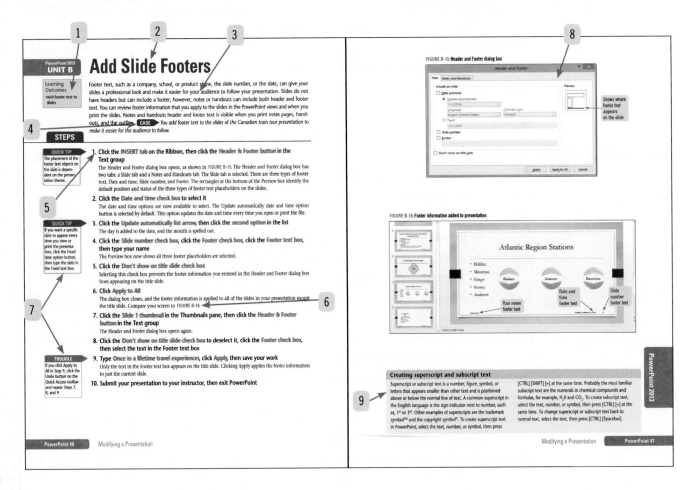

1 New! Learning Outcomes box lists measurable learning goals for which a student is accountable in that lesson.

2 Each two-page lesson focuses on a single skill.

3 Introduction briefly explains why the lesson skill is important.

4 A case scenario motivates the steps and puts learning in context.

5 Step-by-step instructions and brief explanations guide students through each hands-on lesson activity.

6 New! Figure references are now in red bold to help students refer back and forth between the steps and screenshots.

7 Tips and troubleshooting advice, right where you need it—next to the step itself.

8 New! Larger screen shots with green callouts keep students on track as they complete steps.

9 Clues to Use yellow boxes provide useful information related to the lesson skill.

This book is an ideal learning tool for a wide range of learners—the "rookies" will find the clean design easy to follow and focused with only essential information presented, and the "hotshots" will appreciate being able to move quickly through the lessons to find the information they need without reading a lot of text. The design also makes this a great reference after the course is over! See the illustration on the left to learn more about the pedagogical and design elements of a typical lesson.

What's New in this Edition

- **Coverage** — This book helps students learn essential skills using Microsoft PowerPoint 2013, including creating and modifying a presentation, inserting objects, and finalizing a presentation. The Working in the Cloud appendix helps students learn to use SkyDrive to save, share and manage files in the cloud and to use Office Web Apps.

- **New! Learning Outcomes** — Each lesson displays a green Learning Outcomes box that lists skills-based or knowledge-based learning goals for which students are accountable. Each Learning Outcome maps to a variety of learning activities and assessments. (See the *New! Learning Outcomes* section on page xiii for more information.)

- **New! Updated Design** — This edition features many new design improvements to engage students — including larger lesson screenshots with green callouts and a refreshed Unit Opener page.

- **New! Independent Challenge 4: Explore** — This new case-based assessment activity allows students to explore new skills and use creativity to solve a problem or create a project.

- **Covers Microsoft Office 2013 Specialist exam objectives** — Book content is written to cover the exam objectives. Study Guide supplement in the Instructor Resources provides map of where each objective is covered in the book.

Assignments

This book includes a wide variety of high quality assignments you can use for practice and assessment. Assignments include:

- **Concepts Review** — Multiple choice, matching, and screen identification questions.

- **Skills Review** — Step-by-step, hands-on review of every skill covered in the unit.

- **Independent Challenges 1-3** — Case projects requiring critical thinking and application of the unit skills. The Independent Challenges increase in difficulty. The first one in each unit provides the most hand-holding; the subsequent ones provide less guidance and require more critical thinking and independent problem solving.

- **Independent Challenge 4: Explore** — Case projects that let students explore new skills that are related to the core skills covered in the unit and are often more open ended, allowing students to use creativity to complete the assignment.

- **Visual Workshop** — Critical thinking exercises that require students to create a project by loking at a completed solution; they must apply the skills they've learned in the unit and use critical thinking skills to create the project from scratch.

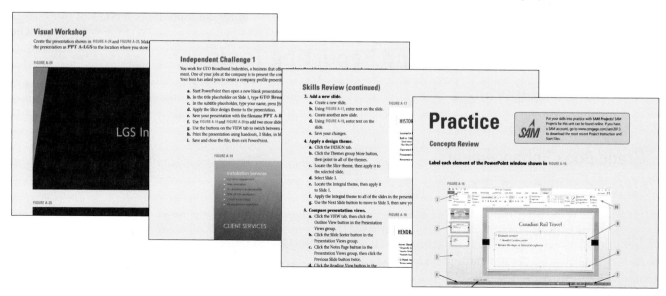

WHAT'S NEW FOR SAM 2013?

Get your students workplace ready with SAM

The market-leading assessment and training solution for Microsoft Office

SAM 2013

Exciting New Features and Content

- ➤ Computer Concepts Trainings and Assessments *(shown on monitor)*
- ➤ Student Assignment Calendar
- ➤ All New SAM Projects
- ➤ Mac Hints
- ➤ More MindTap Readers

More Efficient Course Setup and Management Tools

- ➤ Individual Assignment Tool
- ➤ Video Playback of Student Clickpaths
- ➤ Express Assignment Creation Tool

Improved Grade Book and Reporting Tools

- ➤ Institutional Reporting
- ➤ Frequency Analysis Report
- ➤ Grade Book Enhancements
- ➤ Partial Credit Grading for Projects

SAM's active, hands-on environment helps students master Microsoft Office skills and computer concepts that are essential to academic and career success.

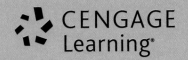

New! Learning Outcomes

Every 2-page lesson in this book now contains a green **Learning Outcomes box** that states the learning goals for that lesson.

- **What is a learning outcome?** A learning outcome states what a student is expected to know or be able to do after completing a lesson. Each learning outcome is skills-based or knowledge-based and is *measurable*. Learning outcomes map to learning activities and assessments.

- **How do students benefit from learning outcomes?** Learning outcomes tell students exactly what skills and knowledge they are *accountable* for learning in that lesson. This helps students study more efficiently and effectively and makes them more active learners.

- **How do instructors benefit from learning outcomes?** Learning outcomes provide clear, measurable, skills-based learning goals that map to various high-quality learning activities and assessments. A **Learning Outcomes Map**, available for each unit in this book, maps every learning outcome to the learning activities and assessments shown below.

Learning Outcomes Map to These Learning Activities:

1. Book lessons: Step-by-step tutorial on one skill presented in a two-page learning format
2. SAM Training: Short animations and hands-on practice activities in simulated environment

Learning Outcomes Map to These Assessments:

1. End-of-Unit Exercises: **Concepts Review** (screen identification, matching, multiple choice); **Skills Review** (hands-on review of each lesson); **Independent Challenges** (hands-on, case-based review of specific skills); **Visual Workshop** (activity that requires student to build a project by looking at a picture of the final solution).
2. Exam View Test Banks: Objective-based questions you can use for online or paper testing.
3. SAM Assessment: Performance-based assessment in a simulated environment.
4. SAM Projects: Auto-graded projects for Word, Excel, Access, and PowerPoint that students create live in the application.
5. Extra Independent Challenges: Extra case-based exercises available in the Instructor Resources that cover various skills.

Learning Outcomes Map

A **Learning Outcomes Map**, contained in the Instructor Resources, provides a listing of learning activities and assessments for each learning outcome in the book.

Learning Outcomes Map
Microsoft PowerPoint 2013 Illustrated
Unit D: Finishing a Presentation

KEY:
IC=Independent Challenge   EIC=Extra Independent Challenge
VW=Visual Workshop

	Concepts Review	Skills Review	IC1	IC2	IC3	IC4	VW	EIC 1	EIC 2	Test Bank	SAM Assessment	SAM Projects	SAM Training
Modify Masters													
Navigate Slide Master view	✓	✓	✓							✓			
Add and modify a picture		✓	✓							✓			
Customize the Background and Theme													
Apply a slide background and change the style		✓		✓	✓	✓	✓			✓	✓		✓
Modify presentation theme	✓	✓		✓	✓		✓			✓			
Use Slide Show Commands													
Preview a slide show	✓	✓		✓	✓	✓	✓			✓	✓		
Navigate a slide show		✓					✓			✓			
Use slide show tools		✓		✓			✓			✓			
Set Slide Transitions and Timings													
Apply and modify a transition	✓	✓	✓	✓		✓				✓	✓	✓	✓
Modify slide timings	✓	✓	✓		✓					✓			
Animate Objects													
Animate obj...				✓									

Instructor Resources

This book comes with a wide array of high-quality technology-based, teaching tools to help you teach and to help students learn. The following teaching tools are available for download at our Instructor Companion Site. Simply search for this text at *login.cengage.com.* An instructor login is required.

- **New! Learning Outcomes Map** — A detailed grid for each unit (in Excel format) shows the learning activities and assessments that map to each learning outcome in that unit.

- **Instructor's Manual** — Available as an electronic file, the Instructor's Manual includes lecture notes with teaching tips for each unit.

- **Sample Syllabus** — Prepare and customize your course easily using this sample course outline.

- **PowerPoint Presentations** — Each unit has a corresponding PowerPoint presentation covering the skills and topics in that unit that you can use in lectures, distribute to your students, or customize to suit your course.

- **Figure Files** — The figures in the text are provided on the Instructor Resources site to help you illustrate key topics or concepts. You can use these to create your own slide shows or learning tools.

- **MOS Exam Study Guide** — provides information on the PowerPoint 2013 Microsoft Office Sprecialist exam; detailed grid lists each exam objective and page numbers of where each is covered in the book.

- **Solution Files** — Solution Files are files that contain the finished project that students create or modify in the lessons or end-of-unit material.

- **Solutions Document** — This document outlines the solutions for the end-of-unit Concepts Review, Skills Review, Independent Challenges and Visual Workshops. An Annotated Solution File and Grading Rubric accompany each file and can be used together for efficient grading.

- **ExamView Test Banks** — ExamView is a powerful testing software package that allows you to create and administer printed, computer (LAN-based), and Internet exams. Our ExamView test banks include questions that correspond to the skills and concepts covered in this text, enabling students to generate detailed study guides that include page references for further review. The computer-based and Internet testing components allow students to take exams at their computers, and also save you time by grading each exam automatically.

Key Facts About Using This Book

Data Files are needed: To complete many of the lessons and end-of-unit assignments, students need to start from partially completed Data Files, which help students learn more efficiently. By starting out with a Data File, students can focus on performing specific tasks without having to create a file from scratch. All Data Files are available as part of the Instructor Resources. Students can also download Data Files themselves for free at cengagebrain.com. (For detailed instructions, go to www.cengage.com/ct/studentdownload.)

System requirements: This book was developed using Microsoft Office 2013 Professional running on Windows 8. Note that Windows 8 is not a requirement for the units on Microsoft Office; Office 2013 runs virtually the same on Windows 7 and Windows 8. Please see Important Notes for Windows 7 Users on the next page for more information.

Screen resolution: This book was written and tested on computers with monitors set at a resolution of 1366 x 768. If your screen shows more or less information than the figures in this book, your monitor is probably set at a higher or lower resolution. If you don't see something on your screen, you might have to scroll down or up to see the object identified in the figure.

Tell Us What You Think!

We want to hear from you! Please email your questions, comments, and suggestions to the Illustrated Series team at: **illustratedseries@cengage.com**

Important Notes for Windows 7 Users

The screenshots in this book show Microsoft Office 2013 running on Windows 8. However, if you are using Microsoft Windows 7, you can still use this book because Office 2013 runs virtually the same on both platforms. There are only two differences that you will encounter if you are using Windows 7. Read this section to understand the differences.

Dialog boxes

If you are a Windows 7 user, dialog boxes shown in this book will look slightly different than what you see on your screen. Dialog boxes for Windows 7 have a light blue title bar, instead of a medium blue title bar. However, beyond this superficial difference in appearance, the options in the dialog boxes across platforms are the same. For instance, the screen shots below in FIGURE 1 and FIGURE 2 show the Font dialog box running on Windows 7 and the Font dialog box running on Windows 8.

FIGURE 1: **Font dialog box in Windows 7**

FIGURE 2: **Font dialog box in Windows 8**

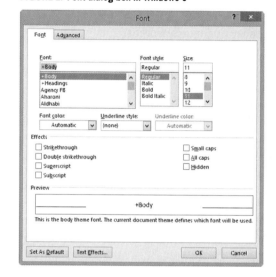

Alternate Steps for Starting an App in Windows 7

Nearly all of the steps in this book work exactly the same for Windows 7 users. However, starting an app (or program/application) requires different steps for Windows 7. The steps below show the Windows 7 steps for starting an app. (Note: Windows 7 alternate steps also appear in red Trouble boxes next to any step in the book that requires starting an app.)

Starting an app (or program/application) using Windows 7

1. Click the **Start button** on the taskbar to open the Start menu.
2. Click **All Programs**, then click the **Microsoft Office 2013 folder**. See Figure 3.
3. Click the app you want to use (such as **PowerPoint 2013**).

FIGURE 3: **Starting an app using Windows 7**

Acknowledgements

Author Acknowledgements

Being a part of the extremely talented and experienced Office Illustrated team makes working on this book that much more enjoyable - many thanks to RBB, CKG, the production group, the testers, and the rest of the Cengage team!

–David W. Beskeen

Advisory Board Acknowledgements

We thank our Illustrated Advisory Board who gave us their opinions and guided our decisions as we developed this edition. They are as follows:

Merlin Amirtharaj, Stanly Community College

Londo Andrews, J. Sargeant Reynolds Community College

Rachelle Hall, Glendale Community College

Terri Helfand, Chaffey Community College

Sheryl Lenhart, Terra Community College

Dr. Jose Nieves, Lord Fairfax Community College

Coming Soon: MindTap

MindTap is a fully online, highly personalized learning experience built upon Cengage Learning content. MindTap combines student learning tools—readings, multimedia, activities and assessments—into a singular Learning Path that guides students through their course. Instructors personalize the experience by customizing authoritative Cengage Learning content and learning tools, including the ability to add SAM trainings, assessments, and projects into the Learning Path via a SAM app that integrates into the MindTap framework seamlessly with Learning Management Systems. Available in 2014.

Getting Started with Microsoft Office 2013

CASE This unit introduces you to the most frequently used programs in Office, as well as common features they all share.

Unit Objectives

After completing this unit, you will be able to:

- Understand the Office 2013 suite
- Start an Office app
- Identify Office 2013 screen elements
- Create and save a file
- Open a file and save it with a new name
- View and print your work
- Get Help, close a file, and exit an app

File You Will Need

OFFICE A-1.xlsx

Understand the Office 2013 Suite

Microsoft Office 2013 is a group of programs--which are also called applications or apps--designed to help you create documents, collaborate with coworkers, and track and analyze information. You use different Office programs to accomplish specific tasks, such as writing a letter or producing a presentation, yet all the programs have a similar look and feel. Microsoft Office 2013 apps feature a common, context-sensitive user interface, so you can get up to speed faster and use advanced features with greater ease. The Office apps are bundled together in a group called a **suite**. The Office suite is available in several configurations, but all include Word, Excel, and PowerPoint. Other configurations include Access, Outlook, Publisher, and other programs. **CASE** *As part of your job, you need to understand how each Office app is best used to complete specific tasks.*

DETAILS

The Office apps covered in this book include:

• **Microsoft Word 2013**

When you need to create any kind of text-based document, such as a memo, newsletter, or multipage report, Word is the program to use. You can easily make your documents look great by inserting eye-catching graphics and using formatting tools such as themes, which are available in most Office programs. **Themes** are predesigned combinations of color and formatting attributes you can apply to a document. The Word document shown in FIGURE A-1 was formatted with the Organic theme.

• **Microsoft Excel 2013**

Excel is the perfect solution when you need to work with numeric values and make calculations. It puts the power of formulas, functions, charts, and other analytical tools into the hands of every user, so you can analyze sales projections, calculate loan payments, and present your findings in a professional manner. The Excel worksheet shown in FIGURE A-1 tracks personal expenses. Because Excel automatically recalculates results whenever a value changes, the information is always up to date. A chart illustrates how the monthly expenses are broken down.

• **Microsoft PowerPoint 2013**

Using PowerPoint, it's easy to create powerful presentations complete with graphics, transitions, and even a soundtrack. Using professionally designed themes and clip art, you can quickly and easily create dynamic slide shows such as the one shown in FIGURE A-1.

• **Microsoft Access 2013**

Access is a relational database program that helps you keep track of large amounts of quantitative data, such as product inventories or employee records. The form shown in FIGURE A-1 was created for a grocery store inventory database. Employees use the form to enter data about each item. Using Access enables employees to quickly find specific information such as price and quantity.

Microsoft Office has benefits beyond the power of each program, including:

• **Common user interface: Improving business processes**

Because the Office suite programs have a similar **interface**, or look and feel, your experience using one program's tools makes it easy to learn those in the other programs. In addition, Office documents are **compatible** with one another, meaning that you can easily incorporate, or **integrate**, an Excel chart into a PowerPoint slide, or an Access table into a Word document.

• **Collaboration: Simplifying how people work together**

Office recognizes the way people do business today, and supports the emphasis on communication and knowledge sharing within companies and across the globe. All Office programs include the capability to incorporate feedback—called **online collaboration**—across the Internet or a company network.

FIGURE A-1: Microsoft Office 2013 documents

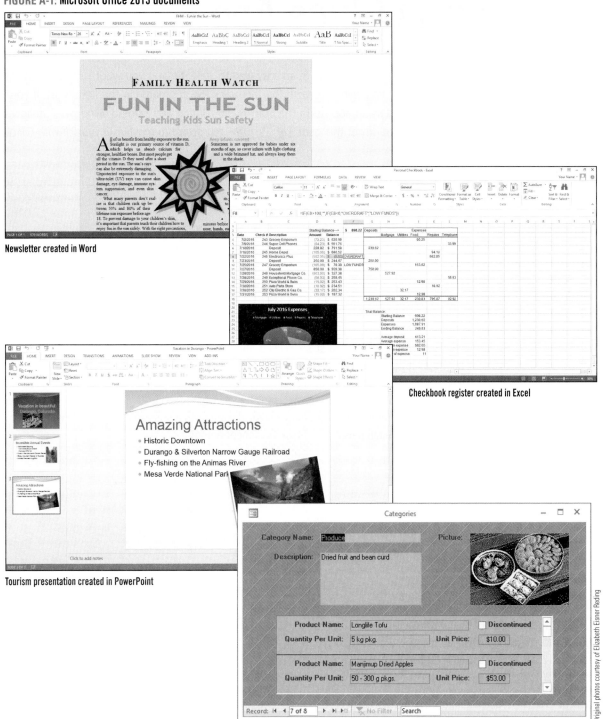

Newsletter created in Word

Checkbook register created in Excel

Tourism presentation created in PowerPoint

Store inventory form created in Access

Original photos courtesy of Elizabeth Eisner Reding

What is Office 365?

Until the release of Microsoft Office 2013, most consumers purchased Microsoft Office in a traditional way: by buying a retail package from a store or downloading it from Microsoft.com. You can still purchase Microsoft Office 2013 in this traditional way--but you can also now purchase it as a subscription service called Microsoft Office 365 (for businesses) and Microsoft Office 365 Home Premium (for consumers). Office 365 requires businesses to pay a subscription fee for each user. Office 365 Home Premium Edition allows households to install Office on up to 5 devices. These subscription versions of Office provide extra services and are optimized for working in the cloud.

Start an Office App

To get started using Microsoft Office, you need to start, or **launch**, the Office app you want to use. If you are running Microsoft Office on Windows 8, an easy way to start the app you want is to go to the Start screen, type the app name you want to search for, then click the app name In the Results list. If you are running Windows 7, you start an app using the Start menu. (If you are running Windows 7, follow the Windows 7 steps at the bottom of this page.) **CASE** ▶ *You decide to familiarize yourself with Office by starting Microsoft Word.*

STEPS

1. **Go to the** Windows 8 Start screen
   Your screen displays a variety of colorful tiles for all the apps on your computer. You could locate the app you want to open by scrolling to the right until you see it, or you can type the app name to search for it.

2. **Type** word
   Your screen now displays "Word 2013" under "Results for 'word'", along with any other app that has "word" as part of its name (such as WordPad). See FIGURE A-2.

3. **Click** Word 2013
   Word 2013 launches, and the Word **start screen** appears, as shown in FIGURE A-3. The start screen is a landing page that appears when you first start an Office app. The left side of this screen displays recent files you have opened. (If you have never opened any files, then there will be no files listed under Recent.) The right side displays images depicting different templates you can use to create different types of documents. A **template** is a file containing professionally designed content that you can easily replace with your own. You can also start from scratch using the Blank Document option.

Starting an app using Windows 7

1. Click the Start button ⊕ on the taskbar
2. Click All Programs on the Start menu, click the Microsoft Office 2013 folder as shown in FIGURE A-4, then click Word 2013

Word 2013 launches, and the Word start screen appears, as shown previously in FIGURE A-3. The start screen is a landing page that appears when you first start an Office app. The left side of this screen displays recent files you have opened. (If you have never opened any files, then there will be no files listed under Recent.) The right side displays images depicting different templates you can use to create different types of documents. A **template** is a file containing professionally designed content that you can easily replace with your own. Using a template to create a document can save time and ensure that your document looks great. You can also start from scratch using the Blank Document option.

Using shortcut keys to move between Office programs

You can switch between open apps using a keyboard shortcut. The [Alt][Tab] keyboard combination lets you either switch quickly to the next open program or file or choose one from a gallery. To switch immediately to the next open program or file, press [Alt][Tab]. To choose from all open programs and files, press and hold [Alt], then press and release [Tab] without releasing [Alt]. A gallery opens on screen, displaying the filename and a thumbnail image of each open program and file, as well as of the desktop. Each time you press [Tab] while holding [Alt], the selection cycles to the next open file or location. Release [Alt] when the program, file, or location you want to activate is selected.

FIGURE A-2: Searching for Word app from the Start screen in Windows 8

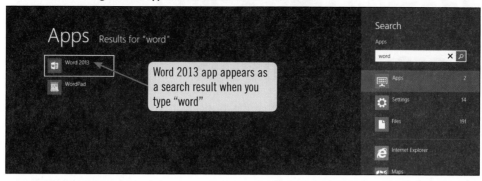

FIGURE A-3: Word start screen

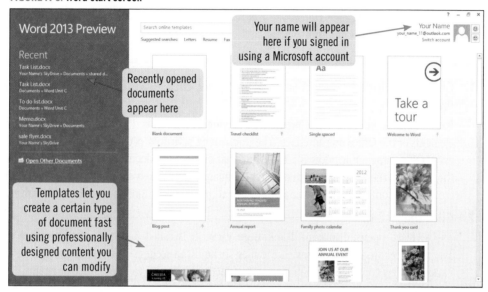

FIGURE A-4: Starting an app using Windows 7

Using the Office Clipboard

You can use the Office Clipboard to cut and copy items from one Office program and paste them into others. The Office Clipboard can store a maximum of 24 items. To access it, open the Office Clipboard task pane by clicking the dialog box launcher 🔲 in the Clipboard group on the HOME tab. Each time you copy a selection, it is saved in the Office Clipboard. Each entry in the

Office Clipboard includes an icon that tells you the program it was created in. To paste an entry, click in the document where you want it to appear, then click the item in the Office Clipboard. To delete an item from the Office Clipboard, right-click the item, then click Delete.

Identify Office 2013 Screen Elements

One of the benefits of using Office is that the programs have much in common, making them easy to learn and making it simple to move from one to another. Individual Office programs have always shared many features, but the innovations in the Office 2013 user interface mean even greater similarity among them all. That means you can also use your knowledge of one program to get up to speed in another. A **user interface** is a collective term for all the ways you interact with a software program. The user interface in Office 2013 provides intuitive ways to choose commands, work with files, and navigate in the program window. **CASE** *Familiarize yourself with some of the common interface elements in Office by examining the PowerPoint program window.*

STEPS

1. **Go to the Windows 8** Start screen, **type** pow, **click** PowerPoint 2013, **then click** Blank Presentation

   PowerPoint becomes the active program displaying a blank slide. Refer to FIGURE A-5 to identify common elements of the Office user interface. The **document window** occupies most of the screen. At the top of every Office program window is a **title bar** that displays the document name and program name. Below the title bar is the **Ribbon**, which displays commands you're likely to need for the current task. Commands are organized onto **tabs**. The tab names appear at the top of the Ribbon, and the active tab appears in front.

2. **Click the** FILE **tab**

   The FILE tab opens, displaying **Backstage view**. It is called Backstage view becausee the commands available here are for working with the files "behind the scenes." The navigation bar on the left side of Backstage view contains commands to perform actions common to most Office programs.

3. **Click the** Back button ⊖ **to close Backstage view and return to the document window, then click the** DESIGN **tab on the Ribbon**

   To display a different tab, click its name. Each tab contains related commands arranged into **groups** to make features easy to find. On the DESIGN tab, the Themes group displays available design themes in a **gallery**, or visual collection of choices you can browse. Many groups contain a **dialog box launcher**, which you can click to open a dialog box or pane from which to choose related commands.

4. **Move the mouse pointer ▷ over the** Ion theme **in the Themes group as shown in** FIGURE A-6, **but** *do not click* **the mouse button**

   The Ion theme is temporarily applied to the slide in the document window. However, because you did not click the theme, you did not permanently change the slide. With the **Live Preview** feature, you can point to a choice, see the results, then decide if you want to make the change. Live Preview is available throughout Office.

5. **Move ▷ away from the Ribbon and towards the slide**

   If you had clicked the Ion theme, it would be applied to this slide. Instead, the slide remains unchanged.

6. **Point to the** Zoom slider ▬▬▬▬▮▬▬▬ + 100% **on the status bar, then drag to the right until the Zoom level reads** 166%

   The slide display is enlarged. Zoom tools are located on the status bar. You can drag the slider or click the Zoom In or Zoom Out buttons to zoom in or out on an area of interest. **Zooming in** (a higher percentage), makes a document appear bigger on screen but less of it fits on the screen at once; **zooming out** (a lower percentage) lets you see more of the document at a reduced size.

7. **Click the** Zoom Out button ▬ **on the status bar to the left of the Zoom slider until the Zoom level reads** 120%

Getting Started with Microsoft Office 2013

FIGURE A-5: PowerPoint program window

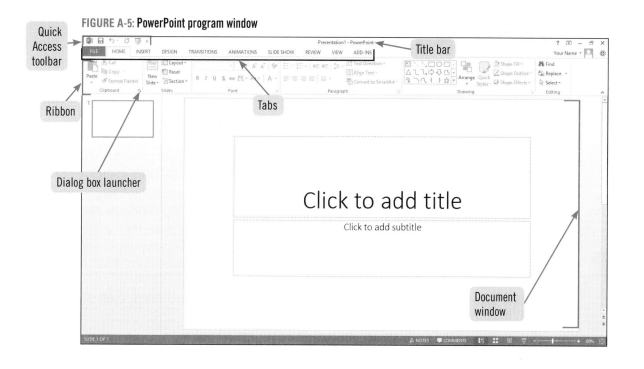

FIGURE A-6: Viewing a theme with Live Preview

Using Backstage view

Backstage view in each Microsoft Office program offers "one stop shopping" for many commonly performed tasks, such as opening and saving a file, printing and previewing a document, defining document properties, sharing information, and exiting a program. Backstage view opens when you click the FILE tab in any Office program, and while features such as the Ribbon, Mini toolbar, and Live Preview all help you work *in* your documents, the FILE tab and Backstage view help you work *with* your documents. You can return to your active document by pressing the Back button.

Create and Save a File

When working in an Office program, one of the first things you need to do is to create and save a file. A **file** is a stored collection of data. Saving a file enables you to work on a project now, then put it away and work on it again later. In some Office programs, including Word, Excel, and PowerPoint, you can open a new file when you start the program, then all you have to do is enter some data and save it. In Access, you must create a file before you enter any data. You should give your files meaningful names and save them in an appropriate location, such as a folder on your hard drive or SkyDrive so they're easy to find. **SkyDrive** is the Microsoft cloud storage system that lets you easily save, share, and access your files from anywhere you have Internet access. See "Saving Files to SkyDrive" for more information on this topic. **CASE** ▶ *Use Word to familiarize yourself with creating and saving a document. First you'll type some notes about a possible location for a corporate meeting, then you'll save the information for later use.*

STEPS

1. **Click the Word program button** ▦ **on the taskbar, click Blank document, then click the Zoom In button** ➕ **until the level is 120%, if necessary**

2. **Type Locations for Corporate Meeting, then press [Enter] twice**
   The text appears in the document window, and the **insertion point** blinks on a new blank line. The insertion point indicates where the next typed text will appear.

3. **Type Las Vegas, NV, press [Enter], type San Diego, CA, press [Enter], type Seattle, WA, press [Enter] twice, then type your name**

4. **Click the Save button** 🖫 **on the Quick Access toolbar**
   Backstage view opens showing various options for saving the file, as shown in **FIGURE A-7**.

5. **Click Computer, then click Browse**
   Because this is the first time you are saving this document, the Save As command is displayed. Once you choose a location where you will save the file, the Save As dialog box displays, as shown in **FIGURE A-8**. Once a file is saved, clicking 🖫 saves any changes to the file *without* opening the Save As dialog box. The Address bar in the Save As dialog box displays the default location for saving the file, but you can change it to any location. The File name field contains a suggested name for the document based on text in the file, but you can enter a different name.

6. **Type OF A-Potential Corporate Meeting Locations**
   The text you type replaces the highlighted text. (The "OF A-" in the filename indicates that the file is created in Office Unit A. You will see similar designations throughout this book when files are named.)

7. **In the Save As dialog box, use the Address bar or Navigation Pane to navigate to the location where you store your Data Files**
   You can store files on your computer, a network drive, your SkyDrive, or any acceptable storage device.

8. **Click Save**
   The Save As dialog box closes, the new file is saved to the location you specified, and the name of the document appears in the title bar, as shown in **FIGURE A-9**. (You may or may not see the file extension ".docx" after the filename.) See **TABLE A-1** for a description of the different types of files you create in Office, and the file extensions associated with each.

TABLE A-1: Common filenames and default file extensions

file created in	is called a	and has the default extension
Word	document	.docx
Excel	workbook	.xlsx
PowerPoint	presentation	.pptx
Access	database	.accdb

Getting Started with Microsoft Office 2013

© 2014 Cengage Learning

FIGURE A-7: Save As screen in Backstage view

FIGURE A-8: Save As dialog box

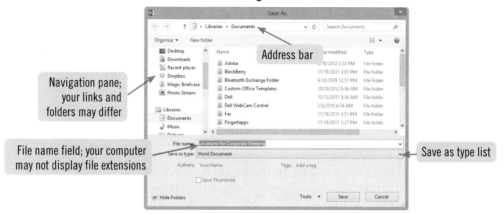

FIGURE A-9: Saved and named Word document

Saving files to SkyDrive

All Office programs include the capability to incorporate feedback—called **online collaboration**—across the Internet or a company network. Using **cloud computing** (work done in a virtual environment), you can take advantage of commonly shared features such as a consistent interface. Using SkyDrive, a free file storage service from Microsoft, you and your colleagues can create and store documents in the cloud and make the documents available anywhere there is Internet access to whomever you choose. To use SkyDrive, you need a free Microsoft Account, which you obtain at the signup.live.com website. You can find more information about SkyDrive in the "Working in the Cloud" appendix. When you are logged into your Microsoft account and you save a file in any of the Office apps, the first option in the Save As screen is your SkyDrive. Double-click your SkyDrive option and the Save As dialog box opens displaying a location in the address bar unique to your SkyDrive account. Type a name in the File name text box, then click Save and your file is saved to your SkyDrive. To sync your files with SkyDrive, you'll need to download and install the SkyDrive for Windows app. Then, when you open Explorer, you'll notice a new folder called SkyDrive has been added to the Users folder. In this folder is a sub-folder called Documents, in which an updated copy of your Office app files resides. This means if your Internet connection fails, you can work on your files offline. The SkyDrive folder also displays Explorer in the list of Favorites folders.

Open a File and Save It with a New Name

In many cases as you work in Office, you start with a blank document, but often you need to use an existing file. It might be a file you or a coworker created earlier as a work in progress, or it could be a complete document that you want to use as the basis for another. For example, you might want to create a budget for this year using the budget you created last year; instead of typing in all the categories and information from scratch, you could open last year's budget, save it with a new name, and just make changes to update it for the current year. By opening the existing file and saving it with the Save As command, you create a duplicate that you can modify to suit your needs, while the original file remains intact. **CASE** ▶ *Use Excel to open an existing workbook file, and save it with a new name so the original remains unchanged.*

STEPS

TROUBLE
If you are running WIndows 7, click the Start button on the taskbar, type excel, then click Excel 2013.

1. **Go to the Windows 8** Start screen, type exc, click Excel 2013, **click** Open Other Workbooks, **click** Computer **on the navigation bar, then click** Browse

   The Open dialog box opens, where you can navigate to any drive or folder accessible to your computer to locate a file. You can click Recent Workbooks on the navigation bar to display a list of recent workbooks; click a file in the list to open it.

2. **In the Open dialog box, navigate to the location where you store your Data Files**

   The files available in the current folder are listed, as shown in FIGURE A-10. This folder displays one file.

TROUBLE
Click Enable Editing on the Protected View bar near the top of your document window if prompted.

3. **Click** OFFICE A-1.xlsx, **then click** Open

   The dialog box closes, and the file opens in Excel. An Excel file is an electronic spreadsheet, so the new file displays a grid of rows and columns you can use to enter and organize data.

4. **Click the** FILE tab, **click** Save As **on the navigation bar, then click** Browse

   The Save As dialog box opens, and the current filename is highlighted in the File name text box. Using the Save As command enables you to create a copy of the current, existing file with a new name. This action preserves the original file and creates a new file that you can modify.

5. **Navigate to the location where you store your Data Files if necessary, type** OF A-Budget for Corporate Meeting **in the File name text box, as shown in** FIGURE A-11, **then click** Save

   A copy of the existing workbook is created with the new name. The original file, Office A-1.xlsx, closes automatically.

6. **Click cell** A19, **type your name, then press [Enter], as shown in** FIGURE A-12

   In Excel, you enter data in cells, which are formed by the intersection of a row and a column. Cell A19 is at the intersection of column A and row 19. When you press [Enter], the cell pointer moves to cell A20.

7. **Click the** Save button 🔲 **on the Quick Access toolbar**

   Your name appears in the workbook, and your changes to the file are saved.

Exploring File Open options

You might have noticed that the Open button in the Open dialog box includes a list arrow to the right of the button. In a dialog box, if a button includes a list arrow you can click the button to invoke the command, or you can click the list arrow to see a list of related commands that you can apply to a selected file in the file list. The Open list arrow includes several related commands, including Open Read-Only and Open as Copy.

Clicking Open Read-Only opens a file that you can only save with a new name; you cannot make changes to the original file. Clicking Open as Copy creates and opens a copy of the selected file and inserts the word "Copy" in the file's title. Like the Save As command, these commands provide additional ways to use copies of existing files while ensuring that original files do not get changed by mistake.

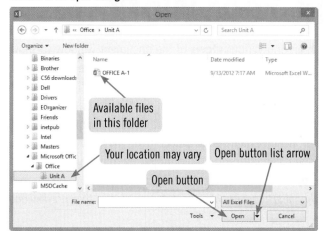

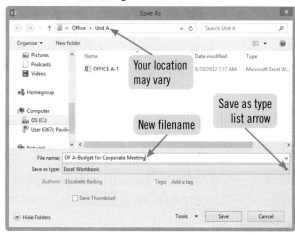

FIGURE A-12: Your name added to the workbook

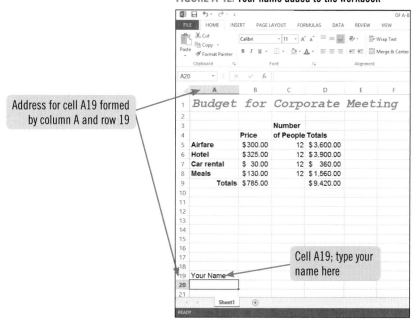

Working in Compatibility Mode

Not everyone upgrades to the newest version of Office. As a general rule, new software versions are **backward compatible**, meaning that documents saved by an older version can be read by newer software. To open documents created in older Office versions, Office 2013 includes a feature called Compatibility Mode. When you use Office 2013 to open a file created in an earlier version of Office, "Compatibility Mode" appears in the title bar, letting you know the file was created in an earlier but usable version of the program. If you are working with someone who may not be using the newest version of the software, you can avoid possible incompatibility problems by saving your file in another, earlier format. To do this in an Office program, click the FILE tab, click Save As on the navigation bar, click the location where you want to save the file, then click Browse. In the Save As dialog box, click the Save as type list arrow in the Save As dialog box, then click an option on the list. For example, if you're working in Excel, click Excel 97-2003 Workbook format in the Save as type list to save an Excel file so it can be opened in Excel 97 or Excel 2003.

View and Print Your Work

Each Microsoft Office program lets you switch among various **views** of the document window to show more or fewer details or a different combination of elements that make it easier to complete certain tasks, such as formatting or reading text. Changing your view of a document does not affect the file in any way, it affects only the way it looks on screen. If your computer is connected to a printer or a print server, you can easily print any Office document using the Print button on the Print tab in Backstage view. Printing can be as simple as **previewing** the document to see exactly what a document will look like when it is printed and then clicking the Print button. Or, you can customize the print job by printing only selected pages. The Backstage view can also be used to share your document with others, or to export it in a different format. **CASE** *Experiment with changing your view of a Word document, and then preview and print your work.*

STEPS

1. **Click the Word program button ▦ on the taskbar**
   Word becomes the active program, and the document fills the screen.

2. **Click the VIEW tab on the Ribbon**
   In most Office programs, the VIEW tab on the Ribbon includes groups and commands for changing your view of the current document. You can also change views using the View buttons on the status bar.

3. **Click the Read Mode button in the Views group on the VIEW tab**
   The view changes to Read Mode view, as shown in FIGURE A-13. This view shows the document in an easy-to-read, distraction-free reading mode. Notice that the Ribbon is no longer visible on screen.

4. **Click the Print Layout button 🗏 on the Status bar**
   You return to Print Layout view, the default view in Word.

5. **Click the FILE tab, then click Print on the navigation bar**
   The Print tab opens in Backstage view. The preview pane on the right side of the window displays a preview of how your document will look when printed. Compare your screen to FIGURE A-14. Options in the Settings section enable you to change margins, orientation, and paper size before printing. To change a setting, click it, and then click a new setting. For instance, to change from Letter paper size to Legal, click Letter in the Settings section, then click Legal on the menu that opens. The document preview updates as you change the settings. You also can use the Settings section to change which pages to print. If your computer is connected to multiple printers, you can click the current printer in the Printer section, then click the one you want to use. The Print section contains the Print button and also enables you to select the number of copies of the document to print.

6. **If your school allows printing, click the Print button in the Print section (otherwise, click the Back button ⊙)**
   If you chose to print, a copy of the document prints, and Backstage view closes.

Customizing the Quick Access toolbar

You can customize the Quick Access toolbar to display your favorite commands. To do so, click the Customize Quick Access Toolbar button ▼ in the title bar, then click the command you want to add. If you don't see the command in the list, click More Commands to open the Quick Access Toolbar tab of the current program's Options dialog box. In the Options dialog box, use the Choose commands from list to choose a category, click the desired command in the list on the left, click Add to add it to the Quick Access toolbar, then click OK. To remove a button from the toolbar, click the name in the list on the right in the Options dialog box, then click Remove. To add a command to the Quick Access toolbar as you work, simply right-click the button on the Ribbon, then click Add to Quick Access Toolbar on the shortcut menu. To move the Quick Access toolbar below the Ribbon, click the Customize Quick Access Toolbar button, and then click Show Below the Ribbon.

FIGURE A-13: Web Layout view

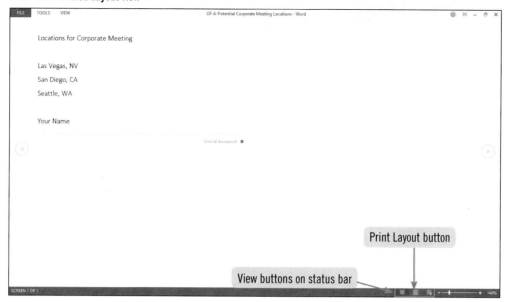

FIGURE A-14: Print settings on the FILE tab

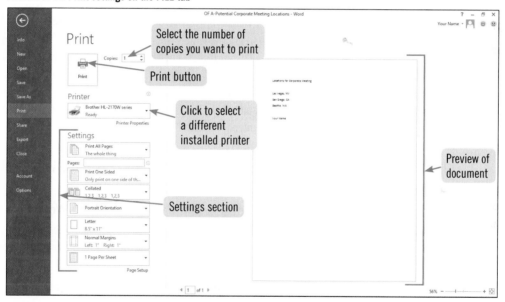

Creating a screen capture

A **screen capture** is a digital image of your screen, as if you took a picture of it with a camera. For instance, you might want to take a screen capture if an error message occurs and you want a Technical Support person to see exactly what's on the screen. You can create a screen capture using features found in Windows 8 or Office 2013. Both Windows 7 and Windows 8 come with the Snipping Tool, a separate program designed to capture whole screens or portions of screens. To open the Snipping Tool, click the Start screen thumbnail, type "sni", then click the Snipping Tool when it appears in the left panel. After opening the Snipping Tool, click New, then drag the pointer on the screen to select the area of the screen you want to capture. When you release the mouse button, the screen capture opens in the Snipping Tool window, and you can save, copy, or send it in an email. In Word, Excel, and PowerPoint 2013, you can capture screens or portions of screens and insert them in the current document using the Screenshot button in the Illustrations group on the INSERT tab. And finally, you can create a screen capture by pressing [PrtScn]. (Keyboards differ, but you may find the [PrtScn] button in or near your keyboard's function keys.) Pressing this key places a digital image of your screen in the Windows temporary storage area known as the **Clipboard**. Open the document where you want the screen capture to appear, click the HOME tab on the Ribbon (if necessary), then click the Paste button in the Clipboard group on the HOME tab. The screen capture is pasted into the document.

Get Help, Close a File, and Exit an App

You can get comprehensive help at any time by pressing [F1] in an Office app or clicking the Help button on the right end of the title bar. You can also get help in the form of a ScreenTip by pointing to almost any icon in the program window. When you're finished working in an Office document, you have a few choices regarding ending your work session. You close a file by clicking the FILE tab, then clicking Close; you exit a program by clicking the Close button on the title bar. Closing a file leaves a program running, while exiting a program closes all the open files in that program as well as the program itself. In all cases, Office reminds you if you try to close a file or exit a program and your document contains unsaved changes. **CASE** ▸ *Explore the Help system in Microsoft Office, and then close your documents and exit any open programs.*

STEPS

1. **Point to the Zoom button in the Zoom group on the VIEW tab of the Ribbon**
   A ScreenTip appears that describes how the Zoom button works and explains where to find other zoom controls.

2. **Click the Microsoft Word Help (F1) button [?] in the upper-right corner of the title bar**
   The Word Help window opens, as shown in **FIGURE A-15**, displaying the home page for help in Word. Each entry is a hyperlink you can click to open a list of topics. The Help window also includes a toolbar of useful Help commands such as printing and increasing the font size for easier readability, and a Search field. If you are not connected to Office.com, a gold band is displayed telling you that you are not connected. Office. com supplements the help content available on your computer with a wide variety of up-to-date topics, templates, and training. If you are not connected to the Internet, the Help window displays only the help content available on your computer.

3. **Click the Learn Word basics link in the Getting started section of the Word Help window**
   The Word Help window changes, and a list of basic tasks appears below the topic.

4. **If necessary, scroll down until the Choose a template topic fills the Word Help window**
   The topic is displayed in the pane of the Help window, as shown in **FIGURE A-16**. The content in the window explains that you can create a document using a template (a pre-formatted document) or just create a blank document.

5. **Click in the Search online help text box, type Delete, then press [Enter]**
   The Word Help window now displays a list of links to topics about different types of deletions that are possible within Word.

6. **Click the Keep Help on Top button [📌] in the upper-right corner (below the Close button)**
   The Pin Help button rotates so the pin point is pointed towards the bottom of the screen: this allows you to read the Help window while you work on your document.

7. **Click the Word document window, then notice the Help window remains visible**

8. **Click a blank area of the Help window, click [📌] to Unpin Help, click the Close button [✕] in the Help window, then click the Close button [✕] in the upper-right corner of the screen**
   Word closes, and the Excel program window is active.

9. **Click the Close button [✕] to exit Excel, click the Close button [✕] to exit the remaining Excel workbook, click the PowerPoint program button [📰] on the taskbar if necessary, then click the Close button [✕] to exit PowerPoint**
   Excel and PowerPoint both close.

FIGURE A-15: Word Help window

FIGURE A-16: Create a document Help topic

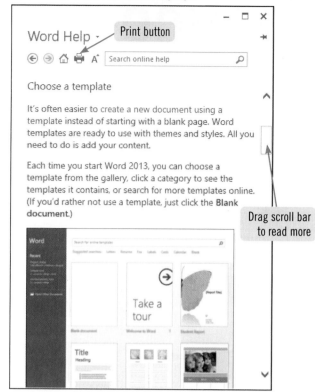

Enabling touch mode

If you are using a touch screen with any of the Office 2013 apps, you can enable the touch mode to give the user interface a more spacious look. Enable touch mode by clicking the Quick Access toolbar list arrow, then clicking Touch/Mouse Mode to select it. Then you'll see the Touch Mode button in the Quick Access toolbar. Click , and you'll see the interface spread out.

Recovering a document

Each Office program has a built-in recovery feature that allows you to open and save files that were open at the time of an interruption such as a power failure. When you restart the program(s) after an interruption, the Document Recovery task pane opens on the left side of your screen displaying both original and recovered versions of the files that were open. If you're not sure which file to open (original or recovered), it's usually better to open the recovered file because it will contain the latest information. You can, however, open and review all versions of the file that were recovered and save the best one. Each file listed in the Document Recovery task pane displays a list arrow with options that allow you to open the file, save it as is, delete it, or show repairs made to it during recovery.

Practice

Concepts Review

Label the elements of the program window shown in FIGURE A-17.

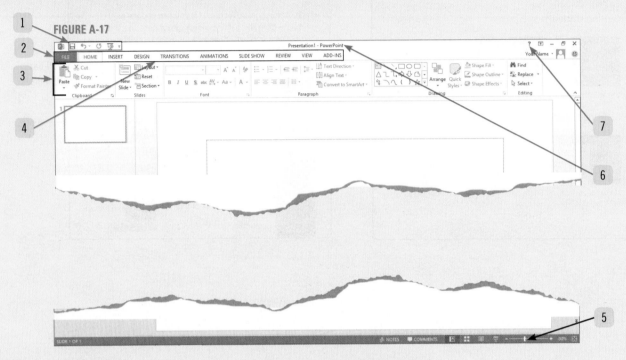

FIGURE A-17

Match each project with the program for which it is best suited.

8. Microsoft Access   a. Corporate convention budget with expense projections
9. Microsoft Excel   b. Presentation for city council meeting
10. Microsoft Word   c. Business cover letter for a job application
11. Microsoft PowerPoint   d. Department store inventory

Independent Challenge 1

You just accepted an administrative position with a local independently owned produce vendor that has recently invested in computers and is now considering purchasing Microsoft Office for the company. You are asked to propose ways Office might help the business. You produce your document in Word.

    a. Start Word, create a new Blank document, then save the document as **OF A-Microsoft Office Document** in the location where you store your Data Files.

    b. Change the zoom factor to 120%, type **Microsoft Word**, press [Enter] twice, type **Microsoft Excel**, press [Enter] twice, type **Microsoft PowerPoint**, press [Enter] twice, type **Microsoft Access**, press [Enter] twice, then type your name.

    c. Click the line beneath each program name, type at least two tasks you can perform using that program (each separated by a comma), then press [Enter].

    d. Save the document, then submit your work to your instructor as directed.

    e. Exit Word.

Creating a Presentation in PowerPoint 2013

Define Presentation Software

Presentation software (also called presentation graphics software) is a computer program you use to organize and present information to others. Presentations are typically in the form of a slide show. Whether you are explaining a new product or moderating a meeting, presentation software can help you effectively communicate your ideas. You can use PowerPoint to create informational slides that you display, speaker notes for the presenter, and handouts for the audience. **CASE** *You need to start working on the Canadian train tours presentation. Because you are only somewhat familiar with PowerPoint, you get to work exploring its capabilities.* FIGURE A-1 *shows how a presentation looks printed as handouts.* FIGURE A-2 *shows how the same presentation might look printed as notes for a speaker.*

DETAILS

You can easily complete the following tasks using PowerPoint:

• **Enter and edit text easily**

  Text editing and formatting commands in PowerPoint are organized by the task you are performing at the time, so you can enter, edit, and format text information simply and efficiently to produce the best results in the least amount of time.

• **Change the appearance of information**

  PowerPoint has many effects that can transform the way text, graphics, and slides appear. By exploring some of these capabilities, you discover how easy it is to change the appearance of your presentation.

• **Organize and arrange information**

  Once you start using PowerPoint, you won't have to spend much time making sure your information is correct and in the right order. With PowerPoint, you can quickly and easily rearrange and modify text, graphics, and slides in your presentation.

• **Include information from other sources**

  Often, when you create presentations, you use information from a variety of sources. With PowerPoint, you can import text, photographs, numerical data, and facts from files created in programs such as Adobe Photoshop, Microsoft Word, Microsoft Excel, and Microsoft Access. You can also import information from other PowerPoint presentations as well as graphic images from a variety of sources such as the Internet, other computers, a digital camera, or other graphics programs. Always be sure you have permission to use any work that you did not create yourself.

• **Present information in a variety of ways**

  With PowerPoint, you can present information using a variety of methods. For example, you can print handout pages or an outline of your presentation for audience members. You can display your presentation as an on-screen slide show using your computer, or if you are presenting to a large group, you can use a video projector and a large screen. If you want to reach an even wider audience, you can broadcast the presentation over the Internet so people anywhere in the world can use a Web browser to view your presentation.

• **Collaborate with others on a presentation**

  PowerPoint makes it easy to collaborate or share a presentation with colleagues and coworkers using the Internet. You can use your email program to send a presentation as an attachment to a colleague for feedback. If you have a number of people that need to work together on a presentation, you can save the presentation to a shared workspace such as a network drive or SkyDrive so authorized users in your group with an Internet connection can access the presentation.

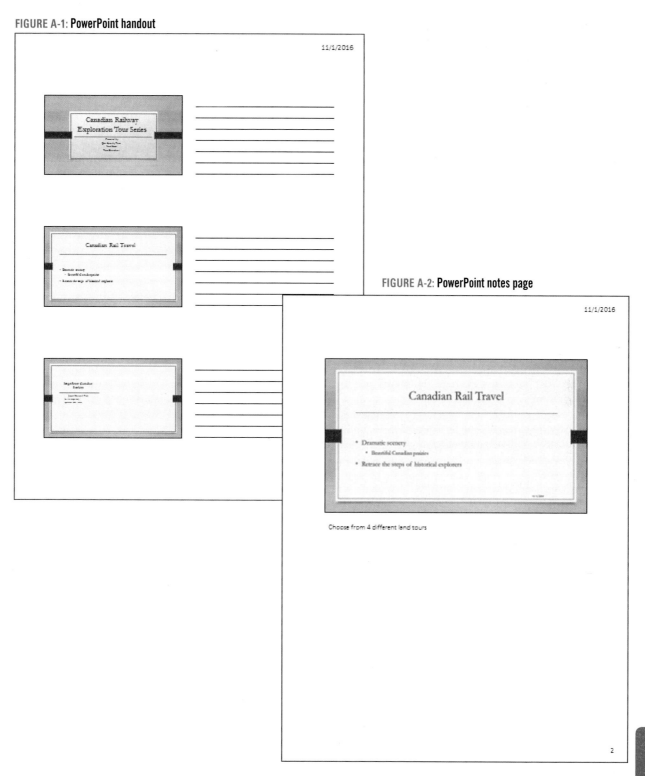

FIGURE A-1: PowerPoint handout

FIGURE A-2: PowerPoint notes page

Using PowerPoint on a touch screen

You can use PowerPoint 2013 on a Windows 8 computer with a touch-enabled monitor or any other compatible touch screen, such as a tablet computer. Using your fingers, you can use typical touch gestures to create, modify and navigate presentations. To enable touch mode capabilities in PowerPoint, you need to add the Touch Mode button to the Quick Access toolbar. Click the Customize Quick Access Toolbar button, click Touch/Mouse Mode, click the Touch/Mouse Mode button on the Quick Access toolbar then click Touch. In Touch mode, additional space is added around all of the buttons and icons in the Ribbon and the status bar to make them easier to touch. Common gestures that you can use in PowerPoint include double-tapping text to edit it and tapping a slide then dragging it to rearrange it in the presentation.

Plan an Effective Presentation

Before you create a presentation, you need to have a general idea of the information you want to communicate. PowerPoint is a powerful and flexible program that gives you the ability to start a presentation simply by entering the text of your message. If you have a specific design in mind that you want to use, you can start the presentation by working on the design. In most cases you'll probably enter the text of your presentation into PowerPoint first and then tailor the design to the message and audience. When preparing your presentation, you need to keep in mind not only who you are giving it to, but also how you are presenting it. For example, if you are giving a presentation using a projector, you need to know what other equipment you will need, such as a sound system and a projector. **CASE** *Use the planning guidelines below to help plan an effective presentation.* FIGURE A-3 *illustrates a storyboard for a well-planned presentation.*

DETAILS

In planning a presentation, it is important to:

- **Determine and outline the message you want to communicate**

  The more time you take developing the message and outline of your presentation, the better your presentation will be in the end. A presentation with a clear message that reads like a story and is illustrated with appropriate visual aids will have the greatest impact on your audience. Start the presentation by giving a general description of Canadian train travel and the types of tours offered by Quest Specialty Travel. See FIGURE A-3.

- **Identify your audience and where and how you are giving the presentation**

  Audience and delivery location are major factors in the type of presentation you create. For example, a presentation you develop for a staff meeting that is held in a conference room would not necessarily need to be as sophisticated or detailed as a presentation that you develop for a large audience held in an auditorium. Room lighting, natural light, screen position, and room layout all affect how the audience responds to your presentation. You might also broadcast your presentation over the Internet to several people who view the presentation on their computers in real time. This presentation will be delivered in a small auditorium to QST's management and sales team.

- **Determine the type of output**

  Output choices for a presentation include black-and-white or color handouts, on-screen slide show, or an online broadcast. Consider the time demands and computer equipment availability as you decide which output types to produce. Because you are speaking in a small auditorium to a large group and have access to a computer and projection equipment, you decide that an on-screen slide show is the best output choice for your presentation.

- **Determine the design**

  Visual appeal, graphics, and presentation design work to communicate your message. You can choose one of the professionally designed themes that come with PowerPoint, modify one of these themes, or create one of your own. You decide to choose one of PowerPoint's design themes to convey the new tour information.

- **Decide what additional materials will be useful in the presentation**

  You need to prepare not only the slides themselves but also supplementary materials, including speaker notes and handouts for the audience. You use speaker notes to help remember key details, and you pass out handouts for the audience to use as a reference during the presentation.

FIGURE A-3: Storyboard of the presentation

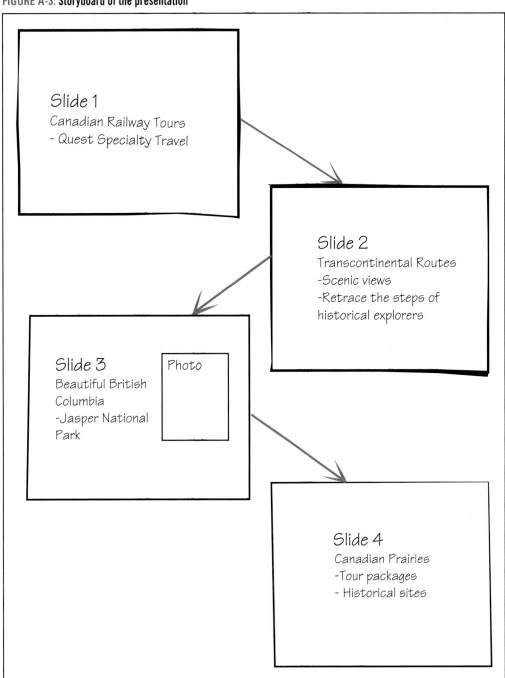

Understanding copyright

Intellectual property is any idea or creation of the human mind. Copyright law is a type of intellectual property law that protects works of authorship, including books, Web pages, computer games, music, artwork, and photographs. Copyright protects the expression of an idea, but not the underlying facts or concepts. In other words, the general subject matter is not protected, but how you express it is, such as when several people photograph the same sunset. Copyright attaches to any original work of authorship as soon as it is created, you do not have to register it with the Copyright Office or display the copyright symbol, ©. Fair use is an exception to copyright and permits the public to use copyrighted material for certain purposes without obtaining prior consent from the owner. Determining whether fair use applies to a work depends on its purpose, the nature of the work, how much of the work you want to copy, and the effect on the work's value. Unauthorized use of protected work (such as downloading a photo or a song from the Web) is known as copyright infringement and can lead to legal action.

Examine the PowerPoint Window

When you first start PowerPoint, you have the ability to choose what kind of presentation you want to use to start—a blank one, or one with a preformatted design. You can also open and work on an existing presentation. PowerPoint has different **views** that allow you to see your presentation in different forms. By default, the PowerPoint window opens in **Normal view**, which is the primary view that you use to write, edit, and design your presentation. Normal view is divided into two areas called **panes**: the pane on the left, called the Thumbnails pane, displays the slides of your presentation as small images, called **slide thumbnails**. The large pane is the Slide pane where you do most of your work on the slide. **CASE** *The PowerPoint window and the specific parts of Normal view are described below.*

STEPS

1. **Start** PowerPoint 2013

   PowerPoint starts and the PowerPoint start screen opens, as shown in **FIGURE A-4**.

2. **Click the** Blank Presentation slide thumbnail

   The PowerPoint window opens in Normal view as shown in **FIGURE A-5**.

DETAILS

Using Figure A-5 as a guide, examine the elements of the PowerPoint window, then find and compare the elements described below:

• The **Ribbon** is a wide band spanning the top of the PowerPoint window that organizes all of PowerPoint's primary commands. Each set of primary commands is identified by a **tab**; for example, the HOME tab is selected by default, as shown in **FIGURE A-5**. Commands are further arranged into **groups** on the Ribbon based on their function. So, for example, text formatting commands such as Bold, Underline, and Italic are located on the HOME tab, in the Font group.

• The **Thumbnails pane**. You can quickly navigate through the slides in your presentation by clicking the slide thumbnails on this pane. You can also add, delete, or rearrange slides using this pane.

• The **Slide pane** displays the current slide in your presentation.

• The **Quick Access toolbar** provides access to common commands such as Save, Undo, Redo, and Start From Beginning. The Quick Access toolbar is always visible no matter which Ribbon tab you select. This toolbar is fully customizable. Click the Customize Quick Access Toolbar button to add or remove buttons.

• The **View Shortcuts** buttons on the status bar allow you to switch quickly between PowerPoint views.

• The **Notes button** on the status bar allows you to open the Notes pane. The Notes pane is used to type text that references a slide's content. You can print these notes and refer to them when you make a presentation or print them as handouts and give them to your audience. The Notes pane is not visible to the audience when you show a slide presentation in Slide Show view.

• The **Comments button** on the status bar allows you to open the Comments pane. In the Comments pane you can create, edit, select, and delete comments.

• The **status bar**, located at the bottom of the PowerPoint window, shows messages about what you are doing and seeing in PowerPoint, including which slide you are viewing and the total number of slides. In addition, the status bar displays the Zoom slider controls, the Fit slide to current window button ⊞, and information on other functionality such as the presentation theme name, signatures and permissions.

• The **Zoom slider** is in the lower-right corner of the status bar and is used to zoom the slide in and out quickly.

FIGURE A-4: PowerPoint start screen

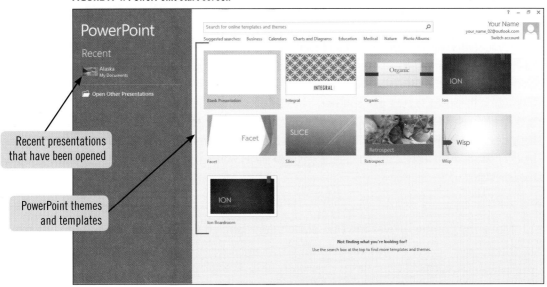

Recent presentations that have been opened

PowerPoint themes and templates

FIGURE A-5: PowerPoint window in Normal view

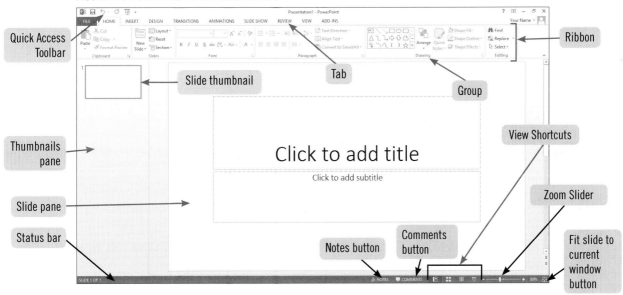

Quick Access Toolbar

Slide thumbnail

Tab

Group

Ribbon

Thumbnails pane

View Shortcuts

Slide pane

Zoom Slider

Status bar

Notes button

Comments button

Fit slide to current window button

Viewing your presentation in gray scale or black and white

Viewing your presentation in gray scale (using shades of gray) or pure black and white is very useful when you are printing a presentation on a black-and-white printer and you want to make sure your presentation prints correctly. To see how your color presentation looks in gray scale or black and white, click the VIEW tab, then click either the Grayscale or Black and White button in the Color/Grayscale group. Depending on which button you select, the Grayscale or the Black and White tab appears, and the Ribbon displays different settings that you can customize. If you don't like the way an individual object looks in black and white or gray scale, you can change its color. Click the object while still in Grayscale or Black and White view, then choose an option in the Change Selected Object group on the Ribbon.

Enter Slide Text

Learning
Outcomes
• Enter slide text
• Change slide text

When you start a blank PowerPoint presentation, an empty title slide appears in Normal view. The title slide has two **text placeholders**—boxes with dotted borders—where you enter text. The top text placeholder on the title slide is the **title placeholder**, labeled "Click to add title". The bottom text placeholder on the title slide is the **subtitle text placeholder**, labeled "Click to add subtitle". To enter text in a placeholder, click the placeholder and then type your text. After you enter text in a placeholder, the placeholder becomes a text object. An **object** is any item on a slide that can be modified. Objects are the building blocks that make up a presentation slide. **CASE** ▶ *Begin working on your presentation by entering text on the title slide.*

STEPS

1. **Move the pointer ⍾ over the title placeholder labeled** Click to add title **in the Slide pane**

   The pointer changes to I when you move the pointer over the placeholder. In PowerPoint, the pointer often changes shape, depending on the task you are trying to accomplish.

2. **Click the** title placeholder **in the Slide pane**

   The **insertion point**, a blinking vertical line, indicates where your text appears when you type in the placeholder. A **selection box** with a dashed line border and **sizing handles** appears around the placeholder, indicating that it is selected and ready to accept text. When a placeholder or object is selected, you can change its shape or size by dragging one of the sizing handles. See **FIGURE A-6**.

3. **Type** Canadian Railway Exploration Tour Series

   PowerPoint wraps the text to a second line and then center-aligns the title text within the title placeholder, which is now a text object. Notice the text also appears on the slide thumbnail on the Thumbnails pane.

4. **Click the** subtitle text placeholder **in the Slide pane**

   The subtitle text placeholder is ready to accept text.

5. **Type** Presented by, **then press** [Enter]

   The insertion point moves to the next line in the text object.

6. **Type** Quest Specialty Tours, **press** [Enter], **type** Adventure Tour Series, **press** [Enter], **type your name, press** [Enter], **then type** Tour Consultant

   Notice the AutoFit Options button ⊞ appears near the text object. The AutoFit Options button on your screen indicates that PowerPoint has automatically decreased the font size of all the text in the text object so it fits inside the text object.

7. **Click the** AutoFit Options button ⊞, **then click** Stop Fitting Text to This Placeholder **on the shortcut menu**

   The text in the text object changes back to its original size and no longer fits inside the text object.

8. **In the subtitle text object, position** I **to the right of** Series, **drag left to select the entire line of text, press** [Backspace], **then click outside the text object in a blank area of the slide**

   The Adventure Tour Series line of text is deleted and the AutoFit Options button menu closes, as shown in **FIGURE A-7**. Clicking a blank area of the slide deselects all selected objects on the slide.

9. **Click the** Save button 🖫 **on the Quick Access toolbar to open Backstage view, then save the presentation as** PPT A-QST **in the location where you store your Data Files**

   In Backstage view, you have the option of saving your presentation to your computer or SkyDrive. Notice that PowerPoint automatically entered the title of the presentation as the filename in the Save As dialog box.

FIGURE A-6: Title text placeholder ready to accept text

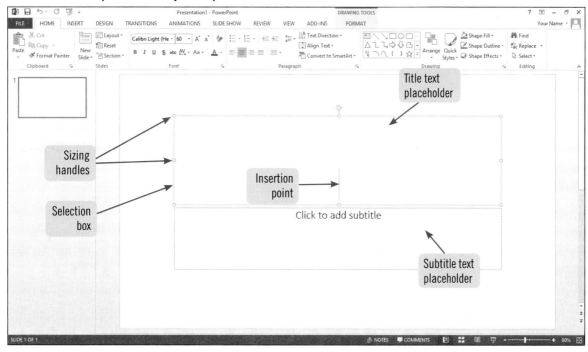

FIGURE A-7: Text on title slide

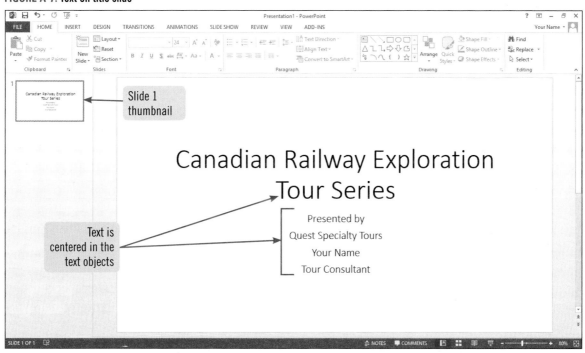

Saving fonts with your presentation

When you create a presentation, it uses the fonts that are installed on your computer. If you need to open the presentation on another computer, the fonts might look different if that computer has a different set of fonts. To preserve the look of your presentation on any computer, you can save, or embed, the fonts in your presentation. Click the FILE tab, then click Options. The PowerPoint Options dialog box opens. Click Save in the left pane, then click the Embed fonts in the file check box. Click the Embed all characters option button, then click OK to close the dialog box. Click Save on the Quick Access toolbar. Now the presentation looks the same on any computer that opens it. Using this option, however, significantly increases the size of your presentation, so only use it when necessary. You can freely embed any TrueType or OpenType font that comes with Windows. You can embed other TrueType fonts only if they have no license restrictions.

Add a New Slide

Learning
Outcomes
• Add a new slide
• Indent text levels
• Modify slide layout

Usually when you add a new slide to a presentation, you have a pretty good idea of what you want the slide to look like. For example, you may want to add a slide that has a title over bulleted text and a picture. To help you add a slide like this quickly and easily, PowerPoint provides nine standard slide layouts. A **slide layout** contains text and object placeholders that are arranged in a specific way on the slide. You have already worked with the Title Slide layout in the previous lesson. In the event that a standard slide layout does not meet your needs, you can modify an existing slide layout or create a new, custom slide layout. **CASE** ➤ *To continue developing the presentation, you create a slide that defines the new tour series.*

STEPS

1. **Click the** New Slide button **in the Slides group on the HOME tab on the Ribbon**

   A new blank slide (now the current slide) appears as the second slide in your presentation, as shown in **FIGURE A-8**. The new slide contains a title placeholder and a content placeholder. A **content placeholder** can be used to insert text or objects such as tables, charts, or pictures. Notice the status bar indicates Slide 2 of 2 and the Thumbnails pane now contains two slide thumbnails.

2. **Type** Canadian Rail Travel, **then click the** bottom content placeholder

   The text you typed appears in the title placeholder, and the insertion point is now at the top of the bottom content placeholder.

3. **Type** Dramatic scenery, **then press** [Enter]

   The insertion point appears directly below the text when you press [Enter], and a new first-level bullet automatically appears.

4. **Press** [Tab]

   The new first-level bullet is indented and becomes a second-level bullet.

QUICK TIP
You can also press [Shift][Tab] to decrease the indent level.

5. **Type** Beautiful Canadian prairies, **press** [Enter], **then click the** Decrease List Level button ⮜☰ **in the Paragraph group**

   The Decrease List Level button changes the second-level bullet into a first-level bullet.

6. **Type** Retrace the steps of historical explorers, **then click the** New Slide list arrow **in the Slides group**

   The Office Theme layout gallery opens. Each slide layout is identified by a descriptive name.

7. **Click the** Content with Caption slide layout, **then type** Magnificent Canadian Rockies

   A new slide with three content placeholders appears as the third slide. The text you typed is the title text for the slide.

8. **Click the lower-left placeholder, type** Jasper National Park, **press** [Enter], **click the** Increase List Level button ☰➤, **type** Visit the Maligne Valley, **press** [Enter], **then type** Spectacular wildlife scenes

   The Increase List Level button moves the insertion point one level to the right. Notice this text placeholder does not use text bullets to identify separate lines of text.

9. **Click a blank area of the slide, then click the** Save button ☐ **on the Quick Access toolbar**

   The Save button saves all of the changes to the file. Compare your screen with **FIGURE A-9**.

FIGURE A-8: New blank slide in Normal view

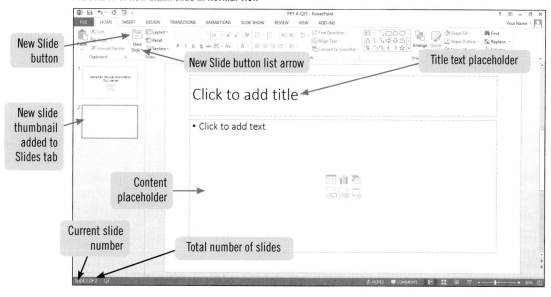

- New Slide button
- New Slide button list arrow
- Title text placeholder
- New slide thumbnail added to Slides tab
- Content placeholder
- Current slide number
- Total number of slides

FIGURE A-9: New slide with Content with Caption slide layout

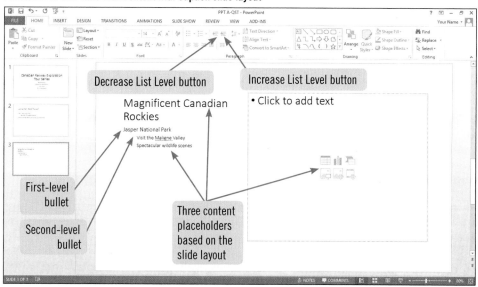

- Decrease List Level button
- Increase List Level button
- First-level bullet
- Second-level bullet
- Three content placeholders based on the slide layout

Entering and printing notes

You can add notes to your slides when there are certain facts you want to remember during a presentation or when there is additional information you want to hand out to your audience. Notes do not appear on the slides when you run a slide show. Use the Notes pane in Normal view or Notes Page view to enter notes for your slides. To open or close the Notes pane, click the Notes button on the status bar. To enter text notes on a slide, click in the Notes pane, then type. If you want to insert graphics as notes, you must use Notes Page view. To open Notes Page view, click the VIEW tab on the Ribbon, then click the Notes Page button in the Presentation Views group. You can print your notes by clicking the FILE tab on the Ribbon to open Backstage view, then clicking Print. Click the Full Page Slides list arrow in the Settings group (this button retains the last setting for what was printed previously so it might differ) to open the gallery, and then click Notes Pages. Once you verify your print settings, click the Print button. If you don't enter any notes in the Notes pane, and print the notes pages, the slides print as large thumbnails with blank space below the thumbnails to hand write notes.

Apply a Design Theme

PowerPoint provides many design themes to help you quickly create a professional and contemporary looking presentation. A **theme** includes a set of 12 coordinated colors for text, fill, line, and shadow, called **theme colors**; a set of fonts for titles and other text, called **theme fonts**; and a set of effects for lines and fills, called **theme effects** to create a cohesive look. Each theme has at least four custom coordinated variants that provides you with additional color options. In most cases, you would apply one theme to an entire presentation; you can, however, apply multiple themes to the same presentation or even a different theme on each presentation slide. You can use a design theme as is, or you can alter individual elements of the theme as needed. Unless you need to use a specific design theme, such as a company theme or product design theme, it is faser and easier to use one of the themes supplied with PowerPoint. If you design a custom theme, you can save it to use in the future. **CASE** ▶ *You decide to change the default design theme in the presentation to a new one.*

STEPS

1. **Click the** Slide 1 thumbnail **on the Thumbnails pane**

   Slide 1, the title slide, appears in the Slide pane.

2. **Click the** DESIGN tab **on the Ribbon, then point to the** Facet theme **in the Themes group as shown in** FIGURE A-10

   The DESIGN tab appears, and a Live Preview of the Facet theme is displayed on the selected slide. A **Live Preview** allows you to see how your changes affect the slides before actually making the change. The Live Preview lasts about 1 minute, and then your slide reverts back to its original state. The first (far left) theme thumbnail identifies the current theme applied to the presentation, in this case, the default design theme called the Office Theme. Depending on your monitor resolution and screen size, you can see between four and 21 design themes in the Themes group.

3. **Slowly move your pointer** ⌖ **over the other design themes, then click the** Themes group down scroll arrow

   A Live Preview of the theme appears on the slide each time you pass your pointer over the theme thumbnails, and a ScreenTip identifies the theme names.

4. **Move** ⌖ **over the** design themes, **then click the** Wisp theme

   The Wisp design theme is applied to all the slides in the presentation. Notice the new slide background color, graphic elements, fonts, and text color. You decide this theme isn't right for this presentation.

5. **Click the** More button ▼ **in the Themes group**

   The Themes gallery window opens. At the top of the gallery window in the This Presentation section is the current theme applied to the presentation. Notice that just the Wisp theme is listed here because when you changed the theme in the last step, you replaced the default theme with the Wisp theme. The Office section identifies all 21 of the standard themes that come with PowerPoint.

6. **Right-click the** Organic theme **in the Office section, then click** Apply to Selected Slides

   The Organic theme is applied only to Slide 1. You like the Organic theme better, and decide to apply it to all slides.

7. **Right-click the** Organic theme **in the Themes group, then click** Apply to All Slides

   The Organic theme is applied to all three slides. Preview the next slides in the presentation to see how it looks.

8. **Click the** Next Slide button ▼ **at the bottom of the vertical scroll bar**

   Compare your screen to FIGURE A-11.

9. **Click the** Previous Slide button ▲ **at the bottom of the vertical scroll bar, then save your changes**

FIGURE A-10: Slide showing a different design theme

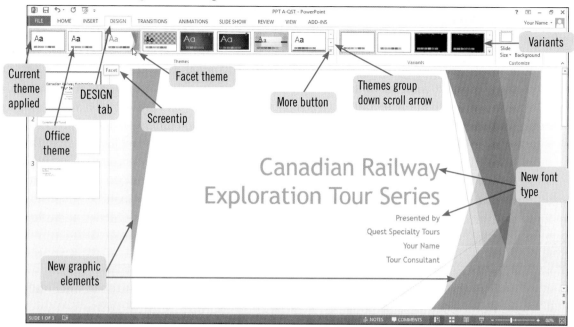

FIGURE A-11: Presentation with Organic theme applied

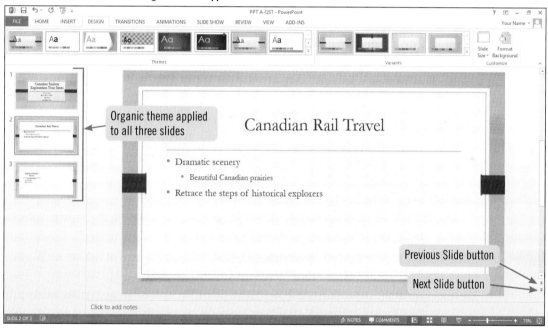

Customizing themes

You are not limited to using the standard themes PowerPoint provides; you can also modify a theme to create your own custom theme. For example, you might want to incorporate your school's or company's colors on the slide background of the presentation or be able to type using fonts your company uses for brand recognition. To change an existing theme, click the VIEW tab on the Ribbon, then click one of the Master buttons in the Master Views group. Click the Theme Colors button, the Theme Fonts button, or the Theme Effects button in the Background group to make changes to the theme, then save this new theme for future use by clicking the Themes button in the Edit Themes group, then click Save Current Theme. You also have the ability to create a new font theme or color theme from scratch by clicking the Theme Fonts button or the Theme Colors button and then clicking Customize Fonts or Customize Colors. You work in the Create New Theme Fonts or Create New Theme Colors dialog box to define the custom theme fonts or colors.

Compare Presentation Views

Learning Outcomes
• Open PowerPoint views

PowerPoint has six primary views: Normal view, Outline view, Slide Sorter view, Notes Page view, Slide Show view, and Reading view. Each PowerPoint view displays your presentation in a different way and is used for different purposes. Normal view is the primary editing view where you add text, graphics, and other elements to the slides. Outline view is the view you use to focus on the text of your presentation. Slide Sorter view is primarily used to rearrange slides; however, you can also add slide effects and design themes in this view. You use Notes Page view to type notes that are important for each slide. Slide Show view displays your presentation over the whole computer screen and is designed to show your presentation to an audience. Similar to Slide Show view, Reading view is designed to view your presentation on a computer screen. To move easily among the PowerPoint views, use the View Shortcuts buttons located on the status bar and the VIEW tab on the Ribbon. **TABLE A-1** provides a brief description of the PowerPoint views. **CASE** ▶ *Examine each of the PowerPoint views, starting with Normal view.*

STEPS

1. **Click the VIEW tab on the Ribbon, then click the Outline View button in the Presentation Views group**

   The presentation text is in the Outline pane on the left side of the window as shown in **FIGURE A-12**. Notice the status bar identifies the number of the slide you are viewing and the total number of slides in the presentation.

2. **Click the small slide icon ☐ next to Slide 2 in the Outline pane, then click the Slide Sorter button ⊞ on the status bar**

   Slide Sorter View opens to display a thumbnail of each slide in the presentation in the window. You can examine the flow of your slides and drag any slide or group of slides to rearrange the order of the slides in the presentation.

3. **Double-click the Slide 1 thumbnail, then click the Reading View button 📖 on the status bar**

   The first slide fills the screen as shown in **FIGURE A-13**. Use Reading view to review your presentation or to show your presentation to someone directly on your computer. The status bar controls at the bottom of the window make it easy to move between slides in this view.

4. **Click the Slide Show button 🖵 on the status bar**

   The first slide fills the entire screen now without the title bar and status bar. In this view, you can practice running through your slides as they would appear in a slide show.

QUICK TIP
You can also press [Enter], [Spacebar], [Page Up], [Page Down], or the arrow keys to advance the slide show.

5. **Click the left mouse button to advance through the slides one at a time until you see a black slide, then click once more to return to Outline view**

   The black slide at the end of the slide show indicates the slide show is finished. At the end of a slide show you automatically return to the slide and PowerPoint view you were in before you ran the slide show, in this case Slide 1 in Outline view.

6. **Click the Notes Page button in the Presentation Views group**

   Notes Page view appears, showing a reduced image of the current slide above a large text placeholder. You can enter text in this placeholder and then print the notes page for your own use.

7. **Click the Normal button in the Presentation Views group, then click the HOME tab on the Ribbon**

FIGURE A-12: Outline view

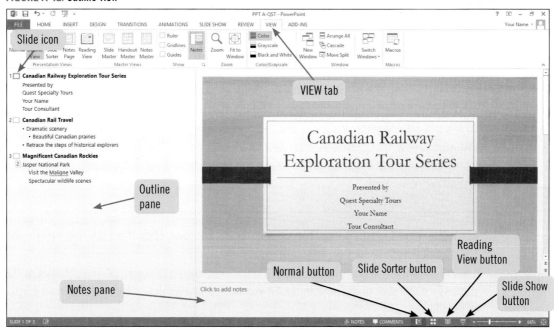

FIGURE A-13: Reading view

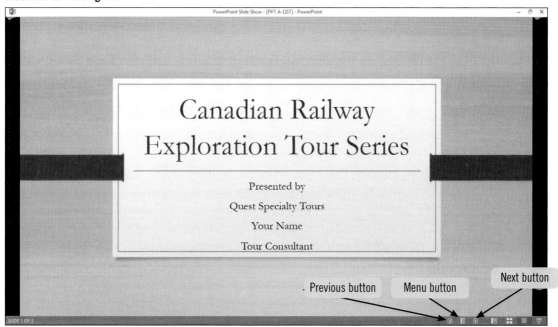

TABLE A-1: PowerPoint views

view name	button	button name	displays
Normal	🖼	Normal	The Slide pane and the thumbnails pane at the same time
Outline View	(no View Shortcuts button)		An outline of the presentation and the Slide pane at the same time
Slide Sorter	▦	Slide Sorter	Thumbnails of all slides
Slide Show	🖵	Slide Show	Your presentation on the whole computer screen
Reading View	📖	Reading View	Your presentation in a large window on your computer screen
Notes Page	(no View Shortcuts button)		A reduced image of the current slide above a large text box

Print a PowerPoint Presentation

You print your presentation when you want to review your work or when you have completed it and want a hard copy. Reviewing your presentation at different stages of development gives you a better perspective of the overall flow and feel of the presentation. You can also preview your presentation to see exactly how each slide looks before you print the presentation. When you are finished working on your presentation, even if it is not yet complete, you can close the presentation file and exit PowerPoint. **CASE** *You are done working on the tour presentation for now. You save and preview the presentation, then you print the slides and notes pages of the presentation so you can review them later. Before leaving for the day, you close the file and exit PowerPoint.*

STEPS

1. **Click the Save button ⊟ on the Quick Access toolbar, click the FILE tab on the Ribbon, then click Print**

   The Print window opens as shown in **FIGURE A-14**. Notice the preview pane on the right side of the window displays the first slide of the presentation. If you do not have a color printer, you will see a grayscale image of the slide.

2. **Click the Next Page button ▷ at the bottom of the Preview pane, then click ▷ again**

   Each slide in the presentation appears in the preview pane.

3. **Click the Print button**

   Each slide in the presentation prints.

4. **Click the FILE tab on the Ribbon, click Print, then click the Full Page Slides button in the Settings group**

   The Print Layout gallery opens. In this gallery you can specify what you want to print (slides, handouts, notes pages, or outline), as well as other print options. To save paper when you are reviewing your slides, you can print in handout format, which lets you print up to nine slides per page. The options you choose in the Print window remain there until you change them or close the presentation.

5. **Click 3 Slides, click the Color button in the Settings group, then click Pure Black and White**

   PowerPoint removes the color and displays the slides as thumbnails next to blank lines as shown in **FIGURE A-15**. Using the Handouts with three slides per page printing option is a great way to print your presentation when you want to provide a way for audience members to take notes. Printing pure black-and-white prints without any gray tones can save printer toner.

6. **Click the Print button**

   The presentation prints one page showing the all the slides of the presentation as thumbnails next to blank lines.

7. **Click the FILE tab on the Ribbon, then click Close**

   If you have made changes to your presentation, a Microsoft PowerPoint alert box opens asking you if you want to save changes you have made to your presentation file.

8. **Click Save, if necessary, to close the alert box**

   Your presentation closes.

9. **Click the Close button ✕ in the Title bar**

   The PowerPoint program closes, and you return to the Windows desktop.

FIGURE A-14: Print window

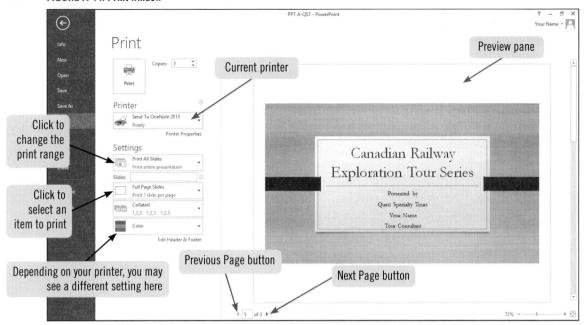

FIGURE A-15: Print window with changed settings

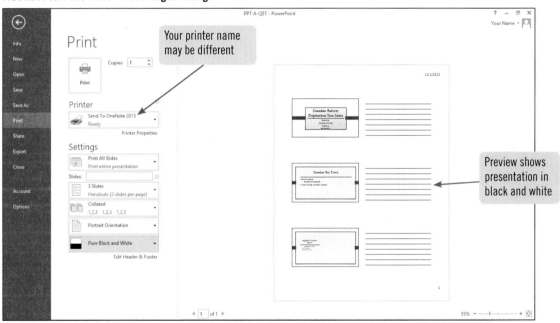

Microsoft Office Web Apps

All Office programs include the capability to incorporate feedback—called online collaboration—across the Internet or a company network. Using **cloud computing** (work done in a virtual environment), you can take advantage of Web programs called Microsoft Office Web Apps, which are simplified versions of the programs found in the Microsoft Office 2013 suite. Because these programs are online, they take up no computer disk space and are accessed using Microsoft SkyDrive, a free service from Microsoft. Using Microsoft SkyDrive, you and your colleagues can create and store documents in the "cloud" and make the documents available to whomever you grant access. To use Microsoft SkyDrive, you need to create a free Microsoft account and establish a Windows Live ID, which you obtain at the Microsoft web site. You can find more information in the "Working in the Cloud" appendix.

Practice

Concepts Review

Label each element of the PowerPoint window shown in FIGURE A-16.

FIGURE A-16

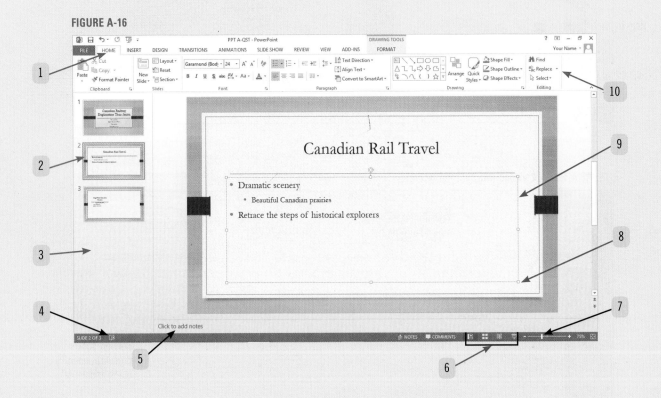

Match each term with the statement that best describes it.

11. **Sizing handle**
12. **Slide Show view**
13. **Theme**
14. **Zoom slider**
15. **Reading view**
16. **Slide Layout**

a. Placeholders arranged in a specific way on the slide
b. Used to change the size of an object
c. A view that is used to review a presentation or to show someone a presentation directly on a computer screen
d. A view that displays a presentation to show to an audience
e. Set of coordinated colors, fonts, and effects
f. Allows you to change the size of the slide in the window

Select the best answer from the list of choices.

17. Which statement about PowerPoint is *not* correct?
- **a.** Graphic images from a digital camera can be inserted into PowerPoint.
- **b.** A presentation can be broadcast over the Internet.
- **c.** You can use PowerPoint to create a database of information.
- **d.** You can import text and numerical data into PowerPoint.

18. Which feature on the status bar allows you to quickly switch between views?
- **a.** Fit slide to current window button
- **b.** Switch view button
- **c.** Zoom Slider
- **d.** View Shortcuts

19. Finish the following sentence: "Copyright attaches to any original work of authorship,...":
- **a.** After you register it with the Copyright Office.
- **b.** As soon as it is created.
- **c.** Under the Fair Use policy.
- **d.** Only when it displays the copyright symbol ©.

20. Other than the Slide pane, where else can you enter slide text?
- **a.** Outline view
- **b.** Slides tab
- **c.** Reading pane
- **d.** Notes Page view

21. According to this unit, what are the building blocks of a presentation?
- **a.** Slides
- **b.** Graphics
- **c.** Placeholders
- **d.** Objects

22. The view that fills the entire screen with each slide in the presentation including the title bar is called:
- **a.** Slide Show view.
- **b.** Fit to window view.
- **c.** Reading view.
- **d.** Normal view.

23. Which of the following is not included in a design theme?
- **a.** Fonts
- **b.** Colors
- **c.** Pictures
- **d.** Normal view

24. What is the function of the slide layout?
- **a.** Puts all your slides in order.
- **b.** Shows you which themes you can apply.
- **c.** Defines how all the elements on a slide are arranged.
- **d.** Enables you to apply a template to the presentation.

Skills Review

1. Examine the PowerPoint window.
- **a.** Start PowerPoint, if necessary then open a new blank presentation.
- **b.** Identify as many elements of the PowerPoint window as you can without referring to the unit material.
- **c.** Be able to describe the purpose or function of each element.
- **d.** For any elements you cannot identify, refer to the unit.

2. Enter slide text.
- **a.** In the Slide pane in Normal view, enter the text **Historic Hendra Stamp Mill & Hotel** in the title placeholder.
- **b.** In the subtitle text placeholder, enter **Nevada Ghost Town Preservation Society**.
- **c.** On the next line of the placeholder, enter your name.
- **d.** Deselect the text object.
- **e.** Save the presentation using the filename **PPT A-Dun Glen** to location where you store your Data Files.

Skills Review (continued)

3. Add a new slide.

  a. Create a new slide.

  b. Using FIGURE A-17, enter text on the slide.

  c. Create another new slide.

  d. Using FIGURE A-18, enter text on the slide.

  e. Save your changes.

4. Apply a design theme.

  a. Click the DESIGN tab.

  b. Click the Themes group More button, then point to all of the themes.

  c. Locate the Slice theme, then apply it to the selected slide.

  d. Select Slide 1.

  e. Locate the Integral theme, then apply it to Slide 1.

  f. Apply the Integral theme to all of the slides in the presentation.

  g. Use the Next Slide button to move to Slide 3, then save your changes.

5. Compare presentation views.

  a. Click the VIEW tab, then click the Outline View button in the Presentation Views group.

  b. Click the Slide Sorter button in the Presentation Views group.

  c. Click the Notes Page button in the Presentation Views group, then click the Previous Slide button twice.

  d. Click the Reading View button in the Presentation Views group, then click the Next button on the status bar.

  e. Click the Normal button on the status bar, then click the Slide Show button.

  f. Advance the slides until a black screen appears, then click to end the presentation.

  g. Save your changes.

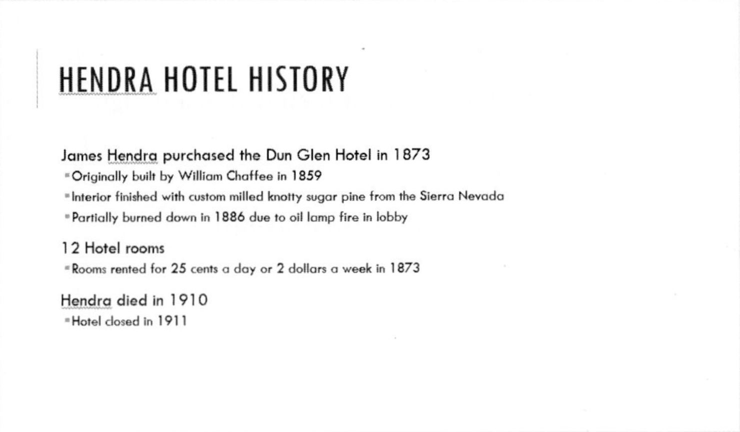

6. Print a PowerPoint presentation.

  a. Print all the slides as handouts, 4 Slides Horizontal, in color.

  b. Print the presentation outline.

  c. Close the file, saving your changes.

  d. Exit PowerPoint.

FIGURE A-17

HISTORIC HENDRA STAMP MILL

Located in Dun Glen, NV

Built in 1866 by James Hendra
- Gold miner and explorer
- Dun Glen NV founding father

Operated from 1866 to 1904

Processed over 1200 tons of material

Removed over $6 million in gold ($143 million today)

FIGURE A-18

HENDRA HOTEL HISTORY

James Hendra purchased the Dun Glen Hotel in 1873
- Originally built by William Chaffee in 1859
- Interior finished with custom milled knotty sugar pine from the Sierra Nevada
- Partially burned down in 1886 due to oil lamp fire in lobby

12 Hotel rooms
- Rooms rented for 25 cents a day or 2 dollars a week in 1873

Hendra died in 1910
- Hotel closed in 1911

Independent Challenge 1

You work for GTO Broadband Industries, a business that offers rural broadband Internet service and network server management. One of your jobs at the company is to present the company's services to local government and community meetings. Your boss has asked you to create a company profile presentation that describes the services GTO offers.

a. Start PowerPoint then open a new blank presentation.

b. In the title placeholder on Slide 1, type **GTO Broadband Industries**.

c. In the subtitle placeholder, type your name, press [Enter], then type today's date.

d. Apply the Slice design theme to the presentation.

e. Save your presentation with the filename **PPT A-Broadband** to the location where you store your Data Files.

f. Use FIGURE A-19 and FIGURE A-20 to add two more slides to your presentation. (*Hint*: Slide 2 uses the Comparison layout.)

g. Use the buttons on the VIEW tab to switch between all of PowerPoint's views.

h. Print the presentation using handouts, 3 Slides, in black and white.

i. Save and close the file, then exit PowerPoint.

FIGURE A-19

FIGURE A-20

PowerPoint 2013

Independent Challenge 2

You have recently been promoted to sales manager at Goodrich Hardwood Industries, which sells and distributes specialty hardwood products used in flooring, cabinets, and furniture. Part of your job is to present company sales figures at a yearly sales meeting. Use the following information as the basis for units of wood sold nationally in your presentation: 425 units cherry, 260 units birch, 146 units hickory, 580 units mahogany, 345 units Brazilian walnut, 230 units American walnut, and 120 units pine. Assume that Goodrich Hardwood has five sales regions throughout the country: West, South, Midwest, Mid Atlantic, and Northeast. Also, assume the sales in each region rose between 1.5% and 4% over last year, and gross sales reached $67 million. The presentation should have at least five slides.

a. Spend some time planning the slides of your presentation. What is the best way to show the information provided? What other information could you add that might be useful for this presentation?

b. Start PowerPoint.

c. Give the presentation an appropriate title on the title slide, and enter today's date and your name in the subtitle placeholder.

d. Add slides and enter appropriate slide text.

e. On the last slide of the presentation, include the following information:

**Goodrich Hardwood Industries
"Your specialty hardwood store"**

f. Apply a design theme. A typical slide might look like the one shown in FIGURE A-21.

g. Switch views. Run through the slide show at least once.

h. Save your presentation with the filename **PPT A-Goodrich** where you store your Data Files.

i. Close the presentation and exit PowerPoint.

FIGURE A-21

TOTAL SALES BY UNIT

580 units – Mahogany
425 units – Cherry
345 units – Brazilian walnut
260 units – Birch
230 units – American walnut
146 units – Hickory
120 units – Pine

Independent Challenge 3

You work for Jamison Corporation, a company in Council Bluffs, Iowa, that is the primary international distributor of products made in Iowa. The marketing manager has asked you to plan and create a PowerPoint presentation that describes the products Iowa exports and the countries that import products made in Iowa. Describe Iowa's top exports, which include tractors, fresh and frozen pork meat, soybeans, corn, and aircraft engine parts. Also include information on top importers of Iowan products: Canada, Mexico, and Japan. Use the Internet, if possible, to research information that will help you formulate your ideas. The presentation should have at least five slides.

a. Spend some time planning the slides of your presentation.

b. Start PowerPoint then open a new blank presentation.

c. Give the presentation an appropriate title on the title slide, and enter today's date and your name in the subtitle placeholder.

d. Add slides and enter appropriate slide text.

e. On the last slide of the presentation, type the following information:

**Jamison Corp.
Council Bluffs, Iowa
*Your Name***

f. Apply a design theme.

g. Switch views. Run through the slide show at least once.

h. Save your presentation with the filename **PPT A-Jamison** to the location where you store your Data Files.

i. Close the presentation and exit PowerPoint.

Independent Challenge 4: Explore

You are a member of the Local Charity Society (LCS), a non-profit organization in Bellingham, Washington. It raises money throughout the year to support community needs such as schools, youth organizations, and other worthy causes. This year LCS has decided to support the Simpson Youth Center by hosting a regional barbeque cook-off, called the Master Pit-master Competition. The competition includes over 20 cooking teams from a five-state region. Create a presentation that describes the event.

a. Spend some time planning the slides of your presentation. Assume the following: the competition is a 2-day event; event advertising will be multistate wide; musical groups will be invited; there will events and games for kids; the event will be held at the county fairgrounds. Use the Internet, if possible, to research information that will help you formulate your ideas.

b. Start PowerPoint then open a new blank presentation.

c. Give the presentation an appropriate title on the title slide, and enter your name and today's date in the subtitle placeholder.

d. Add slides and enter appropriate slide text. You must create at least three slides.

e. Apply a Design Theme. Typical slides might look like the ones shown in FIGURE A-22 and FIGURE A-23.

f. View the presentation.

g. Save your presentation with the filename **PPT A-Pitmaster** to the location where you store your Data Files.

h. Close the presentation and exit PowerPoint.

FIGURE A-22

FIGURE A-23

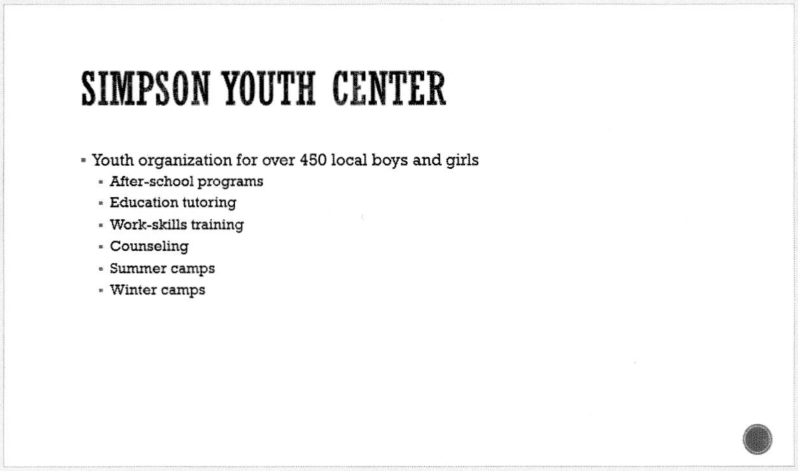

Visual Workshop

Create the presentation shown in FIGURE A-24 and FIGURE A-25. Make sure you include your name on the title slide. Save the presentation as **PPT A-LGS** to the location where you store your Data Files. Print the slides.

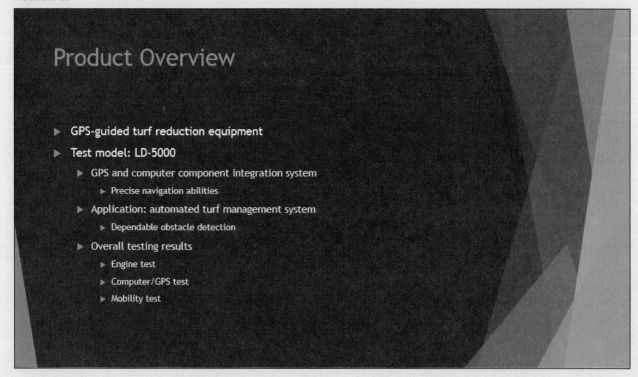

Modifying a Presentation

CASE ▶ You continue working on your Canadian Train tour presentation. In this unit, you'll enter text using Outline view, then you'll format text, create a SmartArt graphic, draw and modify objects, and add slide footer information in the presentation.

Unit Objectives

After completing this unit, you will be able to:

- Enter text in Outline view
- Format text
- Convert text to SmartArt
- Insert and modify shapes
- Rearrange and merge shapes
- Edit and duplicate shapes
- Align and group objects
- Add slide footers

Files You Will Need

PPT B-1.pptx   PPT B-4.pptx
PPT B-2.pptx   PPT B-5.pptx
PPT B-3.pptx

Enter Text in Outline View

Learning Outcomes
- Enter text in Outline view
- Create a new slide

You can enter presentation text by typing directly on the slide in the Slide pane, or, if you need to focus on the text of the presentation, you can enter text in Outline view. Text in Outline view is organized so the headings, or slide titles, appear at the top of the outline. Each subpoint, or each line of bulleted text, appears as one or more indented lines under the title. Each indent in the outline creates another level of bulleted text on the slide. **CASE** *You switch to Outline view to enter text for two more slides for your presentation.*

STEPS

QUICK TIP
To open a PowerPoint 97-2007 presentation in PowerPoint 2013, open the presentation, click the FILE tab, click the Convert button, name the file in the Save As dialog box, then click Save.

1. **Start PowerPoint, open the presentation PPT B-1.pptx from the location where you store your Data Files, then save it as PPT B-QST.pptx**
   A presentation with the new name appears in the PowerPoint window.

2. **Click the Slide 2 thumbnail in the Thumbnails pane, click the New Slide button list arrow in the Slides group, then click Title and Content**
   A new slide, Slide 3, with the Title and Content layout appears as the current slide below Slide 2.

3. **Click the VIEW tab on the Ribbon, then click the Outline View button in the Presentation Views group**
   The text of the presentation appears in the Outline pane next to the Slide pane. The slide icon and the insertion point for Slide 3 are highlighted, indicating it is selected and ready to accept text. Text that you enter next to a slide icon becomes the title for that slide.

4. **Type Atlantic Region Stations, press [Enter], then press [Tab]**
   When you pressed [Enter] after typing the title, you created a new slide. However, because you want to enter bulleted text on Slide 3, you then pressed [Tab] so the text you type will be entered as bullet text on Slide 3. See **FIGURE B-1**.

5. **Type Halifax, press [Enter], type Moncton, press [Enter], type Gaspe, press [Enter], type Sussex, press [Enter], type Amherst, then press [Enter]**
   Each time you press [Enter], the insertion point moves down one line.

6. **Press [Shift][Tab]**
   Because you are working in Outline view, a new slide with the same layout, Slide 4, is created when you press [Shift][Tab].

QUICK TIP
Press [Ctrl][Enter] while the cursor is in the text object to create a new slide with the same layout as the previous slide.

7. **Type Atlantic Region Tour Packages, press [Ctrl][Enter], type Adventure, press [Enter], type Cultural, press [Enter], type Shopping, press [Enter], then type Wildlife**
   Pressing [Ctrl][Enter] while the insertion point is in the title text object moves the cursor into the content placeholder.

8. **Position the pointer on the Slide 3 icon ☐ in the Outline pane**
   The pointer changes to ✛. The Atlantic Region Stations slide, Slide 3, is out of order.

9. **Drag ☐ down until a horizontal indicator line appears above the Slide 5 icon, then release the mouse button**
   The third slide moves down and switches places with the fourth slide as shown in **FIGURE B-2**.

10. **Click the Normal button ▣ on the status bar, then save your work**
    The Outline pane closes, and the Thumbnails pane is now visible in the window.

FIGURE B-1: Outline view showing new slide

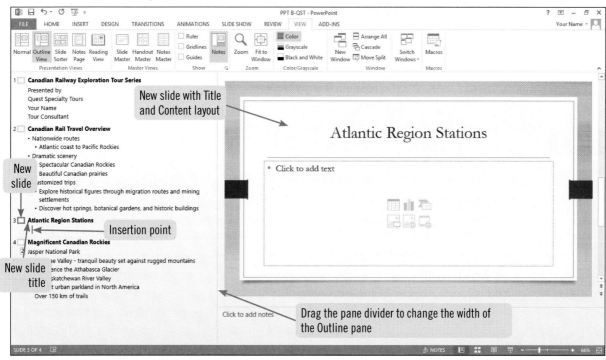

New slide with Title and Content layout

New slide

Insertion point

New slide title

Drag the pane divider to change the width of the Outline pane

FIGURE B-2: Outline view showing moved slide

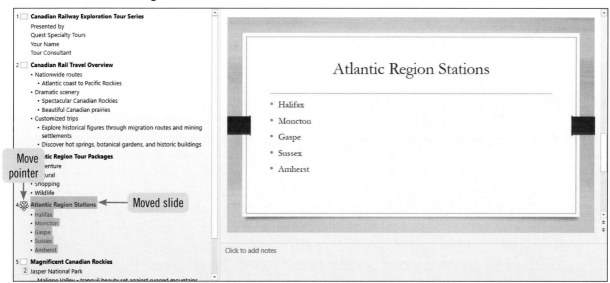

Move pointer

Moved slide

Using proofing tools for other languages

If you have a presentation in another language, how would you check the spelling and grammar of that presentation? Every version of PowerPoint contains a language pack with a primary language, such as English, Italian, or Arabic. Each language pack includes additional languages other than the primary language. For example, the English language pack also includes French and Spanish. So, let's say you have an English version of PowerPoint and you want to check the spelling of a presentation that is written in French. To check the spelling of a French presentation, click a text object on a slide, click the REVIEW tab on the Ribbon, click the Language button in the Language group, then click Set Proofing Language to open the Language dialog box. Click one of the French options from the list, then click OK. Only languages in the list with a spelling symbol are available to use for checking spelling and grammar. Now when you check the spelling, PowerPoint will do so in French. If your version of PowerPoint does not have the language you want to use, you can purchase additional language packs from Microsoft.

Format Text

Once you have entered and edited the text in your presentation, you can modify the way the text looks to emphasize your message. Important text should be highlighted in some way to distinguish it from other text or objects on the slide. For example, if you have two text objects on the same slide, you could draw attention to one text object by changing its color, font, or size. **CASE** *You decide to format the text on Slide 2 of the presentation.*

STEPS

1. **Click the HOME tab on the Ribbon, click the Slide 2 thumbnail in the Thumbnails pane, then double-click Rail in the title text object**

   The word "Rail" is selected, and a Mini toolbar appears above the text. The **Mini toolbar** contains basic text-formatting commands, such as bold and italic, and appears when you select text using the mouse. This toolbar makes it quick and easy to format text, especially when the HOME tab is closed.

2. **Move ⌖ over the Mini toolbar, click the Font Color list arrow 🅰▾, then click the Dark Red color box under Standard Colors**

   The text changes color to dark red as shown in FIGURE B-3. When you click the Font Color list arrow, the Font Color gallery appears showing the Theme Colors and Standard Colors. ScreenTips help identify font colors. Notice that the Font Color button on the Mini toolbar and the Font Color button in the Font group on the HOME tab change color to reflect the new color choice, which is now the active color.

3. **Move the pointer over the title text object border until the pointer changes to ⌖, then click the border**

   The border changes from a dashed to a solid line as you move the pointer over the text object border. The entire title text object is selected, and changes you make now affect all of the text in the text object. When the whole text object is selected, you can change its size, shape, and other attributes. Changing the color of the text helps emphasize it.

4. **Click the Font Color button 🅰 in the Font group**

   All of the text in the title text object changes to the current active color, dark red.

5. **Click the Font list arrow in the Font group**

   A list of available fonts opens with Garamond, the current font used in the title text object, selected at the top of the list in the Theme Fonts section.

6. **Scroll down the alphabetical list, then click Castellar in the All Fonts section**

   The Castellar font replaces the original font in the title text object. Notice that as you move the pointer over the font names in the font list the text on the slide displays a Live Preview of the different font choices.

7. **Click the Underline button 🆄 in the Font group, then click the Increase Font Size button 🅰ᐞ in the Font group**

   All of the text now displays an underline and increases in size to 44.

8. **Click the Character Spacing button ᴬⱽ▾ in the Font group, then click Very Loose**

   The spacing between the letters in the title increases. Compare your screen to FIGURE B-4.

9. **Click a blank area of the slide outside the text object to deselect it, then save your work**

   Clicking a blank area of the slide deselects all objects that are selected.

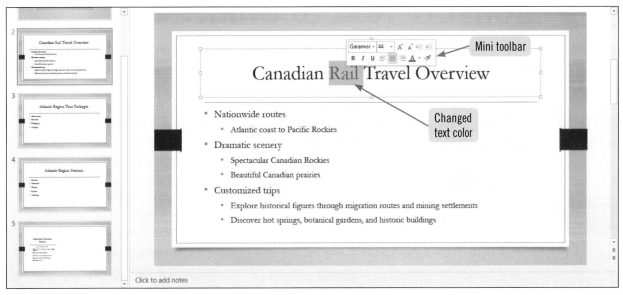

Replacing text and fonts

As you review your presentation, you may decide to replace certain text or fonts throughout the entire presentation using the Replace command. Text can be a word, phrase, or sentence. To replace specific text, click the HOME tab on the Ribbon, then click the Replace button in the Editing group. In the Replace dialog box, enter the text you want to replace, then enter the text you want to use as its replacement. You can also use the Replace command to replace one font for another. Simply click the Replace button list arrow in the Editing group, then click Replace Fonts to open the Replace Font dialog box.

Convert Text to SmartArt

Learning
Outcomes
• Create a SmartArt
graphic
• Modify the
SmartArt design

Sometimes when you are working with text it just doesn't capture your attention, no matter how you dress it up with color or other formatting attributes. The ability to convert text to a SmartArt graphic increases your ability to create dynamic-looking text. A **SmartArt** graphic is a professional-quality diagram that visually illustrates text. There are eight categories, or types, of SmartArt graphics that incorporate graphics to illustrate text differently. For example, you can show steps in a process or timeline, show proportional relationships, or show how parts relate to a whole. You can create a SmartArt graphic from scratch or create one by converting existing text you have entered on a slide with a few simple clicks of the mouse. **CASE** *You want the presentation to appear visually dynamic so you convert the text on Slide 3 to a SmartArt graphic.*

STEPS

1. **Click the Slide 3 thumbnail in the Thumbnails pane, click Adventure in the text object, then click the Convert to SmartArt Graphic button in the Paragraph group**

   A gallery of SmartArt graphic layouts opens. As with many features in PowerPoint, you can preview how your text will look prior to applying the SmartArt graphic layout by using PowerPoint's Live Preview feature. You can review each SmartArt graphic layout and see how it changes the appearance of the text.

2. **Move ⇗ over the SmartArt graphic layouts in the gallery**

   Notice how the text becomes part of the graphic and the color and font changes each time you move the pointer over a different graphic layout. SmartArt graphic names appear in ScreenTips.

TROUBLE
If the Text pane is
not open as shown in
Figure B-5, click the
Text pane control on
the SmartArt graphic.

3. **Click the Vertical Picture Accent List layout in the SmartArt graphics gallery**

   A SmartArt graphic appears on the slide in place of the text object, and a new SMARTART TOOLS DESIGN tab opens on the Ribbon as shown in **FIGURE B-5**. A SmartArt graphic consists of two parts: the SmartArt graphic itself and a Text pane where you type and edit text. This graphic also has placeholders where you can add pictures to the SmartArt graphic.

4. **Click each bullet point in the Text pane, then click the Text pane control button [▷]**

   Notice that each time you select a bullet point in the text pane, a selection box appears around the text objects in the SmartArt graphic. The Text pane control opens and closes the Text pane. You can also open and close the Text pane using the Text Pane button in the Create Graphic group.

QUICK TIP
Text objects in the
SmartArt graphic can
be moved and edited
like any other text
object in PowerPoint.

5. **Click the More button [▼] in the Layouts group, click More Layouts to open the Choose a SmartArt Graphic dialog box, click Relationship, click the Basic Venn layout icon, then click OK**

   The SmartArt graphic changes to the new graphic layout. You can radically change how the SmartArt graphic looks by applying a SmartArt Style. A **SmartArt Style** is a preset combination of simple and 3-D formatting options that follows the presentation theme.

6. **Move ⇗ slowly over the styles in the SmartArt Styles group, then click the More button [▼] in the SmartArt Styles group**

   A Live Preview of each style is displayed on the SmartArt graphic. The SmartArt styles are organized into sections; the top group offers suggestions for the best match for the document, and the bottom group shows you all of the possible 3-D styles that are available.

QUICK TIP
Click the Convert
button in the Reset
group, then click
Convert to Text to
revert the SmartArt
graphic to a standard
text object.

7. **Move ⇗ over the styles in the gallery, then click Cartoon in the 3-D section**

   Notice how this new style adds a black outline and shading to each object to achieve the 3-D effect.

8. **Click a blank area of the slide outside the SmartArt graphic object to deselect it, then save your work**

   Compare your screen to **FIGURE B-6**.

FIGURE B-5: Text converted to a SmartArt graphic

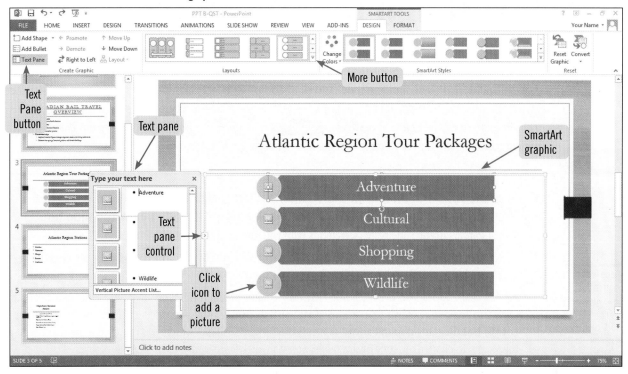

FIGURE B-6: Final SmartArt graphic

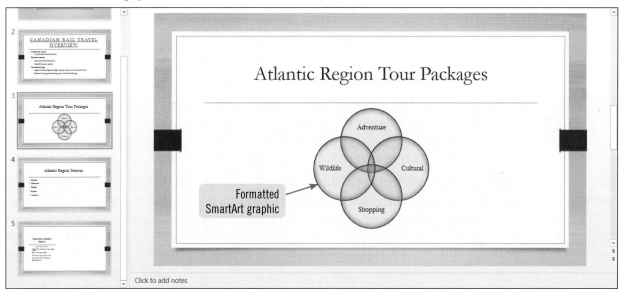

Choosing SmartArt graphics

When choosing a SmartArt graphic to use on your slide, remember that you want the SmartArt graphic to communicate the message of the text effectively; not every SmartArt graphic layout achieves that goal. You must consider the type of text you want to illustrate. For example, does the text show steps in a process, does it show a continual process, or does it show nonsequential information? The answer to this question will dictate the type of SmartArt graphic layout you should choose. Also, the amount of text you want to illustrate will have an effect on the SmartArt graphic layout you choose. Most of the time key points will be the text you use in a SmartArt graphic. Finally, some SmartArt graphic layouts are limited by the number of shapes they can accommodate, so be sure to choose a graphic layout that can illustrate your text appropriately. Experiment with the SmartArt graphic layouts until you find the right one, and have fun in the process!

Insert and Modify Shapes

In PowerPoint you can insert many different types of shapes including lines, geometric figures, arrows, stars, callouts, and banners to enhance your presentation. You can modify many aspects of a shape including its fill color, line color, and line style, as well as add other effects like shadow and 3-D effects. Another way to alter the way a shape looks is to apply a Quick Style. A **Quick Style** is a set of formatting options, including line style, fill color, and effects. **CASE** ▶ *You decide to draw some shapes on Slide 4 of your presentation that identify the Atlantic regional train stations.*

STEPS

1. **Click the** Slide 4 thumbnail **in the Thumbnails pane, click the** Oval button ◯ **in the Drawing group, then position** ✛ **in the blank area of the slide below the slide title**

   Slide 4 appears in the Slide pane. ScreenTips help you identify the shapes.

2. **Press and hold** [Shift]**, drag** ✛ **down and to the right to create the shape, as shown in** FIGURE B-7**, release the mouse button, then release** [Shift]

   A circle shape appears on the slide, filled with the default theme color. Pressing [Shift] while you create the object maintains the object proportions as you change its size, so you create a circle using the oval tool. A **rotate handle**—small round arrow—appears on top of the shape, which you can drag to manually rotate the shape. To change the style of the shape, apply a Quick Style from the Shape Styles group.

3. **Click the** DRAWING TOOLS FORMAT **tab on the Ribbon, click the** More button ▼ **in the Shape Styles group, move** ⬚ **over the styles in the gallery to review the effects on the shape, then click** Subtle Effect - Blue-Grey, Accent 3

   A blue Quick Style with coordinated gradient fill, line, and shadow color is applied to the shape.

4. **Click the** Shape Outline list arrow **in the Shape Styles group, point to** Weight**, move** ⬚ **over the line weight options to review the effect on the shape, then click** 3 pt

   The outline weight (or width) increases and is easier to see now.

5. **Click the** Shape Effects button **in the Shape Styles group, point to** Preset**, move** ⬚ **over the effect options to review the effect on the shape, then click** Preset 3

   Lighting and shadow effects are added to the shape to give it a three-dimensional appearance. You can change the shape to any other shape in the shapes gallery.

6. **Click the** Edit Shape button **in the Insert Shapes group, point to** Change Shape **to open the shapes gallery, then click the** Teardrop button ◯ **in the Basic Shapes section**

   The circle shape changes to a teardrop shape and a new yellow handle—called an **adjustment handle**—appears in the upper-right corner of the shape. Some shapes have an adjustment handle that can be moved to change the most prominent feature of an object, in this case the end of the teardrop. You can rotate the shape to make the shape look different.

7. **Click the** Rotate button **in the Arrange group, move** ⬚ **over the** rotation options **to review the effect on the shape, then click** Flip Vertical

   Notice that the rotate handle is now on the bottom of the shape indicating that the shape has flipped vertically, or rotated 180 degrees, as shown in FIGURE B-8. You prefer the circle shape, and you decide the shape looks better rotated back the way it was before.

8. **Click the** Undo button list arrow ↺ ▾ **in the Quick Access Toolbar, click** Change Shape**, click a blank area of the slide, then save your work**

   The last two commands you performed are undone, and the shape changes back to a circle and is flipped back to its original position. Clicking a blank area of the slide deselects all objects that are selected.

FIGURE B-7: Oval shape added to slide

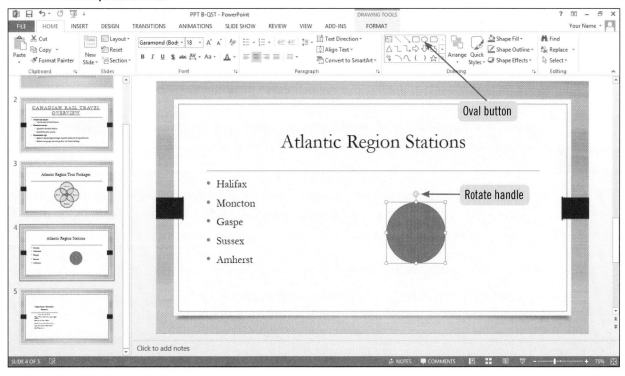

FIGURE B-8: Rotated teardrop shape

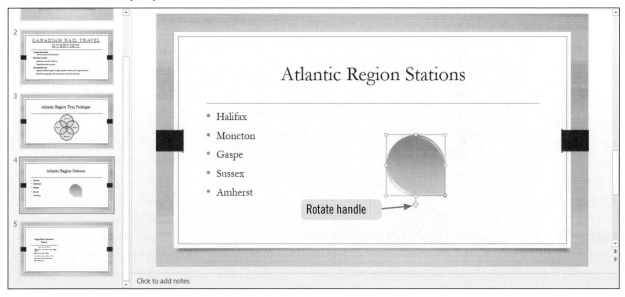

Use the Eyedropper to match colors

As you develop your presentation and work with different shapes and pictures, sometimes from other sources, there may be a certain color that is not in the theme colors of the presentation that you want to capture and apply to objects in your presentation. To capture a color on a specific slide, select any object on the slide, click any button list arrow with a color feature, such as the Shape Fill button or the Shape Outline button on the DRAWING TOOLS FORMAT tab, then click Eyedropper. Move the over the color you want to capture and pause, or hover. As you hover over a color, a Live Preview of the color appears and the RGB (Red Green Blue) values, called coordinates, appear in a ScreenTip. Click when you see the color you want to capture. The new color now appears in any color gallery under Recent Colors. If you decide not to capture a new color, press [Esc] to close the Eyedropper without making any change.

Rearrange and Merge Shapes

Learning
Outcomes
• Reorder shapes
• Combine shapes
  together

Every object on a slide, whether it is a shape, a picture, a text object, or any other object, is placed, or stacked, on the slide in the order it was created, like pieces of paper placed one on top of another. Each object on a slide can be moved up or down in the stack depending how you want the objects to look on the slide. **Merging** shapes, which combines multiple shapes together, provides you the potential to create a variety of unique geometric shapes that are not available in the Shapes gallery. **CASE** *You create a diamond shape on Slide 4 and then merge it with the circle shape.*

STEPS

1. **Click Gaspe in the text object, position ⬚ over the right-middle sizing handle, ⬚ changes to ⬅➡, then drag the sizing handle to the left until the right border of the text object is under the first word in the title text object**

   The width of the text object decreases. When you position ⬚ over a sizing handle, it changes to ⬅➡. This pointer points in different directions depending on which sizing handle it is over.

2. **Click the More button ▼ in the Drawing group, click the Diamond button ◇ in the Basic Shapes section, then drag down and to the right to create the shape**

   Compare your screen to FIGURE B-9. A diamond shape appears on the slide, filled with the default theme color. You can move shapes by dragging them on the slide.

TROUBLE
If Smart Guides do not appear, right-click a blank area of the slide, point to Grid and Guides, then click Smart Guides.

3. **Drag the diamond shape over the circle shape, then use the Smart Guides that appear to position the diamond shape in the center of the circle shape where the guides intersect**

   Smart Guides, help you position objects relative to each other and determine equal distances between objects.

4. **Click the Select button in the Editing group, click Selection Pane, then click the Send Backward button ▼ in the Selection pane once**

   The Selection pane opens on the right side of the window showing the four objects on the slide and the order they are stacked on the slide. The Send Backward and Bring Forward buttons let you change the stacking order. The diamond shape moves back one position in the stack behind the circle shape.

5. **Press [SHIFT], click the circle shape on the slide, release [SHIFT] to select both shapes, click the DRAWING TOOLS FORMAT tab on the Ribbon, click the Merge Shapes button in the Insert Shapes group, then point to Union**

   The two shapes appear to merge, or combine, together to form one shape. The merged shape assumes the theme and formatting style of the diamond shape because it was selected first.

QUICK TIP
To move an object to the top of the stack, click the Bring Forward arrow, then click Bring to Front. To move an object to the bottom of the stack, click the Send Backward arrow, then click Send to Back.

6. **Move ⬚ over the other merge shapes options to review the effect on the shape, click a blank area of the slide twice, click the diamond shape, then click the Bring Forward list arrow in the Arrange group on the DRAWING TOOLS FORMAT tab once**

   Each merge option produces a different result. The diamond shape moves back to the top of the stack. Now, you want to see what happens when you select the circle shape first before you merge the two shapes together.

7. **Click the circle shape, press [SHIFT], click the diamond shape, click the Merge Shapes button in the Insert Shapes group, then point to Union**

   The merged shape adopts the theme and formatting style of the circle shape.

8. **Point to each of the merge shapes options, then click Subtract**

   The two shapes merge into one shape. This merge option deletes the area of all shapes from the first shape you selected, so in this case the area of the diamond shape is deleted from the circle shape. The merged shape is identified as Freeform 6 in the Selection pane. See FIGURE B-10.

9. **Click the Selection Pane button in the Arrange group, click a blank area of the slide, then save your work**

FIGURE B-9: Diamond shape added to slide

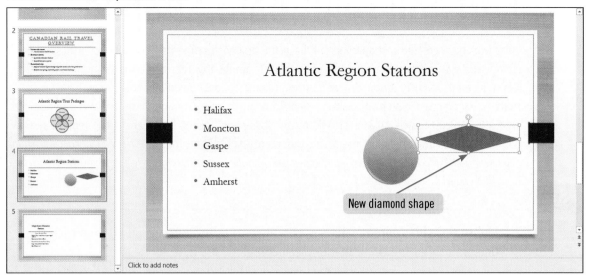

FIGURE B-10: New Merged shape

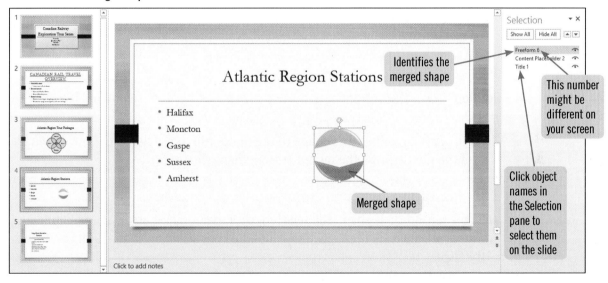

Changing the size and position of shapes

Usually when you resize a shape you can simply drag one of the sizing handles around the outside of the shape, but sometimes you may need to resize a shape more precisely. When you select a shape, the DRAWING TOOLS FORMAT tab appears on the Ribbon, offering you many different formatting options including some sizing commands located in the Size group.

The Width and Height commands in the Size group allow you to change the width and height of a shape. You also have the option to open the Format Shape pane, which allows you to change the size of a shape, as well as the rotation, scale, and position of a shape on the slide.

Edit and Duplicate Shapes

Once you have created a shape you still have the ability to refine its basic characteristics, which helps change the size and appearance of the shape. For example, if you create a shape and it is too large, you can reduce its size by dragging any of its sizing handles. Most PowerPoint shapes can have text attached to them. All shapes can be moved and copied. To help you resize and move shapes and other objects precisely, PowerPoint has rulers you can add to the Slide pane. Rulers display the measurement system your computer uses, either inches or metric measurements. **CASE** ▶ *You want three identical circle shapes on Slide 4. You first add the ruler to the slide to help you change the size of the circle shape you've already created, and then you make copies of it.*

STEPS

1. **Right-click a blank area of Slide 4, click Ruler on the shortcut menu, then click the bottom part of the circle shape to select it**

   Rulers appear on the left and top of the Slide pane. Unless the ruler has been changed to metric measurements, it is divided into inches and half-inch and eighth-inch marks. Notice the current location of the ▷ is identified on both rulers by a small dotted red line in the ruler.

2. **Press [Shift], drag the lower-right sizing handle on the circle shape up and to the left approximately 1/4", release the mouse button, then release [Shift]**

   The distance of a quarter-inch on the ruler is the distance between two lines. The circle shape is now slightly smaller in diameter.

3. **Position ▷ over the selected circle shape so it changes to ⁺↖, then drag the circle shape to the Smart Guides on the slide as shown in FIGURE B-11**

   PowerPoint uses a series of evenly spaced horizontal and vertical lines—called **gridlines**—to align objects, which force objects to "snap" to the grid.

4. **Position ⁺↖ over the bottom part of the circle shape, then press and hold [Ctrl]**

   The pointer changes to ↖₊, indicating that PowerPoint makes a copy of the shape when you drag the mouse.

5. **Holding [Ctrl], drag the circle shape to the right until the circle shape copy is in a blank area of the slide, release the mouse button, then release [Ctrl]**

   An identical copy of the circle shape appears on the slide and Smart Guides appear above and below the shape as you drag the new shape to the right, which helps you align the shapes.

6. **With the second circle shape still selected, click the Copy list arrow in the Clipboard group, click Duplicate, then move the duplicated circle shape to the right in a blank area of the slide**

   You have duplicated the circle shape twice and now have three shapes on the slide.

7. **Click the VIEW tab on the Ribbon, click the Ruler check box in the Show group, click the HOME tab, then type Excursions**

   The ruler closes, and the text you type appears in the selected circle shape and becomes a part of the shape. Now if you move or rotate the shape, the text moves with it. Compare your screen with FIGURE B-12.

8. **Click the middle circle shape, type Getaways, click the left circle shape, type Holidays, click in a blank area of the slide, then save your work**

   All three circle shapes include text.

FIGURE B-11: Merged shape moved on slide

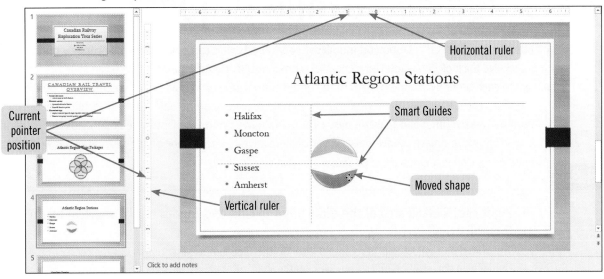

FIGURE B-12: Duplicated shapes

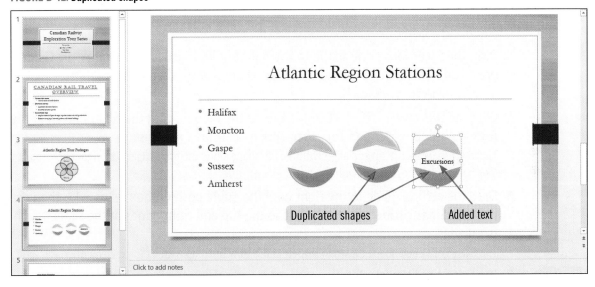

Editing points of a shape

If you want to customize the form (or outline) of any shape in the shapes gallery, you can modify its edit points. To display a shape's edit points, select the shape you want to modify, click the DRAWING TOOLS FORMAT tab on the Ribbon, click the Edit Shape button in the Insert Shapes group, then click Edit Points. Black edit points appear on the shape. To change the form of a shape, drag a black edit point. When you click a black edit point white square edit points appear on either side of the black edit point, which allow you to change the curvature of a line between two black edit points. When you are finished with your custom shape, you can save it as picture and reuse it in other presentations or other files. To save the shape as a picture, right-click the shape, then click Save as Picture.

Align and Group Objects

Learning Outcomes
- Move shapes using guides
- Align and group shapes
- Distribute shapes

After you are finished creating and modifying your objects, you can position them accurately on the slide to achieve the look you want. Using the Align commands in the Arrange group, you can align objects relative to each other by snapping them to the gridlines on a slide or to guides that you manually position on the slide. The Group command groups two or more objects into one object, which secures their relative position to each other and makes it easy to edit and move them. The Distribute commands on the Align list evenly space objects horizontally or vertically relative to each other or the slide. **CASE** *You are ready to position and group the circle shapes on Slide 4 to finish the slide.*

STEPS

1. **Right-click a blank area of the slide, point to Grid and Guides on the shortcut menu, then click Guides**

   The PowerPoint guides appear as dotted lines on the slide and usually intersect at the center of the slide. Guides help you position objects precisely on the slide.

2. **Position ⟋ over the horizontal guide in a blank area of the slide, notice the pointer change to ÷, press and hold the mouse button until the pointer changes to a measurement guide box, then drag the guide up until the guide position box reads .42**

QUICK TIP
To set the formatting of a shape as the default, right-click the shape, then click Set as Default Shape on the Shortcut menu.

3. **Drag the vertical guide to the left until the guide position box reads 2.92, then drag the Holidays circle shape so the top and left edges of the shape touch the guides as shown in FIGURE B-13**

   The Holidays circle shape attaches or "snaps" to the guides.

4. **Drag the Excursions circle shape to the right until it touches a vertical Smart Guide, press and hold [Shift], click the other two circle shapes, then release [Shift]**

   All three shapes are now selected.

5. **Click the DRAWING TOOLS FORMAT tab on the Ribbon, click the Align button in the Arrange group, click Align Top, then click a blank area of the slide**

   The lower shapes move up and align with the top shape along their top edges. The right circle shape would look better if it were lined up with the line under the title.

6. **Drag the vertical guide to the right until the guide position box reads 5.17, then drag the Excursions circle shape to the left so the top and right edges of the shape touch the guides**

   The Excursions circle shape moves to the left and is now lined up with a design element on the slide.

QUICK TIP
To quickly add a new guide to the slide, press [Ctrl], then drag an existing guide. The original guide remains in place. Drag a guide off the slide to delete it.

7. **Press and hold [Shift], click the other two circle shapes, release [Shift], click the DRAWING TOOLS FORMAT tab, then click the Align button in the Arrange group**

8. **Click Distribute Horizontally, click the Group button in the Arrange group, then click Group**

   The shapes are now distributed equally between themselves and grouped together to form one object without losing their individual attributes, as shown in FIGURE B-14. Notice that the sizing handles and rotate handle now appear on the outer edge of the grouped object, not around each individual object.

9. **Drag the horizontal guide to the middle of the slide until its guide position box reads 0.00, then drag the vertical guide to the middle of the slide until its guide position box reads 0.00**

10. **Click the VIEW tab on the Ribbon, click the Guides check box in the Show group, click a blank area of the slide, then save your work**

    The guides are no longer displayed on the slide

Modifying a Presentation

FIGURE B-13: Repositioned shape

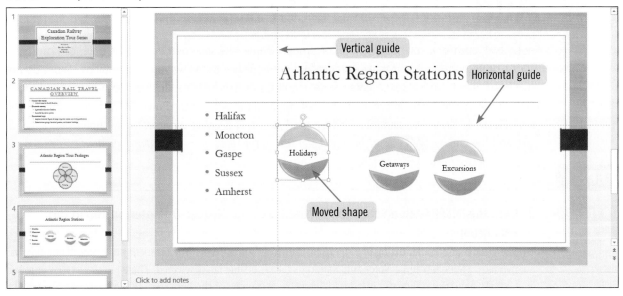

FIGURE B-14: Aligned and grouped shapes

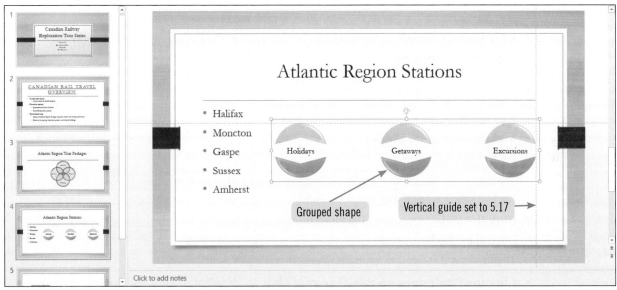

Distributing objects

There are two ways to distribute objects in PowerPoint: relative to each other and relative to the slide edge. If you choose to distribute objects relative to each other, PowerPoint evenly divides the empty space between all of the selected objects. When distributing objects in relation to the slide, PowerPoint evenly splits the empty space from slide edge to slide edge between the selected objects. To distribute objects relative to each other, click the Align button in the Arrange group on the DRAWING TOOLS FORMAT tab, then click Align Selected Objects. To distribute objects relative to the slide, click the Align button in the Arrange group on the DRAWING TOOLS FORMAT tab, then click Align to Slide.

Add Slide Footers

Footer text, such as a company, school, or product name, the slide number, or the date, can give your slides a professional look and make it easier for your audience to follow your presentation. Slides do not have headers but can include a footer; however, notes or handouts can include both header and footer text. You can review footer information that you apply to the slides in the PowerPoint views and when you print the slides. Notes and handouts header and footer text is visible when you print notes pages, handouts, and the outline. **CASE** *You add footer text to the slides of the Canadian train tour presentation to make it easier for the audience to follow.*

STEPS

QUICK TIP
The placement of the footer text objects on the slide is dependent on the presentation theme.

1. **Click the INSERT tab on the Ribbon, then click the Header & Footer button in the Text group**

   The Header and Footer dialog box opens, as shown in **FIGURE B-15**. The Header and Footer dialog box has two tabs: a Slide tab and a Notes and Handouts tab. The Slide tab is selected. There are three types of footer text, Date and time, Slide number, and Footer. The rectangles at the bottom of the Preview box identify the default position and status of the three types of footer text placeholders on the slides.

2. **Click the Date and time check box to select it**

   The date and time options are now available to select. The Update automatically date and time option button is selected by default. This option updates the date and time every time you open or print the file.

QUICK TIP
If you want a specific date to appear every time you view or print the presentation, click the Fixed date option button, then type the date in the Fixed text box.

3. **Click the Update automatically list arrow, then click the second option in the list**

   The day is added to the date, and the month is spelled out.

4. **Click the Slide number check box, click the Footer check box, click the Footer text box, then type your name**

   The Preview box now shows all three footer placeholders are selected.

5. **Click the Don't show on title slide check box**

   Selecting this check box prevents the footer information you entered in the Header and Footer dialog box from appearing on the title slide.

6. **Click Apply to All**

   The dialog box closes, and the footer information is applied to all of the slides in your presentation except the title slide. Compare your screen to **FIGURE B-16**.

7. **Click the Slide 1 thumbnail in the Thumbnails pane, then click the Header & Footer button in the Text group**

   The Header and Footer dialog box opens again.

8. **Click the Don't show on title slide check box to deselect it, click the Footer check box, then select the text in the Footer text box**

TROUBLE
If you click Apply to All in Step 9, click the Undo button on the Quick Access toolbar and repeat Steps 7, 8, and 9.

9. **Type Once in a lifetime travel experiences, click Apply, then save your work**

   Only the text in the Footer text box appears on the title slide. Clicking Apply applies the footer information to just the current slide.

10. **Submit your presentation to your instructor, then exit PowerPoint**

FIGURE B-15: Header and Footer dialog box

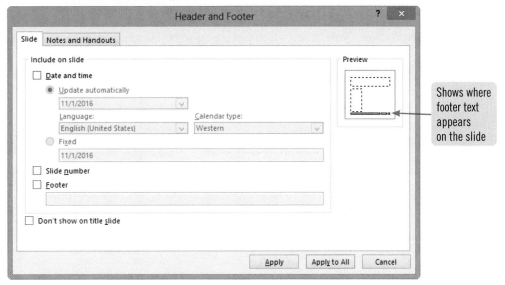

FIGURE B-16: Footer information added to presentation

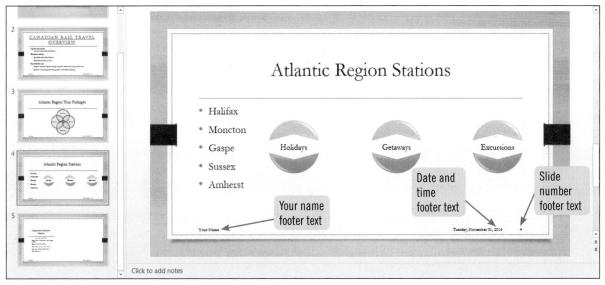

Creating superscript and subscript text

Superscript or subscript text is a number, figure, symbol, or letters that appears smaller than other text and is positioned above or below the normal line of text. A common superscript in the English language is the sign indicator next to number, such as, 1st or 3rd. Other examples of superscripts are the trademark symbol™ and the copyright symbol©. To create superscript text in PowerPoint, select the text, number, or symbol, then press [CTRL] [SHIFT] [+] at the same time. Probably the most familiar subscript text are the numerals in chemical compounds and formulas, for example, H_2O and CO_2. To create subscript text, select the text, number, or symbol, then press [CTRL] [=] at the same time. To change superscript or subscript text back to normal text, select the text, then press [CTRL] [Spacebar].

PowerPoint 2013

Practice

Put your skills into practice with **SAM Projects**! SAM Projects for this unit can be found online. If you have a SAM account, go to www.cengage.com/sam2013 to download the most recent Project Instruction and Start Files.

Concepts Review

Label each element of the PowerPoint window shown in FIGURE B-17.

FIGURE B-17

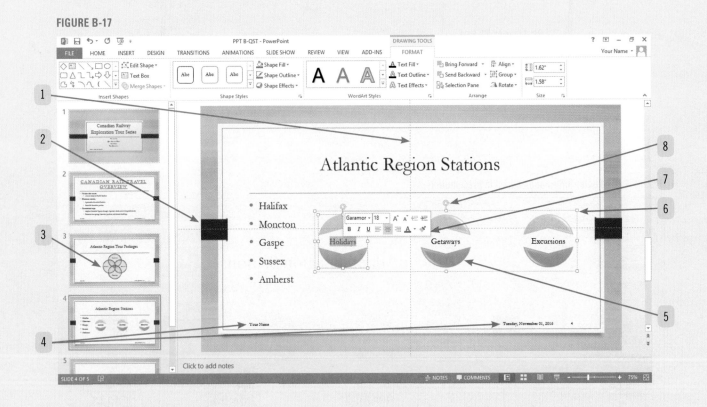

Match each term with the statement that best describes it.

9. **SmartArt graphic**
10. **Merge**
11. **Adjustment handle**
12. **Smart Guides**
13. **Quick Style**
14. **Rotate handle**

a. A diagram that visually illustrates text
b. A preset combination of formatting options you apply to an object
c. Combines multiple shapes together into one shape
d. Yellow handle that changes the most prominent feature of an object
e. Short red dashed lines that appear on the slide
f. Use to drag to turn an object

Select the best answer from the list of choices.

15. What appears just above text when it is selected?

   a. AutoFit Options button   **c.** QuickStyles

   b. Mini toolbar   **d.** Option button

16. Which of the following statements is *not* true about Outline view?

   a. It is organized using headings and subpoints.

   b. Pressing [Enter] moves the insertion point down one line.

   c. Each line of indented text creates a new slide title.

   d. Headings are the same as slide titles.

17. Why would you use the Eyedropper tool?

   a. To save a 3-D effect for future use   **c.** To soften the edges of a shape

   b. To pick up font styles from a text object   **d.** To add a new color to the color gallery

18. Which of the following statements about merged shapes is *not* true?

   a. A merged shape is a combination of multiple shapes.

   b. Merged shapes are unique geometric shapes found in the shapes gallery.

   c. A merged shape assumes the theme of the shape that is selected first.

   d. The stacking order of shapes changes the way a merged shape looks.

19. A professional-quality diagram that visually illustrates text best describes which of the following?

   a. A SmartArt graphic   **c.** A merged shape

   b. A SmartArt Style   **d.** A subscript

20. What do objects snap to when you move them?

   a. Shape edges   **c.** Gridlines

   b. Anchor points   **d.** Slide edges

21. What is *not* true about grouped objects?

   a. Each object is distributed relative to the slide edges.

   b. Grouped objects have one rotate handle.

   c. Grouped objects act as one object but maintain their individual attributes.

   d. Sizing handles appear around the grouped object.

Skills Review

1. Enter text in Outline view.

   a. Open the presentation PPT B-2. pptx from the location where you store your Data Files, then save it as **PPT B-ProPool**. The completed presentation is shown in **FIGURE B-18**.

   b. Create a new slide after Slide 2 with the Title and Content layout.

   c. Open Outline view, then type **Use and Application**.

   d. Press [Enter], press [Tab], type **City water utilities**, press [Enter], type **State water districts**, press [Enter], type **Private water sources**, press [Enter], then type **Commercial pools**.

FIGURE B-18

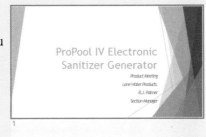

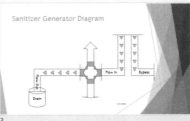

PowerPoint 2013

Skills Review (continued)

   e. Move Slide 3 below Slide 4, then, switch back to Normal view.

   f. Click the HOME tab, then save your changes.

2. Format text.

   a. Go to Slide 1.

   b. Select the name R.J. Palmer, then move the pointer over the Mini toolbar.

   c. Click the Font Color list arrow, then click Red under Standard Colors.

   d. Select the text object, then change all of the text to the color Red.

   e. Click the Font Size list arrow, then click 24.

   f. Click the Italic button.

   g. Click the Character Spacing button, then click Very Tight.

   h. Save your changes.

3. Convert text to SmartArt.

   a. Click the text object on Slide 4.

   b. Click the Convert to SmartArt Graphic button, then apply the Basic Cycle graphic layout to the text object.

   c. Click the More button in the Layouts group, click More Layouts, click Matrix in the Choose a SmartArt Graphic dialog box, click Grid Matrix, then click OK.

   d. Click the More button in the SmartArt Styles group, then apply the Moderate Effect style from the Best Match for Document group to the graphic.

   e. Close the text pane if necessary, then click outside the SmartArt graphic in a blank part of the slide.

   f. Save your changes.

4. Insert and modify shapes.

   a. Go to Slide 3, then add rulers to the Slide pane.

   b. Click the More button in the Drawing group to open the Shapes gallery, click the Plus button in the Equation Shapes section, press [Shift], then draw a two inch shape in a blank area of the slide.

   c. On the DRAWING TOOLS FORMAT tab, click the More button in the Shape Styles group, then click Colored Fill – Green, Accent 6.

   d. Click the Shape Effects button, point to Shadow, then click Offset Diagonal Bottom Right.

   e. Click the Shape Outline list arrow, then click Black, Text 1, Lighter 50% in the Theme Colors section.

   f. Drag the Plus shape to the small open area in the middle of the diagram, adjust the shape if needed to make it fit in the space as shown in **FIGURE B-19**, then save your changes.

FIGURE B-19

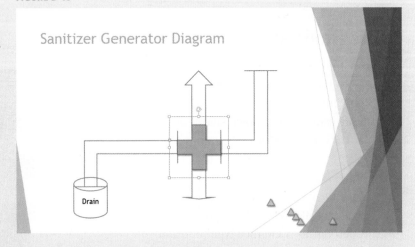

5. Rearrange and merge shapes.

   a. Click the title text object on Slide 3, then drag the bottom-middle sizing handle up to fit the text in the text object.

   b. Click the More button in the Insert Shapes group, click the Hexagon button in the Basic Shapes section, press and hold [Shift], then draw a 1-inch shape.

   c. Drag the hexagon shape over top of the plus shape and center it, then open the Selection pane.

   d. Send the hexagon shape back one level, press [Shift], click the plus shape, then click the Merge Shapes button in the Insert Shapes group on the DRAWING TOOLS FORMAT tab.

e. Point to each of the merge shapes options, click a blank area of the slide twice, then click the plus shape.

f. Send the plus shape back one level, press [Shift], click the hexagon shape, click the Merge Shapes button, then click Combine.

g. Close the Selection pane, then save your work.

6. Edit and duplicate shapes.

a. Select the up-angled shape to the right of the merged shape, then using [Ctrl] make one copy of the shape.

b. Use Smart Guides to align the new up-angled shape just to the right of the original shape.

c. Click the Rotate button in the Arrange group, click Flip Vertical, click the Undo button, click the Rotate button, then click Flip Horizontal.

d. Type **Bypass**, click the up-angled shape to the right of the merged shape, type **Flow In**, click the down-angled shape to the left of the merged shape, then type **Flow Out**.

e. Click the arrow shape above the merged shape, then drag the top-middle sizing handle down 1/2 inch.

f. Click a blank area of the slide, add the guides to the Slide pane, then save your changes.

7. Align and group objects.

a. Move the vertical guide to the left until 3.83 appears, drag a selection box to select the five small green triangle shapes at the bottom of the slide, then click the DRAWING TOOLS FORMAT tab.

b. Click the Align button in the Arrange group, click Align Middle, click the Align button, then click Distribute Horizontally.

c. Click the Rotate button in the Arrange group, click Rotate Left 90º, click the Group button in the Arrange group, then click Group.

d. Move the grouped triangle shape object to the guide in the blank space on the down-angled shape to the left of the merged shape.

e. Duplicate the grouped triangle shape object, then rotate the new object to the left 90º.

f. Duplicate the rotated grouped triangle shape object, then move the two new triangle shape objects on the slide as shown in FIGURE B-20.

g. Set the guides back to 0.00, remove the guides from your screen, remove the rulers, then save your work.

FIGURE B-20

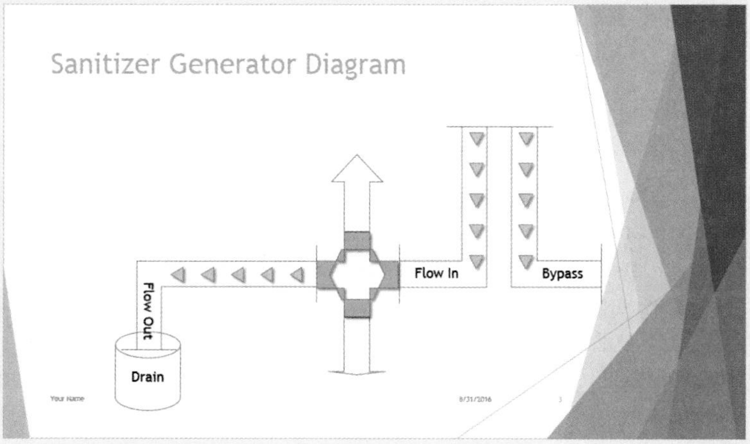

8. Add slide footers.

a. Open the Header and Footer dialog box.

b. On the Slide tab, click the Date and time check box to select it, then click the Fixed option button.

c. Add the slide number to the footer.

d. Type your name in the Footer text box.

e. Apply the footer to all of the slides except the title slide.

f. Open the Header and Footer dialog box again, then click the Notes and Handouts tab.

g. Click the Date and time check box, then type today's date in the Fixed text box.

h. Type the name of your class in the Header text box, then click the Page number check box.

i. Type your name in the Footer text box.

j. Apply the header and footer information to all the notes and handouts, then save your changes.

k. Submit your presentation to your instructor, close the presentation, then exit PowerPoint.

Independent Challenge 1

You are the director of the Performing Arts Center in Baton Rouge, Louisiana, and one of your many duties is to raise funds to cover operation costs. One of the primary ways you do this is by speaking to businesses, community clubs, and other organizations throughout the region. Every year you speak to many organizations, where you give a short presentation detailing what the theater center plans to do for the coming season. You need to continue working on the presentation you started already.

a. Start PowerPoint, open the presentation PPT B-3.pptx from the location where you store your Data Files, and save it as **PPT B-Center**.

b. Use Outline view to enter the following as bulleted text on the Commitment to Excellence slide:
    Excellence
    Testing
    Study
    Diligence

c. Apply the Ion Boardroom design theme to the presentation.

d. Change the font color of each play name on Slide 3 to Orange, Accent 4.

e. Change the bulleted text on Slide 5 to the Vertical Box List SmartArt Graphic, then apply the Inset SmartArt style.

f. Add your name and slide number as a footer on the slides, then save your changes.

g. Submit your presentation to your instructor, close your presentation, then exit PowerPoint.

Independent Challenge 2

You are a manager for RC Investments Inc., a financial services company. You have been asked by your boss to develop a presentation outlining important details and aspects of the mortgage process to be used at a financial seminar.

a. Start PowerPoint, open the presentation PPT B-4.pptx from the location where you store your Data Files, and save it as **PPT B-RC Investments**.

b. Apply an Office Theme Dark design theme to the presentation.

c. On Slide 4 select the three shapes, Banks, Mortgage Bankers, and Private Investors, release [Shift], then using the Align command distribute them vertically and align them to their left edges.

d. Select the blank shape, type **Borrower**, press [Shift], select the Mortgage Broker and Mortgage Bankers shapes, release [Shift], then using the Align command distribute them horizontally and align them to the middle.

e. Select all of the shapes, then apply Moderate Effect – Orange, Accent 2 from the Shape Styles group.

f. Create a diamond shape, then merge it with the Borrower shape as shown in FIGURE B-21.

g. Using the Arrow shape from the Shapes gallery, draw a 4 1/2-pt arrow between all of the shapes. (*Hint*: Draw one arrow shape, change the line weight using the Shape Outline list arrow, then duplicate the shape.)

FIGURE B-21

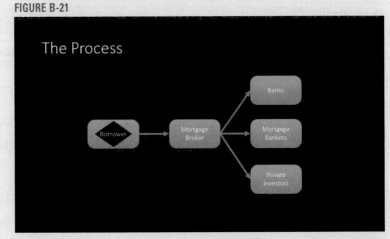

h. Group all the shapes together.

i. Add the page number and your name as a footer on the notes and handouts, then save your changes.

j. Submit your presentation to your instructor, close your presentation, then exit PowerPoint.

Independent Challenge 3

You are an independent distributor of natural foods in Eugene, Oregon. Your business, Coast Natural Foods, has grown progressively since its inception 10 years ago, but sales have leveled off over the last 12 months. In an effort to stimulate growth, you decide to purchase Gemco Foods Inc., a natural food dealer in Idaho and Washington, which would allow your company to begin expanding into surrounding states. Use PowerPoint to develop a presentation you can use to gain a financial backer for the acquisition. Create your own information for the presentation.

a. Start PowerPoint, create a new presentation, then apply the Wisp design theme to the presentation.

b. Type **A Plan for Growth** as the main title on the title slide, and **Coast Natural Foods** as the subtitle.

c. Save the presentation as **PPT B-Natural Foods** to the location where you store your Data Files.

d. Add five more slides with the following titles: Slide 2, **History**; Slide 3, **Trends**; Slide 4, **Growth**; Slide 5, **Funding**; Slide 6, **Management Team**.

e. Enter appropriate text into the text placeholders of the slides. Use both the Slide pane and Outline view to enter text.

f. Convert text on one slide to a SmartArt graphic, then apply the SmartArt graphic style Inset Effect.

g. Create two shapes, format the shapes, then merge the shapes together.

h. View the presentation as a slide show, then view the slides in Slide Sorter view.

i. Add the slide number and your name as a footer on the slides, then save your changes.

j. Submit your presentation to your instructor, close your presentation, then exit PowerPoint.

Independent Challenge 4: Explore

Your computer instructor at Tri-Cities College has been asked by the department head to convert her Computer Basics 101 course into an accelerated night course designed for adult students. Your instructor has asked you to help her create a presentation for the class that she can post on the Internet. Most of the basic text information is already on the slides, you primarily need to add a theme and other object formatting.

a. Start PowerPoint, open the presentation PPT B-5.pptx from the location where you store your Data Files, and save it as **PPT B-Computer 101**.

b. Add a new slide after the Course Facts slide with the same layout, type **Course Details** in the title text placeholder, then enter the following as bulleted text in Outline view:

Information systems
Networking
Applied methods
Technology solutions
Software design
Applications

c. Apply the Savon design theme to the presentation.

d. Select the title text object on Slide 1 (*Hint*: Press [Shift] to select the whole object), then change the text color to Orange.

e. Change the font of the title text object to FELIX TITLING, then decrease the font size to 40.

f. Click the subtitle text object on Slide 1, then change the character spacing to Loose.

g. Change the text on Slide 4 to a SmartArt graphic. Use an appropriate diagram type for a list.

h. Change the style of the SmartArt diagram using one of the SmartArt Styles, then view the presentation in Slide Show view.

i. Add the slide number and your name as a footer on the notes and handouts, then save your changes.

j. Submit your presentation to your instructor, close your presentation, then exit PowerPoint.

Visual Workshop

Create the presentation shown in **FIGURE B-22** and **FIGURE B-23**. Add today's date as the date on the title slide. Save the presentation as **PPT B-Ohio Trade** to the location where you store your Data Files. (*Hint*: The SmartArt style used for the SmartArt is a 3D style.) Review your slides in Slide Show view, then add your name as a footer to the notes and handouts. Submit your presentation to your instructor, save your changes, close the presentation, then exit PowerPoint.

FIGURE B-22

FIGURE B-23

Inserting Objects into a Presentation

CASE   In this unit, you continue working on the presentation by inserting text from Microsoft Word and visual elements, including a photograph, table, and a chart, into the presentation. You format these objects using PowerPoint's powerful object-editing features.

Unit Objectives

After completing this unit, you will be able to:

- Insert text from Microsoft Word
- Insert and style a picture
- Insert a text box
- Insert a chart
- Enter and edit chart data
- Insert slides from other presentations
- Insert a table
- Insert and format WordArt

Files You Will Need

PPT C-1.pptx	PPT C-10.pptx
PPT C-2.docx	PPT C-11.pptx
PPT C-3.jpg	PPT C-12.jpg
PPT C-4.pptx	PPT C-13.pptx
PPT C-5.pptx	PPT C-14.docx
PPT C-6.docx	PPT C-15.jpg
PPT C-7.jpg	PPT C-16.jpg
PPT C-8.pptx	PPT C-17.jpg
PPT C-9.pptx	PPT C-18.jpg

Insert Text from Microsoft Word

Learning Outcomes
• Create slides using Outline view
• Move and delete slides

It is easy to insert documents saved in Microsoft Word format (.docx), Rich Text Format (.rtf), plain text format (.txt), and HTML format (.htm) into a PowerPoint presentation. If you have an outline saved in a document file, you can import it into PowerPoint to create a new presentation or create additional slides in an existing presentation. When you import a document into a presentation, PowerPoint creates an outline structure based on the styles in the document. For example, a Heading 1 style in the Word document becomes a slide title and a Heading 2 style becomes the first level of text in a bulleted list. If you insert a plain text format document into a presentation, PowerPoint creates an outline based on the tabs at the beginning of the document's paragraphs. Paragraphs without tabs become slide titles, and paragraphs with one tab indent become first-level text in bulleted lists. **CASE** *You have a Microsoft Word document with information about intercontinental Canadian train routes that you want to insert into your presentation to create several new slides.*

STEPS

QUICK TIP
While in Normal view you can click the Normal button in the status bar to go to Outline view.

1. **Start PowerPoint, open the presentation PPT C-1.pptx from the location where you store your Data Files, save it as PPT C-QST, click the VIEW tab on the Ribbon, then click the Outline View button in the Presentation Views group**

2. **Click the Slide 4 icon ▢ in the Outline pane, click the HOME tab on the Ribbon, click the New Slide button list arrow in the Slides group, then click Slides from Outline**

    Slide 4 appears in the Slide pane. The Insert Outline dialog box opens. Before you insert an outline into a presentation, you need to determine where you want the new slides to be placed. You want the text from the Word document inserted as new slides after Slide 4.

3. **Navigate to the location where you store your Data Files, click the Word document file PPT C-2.docx, then click Insert**

    Six new slides (5, 6, 7, 8, 9 and 10) are added to the presentation, and the new Slide 5 appears in the Slide pane. See **FIGURE C-1**.

4. **Click the down scroll arrow ▼ in the Outline pane and read the text for all the new slides, then click the Normal button ▣ on the status bar**

    The information on Slides 5 and 6 refer to obsolete train routes and are not needed for this presentation.

5. **Press [Shift], click the Slide 6 thumbnail in the Thumbnails pane, then click the Cut button in the Clipboard group**

    Slides 5 and 6 are deleted, and the next slide down (Explorer's Trail West) becomes the new Slide 5 and appears in the Slide pane.

6. **Click the Slide 6 thumbnail in the Thumbnails pane, then drag it above Slide 5**

    Slide 6 and Slide 5 change places. All of the new slides in the presentation now follow the same theme. You want the text of the inserted outline to adopt the theme fonts of the presentation.

QUICK TIP
You can also use Slide Sorter view to move slides around in the presentation.

7. **Press [Shift], click the Slide 8 thumbnail in the Thumbnails pane, release [Shift], click the Reset button in the Slides group, then click the Save button ▣ on the Quick Access toolbar**

    Notice the font type and formatting attributes of the slide text changes to reflect the current theme fonts for the presentation. The Reset button resets the slide placeholders to their default position, size, and text formatting based on the Organic presentation design theme. Compare your screen to **FIGURE C-2**.

FIGURE C-1: Outline pane showing imported text

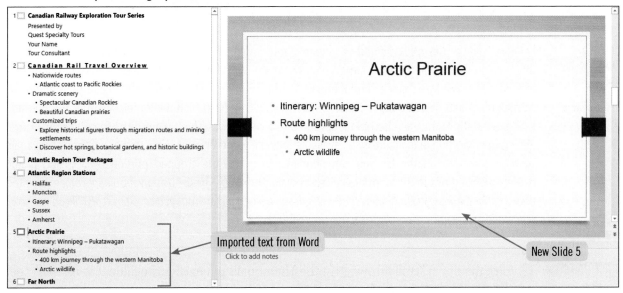

FIGURE C-2: Slides reset to Organic theme default settings

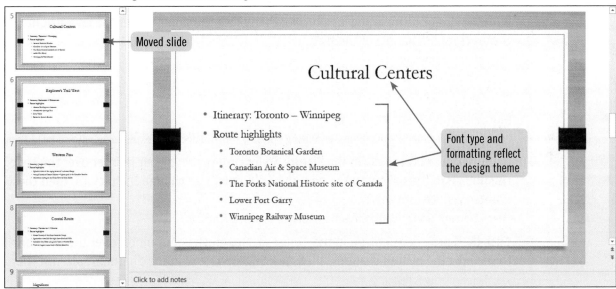

Sending a presentation using email

You can send a copy of a presentation over the Internet to a reviewer to edit and add comments. You can use Microsoft Outlook to send your presentation. Although your email program allows you to attach files, you can send a presentation using Outlook from within PowerPoint. Click the FILE tab, click Share, click Email in the center pane, then click Send as Attachment. Outlook opens and automatically creates an email with a copy of the presentation attached to it. You can also attach and send a PDF copy or an XPS copy of the presentation using your email program. Both of these file formats preserve document formatting, enable file sharing, and can be viewed online and printed.

Insert and Style a Picture

Learning
Outcomes
• Insert and format
a picture
• Resize and move a
picture

In PowerPoint, a **picture** is defined as a digital photograph, a piece of line art or clip art, or other artwork that is created in another program. PowerPoint gives you the ability to insert 14 different types of pictures including JPEG File Interchange Format and BMP Windows Bitmap files into a PowerPoint presentation. As with all objects in PowerPoint, you can format and style inserted pictures to help them fit the theme of your presentation. You can also hide a portion of the picture you don't want to be seen by **cropping** it. The cropped portion of a picture is still available to you if you ever want to show that part of picture again. To reduce the size of the file you can permanently delete the cropped portion by applying picture compression settings in the Compress Pictures dialog box. **CASE** ▶ *Using your digital camera, you took photographs during your train tours. In this lesson you insert a picture that you saved as a JPG file on your computer, and then you crop and style it to best fit the slide.*

STEPS

1. **Click the down scroll arrow ▼ in the Thumbnails pane, click the Slide 9 thumbnail, then click the Pictures icon 🖻 in the content placeholder on the slide**

   The Insert Picture dialog box opens displaying the pictures available in the default Pictures library.

2. **Navigate to location where you store your Data Files, select the picture file PPT C-3.jpg, then click Insert**

   The picture fills the content placeholder on the slide, and the PICTURE TOOLS FORMAT tab opens on the Ribbon. The picture would look better if you cropped some of the image.

3. **Click the Crop button in the Size group, then place the pointer over the lower-right corner cropping handle of the picture**

   The pointer changes to ⌐. When the Crop button is active, cropping handles appear next to the sizing handles on the selected object.

4. **Drag the corner of the picture up and to the left as shown in FIGURE C-3, release the mouse button, then press [Esc]**

   PowerPoint has a number of picture formatting options, and you decide to experiment with some of them.

5. **Click the More button ▼ in the Picture Styles group, move your pointer over the style thumbnails in the gallery to see how the different styles change the picture, then click Rotated, White (3rd row)**

   The picture now has a white frame and is rotated slightly to the left.

6. **Click the Corrections button in the Adjust group, move your pointer over the thumbnails to see how the picture changes, then click Sharpen: 50% in the Sharpen/Soften section**

   The picture clarity is better.

7. **Click the Artistic Effects button in the Adjust group, move your pointer over the thumbnails to see how the picture changes, then click a blank area of the slide**

   The artistic effects are all interesting, but none of them will work well for this picture.

8. **Drag the picture to the center of the blank area of the slide, click a blank area on the slide, then save your changes**

   Compare your screen to FIGURE C-4.

Inserting Objects into a Presentation

FIGURE C-3: Using the cropping pointer to crop a picture

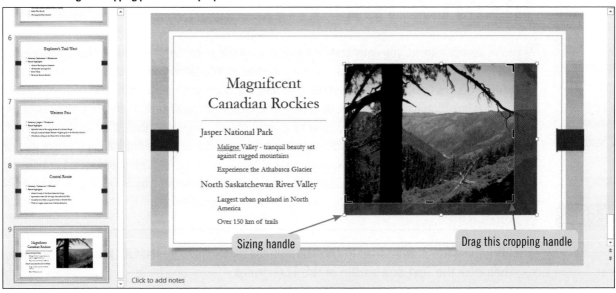

FIGURE C-4: Cropped and styled picture

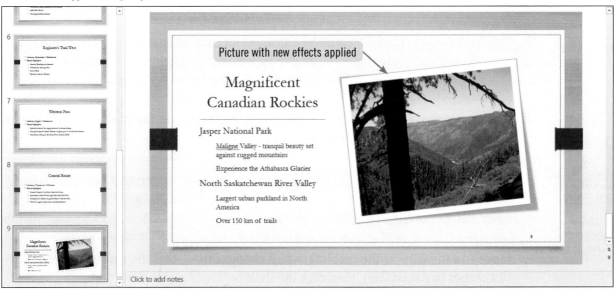

Saving slides as graphics

You can save PowerPoint slides as graphics and later use them in other presentations, in graphics programs, and on Web pages. Display the slide you want to save, click the FILE tab, then click Save As. Select the location where you want to save the file. In the Save As dialog box, click the Save as type list arrow, select the desired graphics format, then name the file. Graphics format choices include GIF Graphics Interchange Format (*.gif), JPEG File Interchange Format (*.jpg), PNG Portable Network Graphics Format (*.png), TIFF Tag Image File Format (*.tif), and Device Independent Bitmap (*.bmp). Click Save, then click the desired option when the alert box appears asking if you want to save all the slides or only the current slide.

Insert a Text Box

Learning Outcomes
• Insert a text box
• Format text in a text box
• Resize and move a text box

As you've already learned, you enter text on a slide using a title or content placeholder that is arranged on the slide based on a slide layout. Every so often you need additional text on a slide where the traditional placeholder does not place text effectively for your message. You can create an individual text box by clicking the Text Box button in the Text group on the INSERT tab on the Ribbon. There are two types of text boxes that you can create: a text label, used for a small phrase where text doesn't automatically wrap to the next line inside the box, and a word-processing box, used for a sentence or paragraph where the text wraps inside the boundaries of the box. Either type of text box can be formatted and edited just like any other text object. **CASE** *You decide to add a text box to the SmartArt graphic on Slide 3. You create a word-processing box on the slide, enter text, edit text, and then format the text.*

STEPS

1. **Click the Slide 3 thumbnail in the Thumbnails pane, click the INSERT tab on the Ribbon, then click the Text Box button in the Text group**
   The pointer changes to ↓.

QUICK TIP
To create a text label, click the Text Box button, position the pointer on the slide, click once, then enter your text.

2. **Move ↓ to the blank area of the slide to the left of the SmartArt graphic, then drag the pointer ─┼─ down and toward the right about 3" to create a text box**
   When you begin dragging, an outline of the text box appears, indicating the size of the text box you are drawing. After you release the mouse button, a blinking insertion point appears inside the text box, in this case a word-processing box, indicating that you can enter text.

3. **Type Each package can be tailored for a quick all-inclusive getaway or an extended holiday**
   Notice the text box increases in size as your text wraps to additional lines inside the text box. Your screen should look similar to FIGURE C-5. After entering the text, you realize the sentence could be clearer if written differently.

4. **Drag I over the phrase all-inclusive to select it, position ▷ on top of the selected phrase, then press and hold the left mouse button**
   The pointer changes to ▷.

TROUBLE
If there is no space after the word "inclusive," click after the word, then press [Spacebar].

5. **Drag the selected words to the left of the word "package" in the text box, then release the mouse button**
   A grey insertion line appears as you drag, indicating where PowerPoint places the text when you release the mouse button. The phrase "all-inclusive" moves before the word "package" and is still selected.

6. **Move I to the edge of the text box, which changes to ⌖, click the text box border (it changes to a solid line), then click the Italic button I in the Font group**
   All of the text in the text box is italicized.

QUICK TIP
Click the Shape Outline list arrow in the Drawing group, then click Weight or Dashes to change the outline width or style of a text object.

7. **Click the Shape Fill list arrow in the Drawing group, click the Blue-Gray, Accent 3, Lighter 60% color box, click the Shape Outline list arrow in the Drawing group, then click the Orange, Accent 5 color box**
   The text object is now filled with a light blue color and has a light orange outline.

8. **Drag the right-middle sizing handle of the text box to the right until all the text fits on two lines, position ⌖ over the text box edge, then drag the text box to the Smart Guide on the slide as shown in FIGURE C-6**

9. **Click the Reading View button ▥ on the status bar, review the slide, press [Esc], then save your changes**

FIGURE C-5: New text object

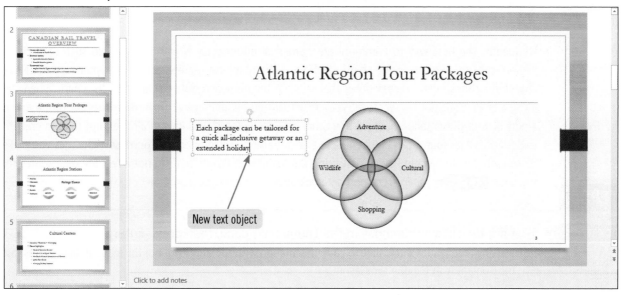

FIGURE C-6: Formatted text object

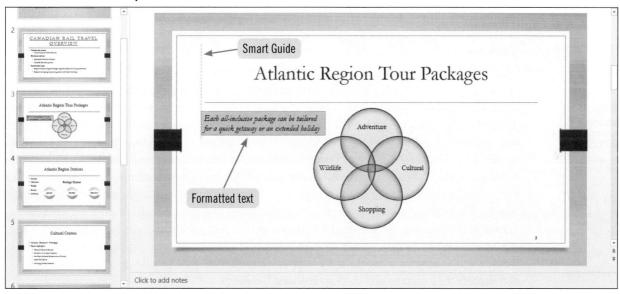

Changing text box defaults

You can change the default formatting characteristics of text boxes you create using the Text Box button on the INSERT tab. To change the formatting defaults for text boxes, select an existing formatted text box, or create a new one and format it using any of PowerPoint's formatting commands. When you are ready to change the text box defaults, press [Shift], right-click the formatted text box, release [Shift], then click Set as Default Text Box on the shortcut menu. Any new text boxes you create now will display the formatting characteristics of this formatted text box.

Insert a Chart

Learning Outcomes
- Insert a new chart on a slide

Frequently, the best way to communicate numerical information is with a visual aid such as a chart. PowerPoint uses Excel to create charts. A **chart** is the graphical representation of numerical data. Every chart has a corresponding **worksheet** that contains the numerical data displayed by the chart. When you insert a chart object into PowerPoint, you are actually embedding it. An **embedded object** is one that is a part of your presentation (just like any other object you insert into PowerPoint) except that an embedded object's data source can be opened, in this case using Excel, for editing purposes. Changes you make to an embedded object in PowerPoint using the features in PowerPoint do not affect the data source for the data. **CASE** *You insert a chart on a new slide.*

STEPS

QUICK TIP
Right-click a slide in the Thumbnails pane, then click Duplicate Slide to create an exact copy of the slide.

1. **Click the Slide 9 thumbnail in the Thumbnails pane, then press [Enter]**
   Pressing [Enter] adds a new slide to your presentation with the slide layout of the selected slide, in this case the Content with Caption slide layout.

2. **Click the HOME tab on the Ribbon, click the Layout button in the Slides group, then click Title and Content**
   The slide layout changes to the Title and Content layout.

3. **Click the Title placeholder, type Customer Survey, then click the Insert Chart icon in the Content placeholder**
   The Insert Chart dialog box opens as shown in FIGURE C-7. Each chart type includes a number of 2D and 3D styles. The Clustered Column chart is the default 2D chart style. For a brief explanation of chart types, refer to TABLE C-1.

QUICK TIP
You can also add a chart to a slide by clicking the Chart button in the Illustrations group on the INSERT tab.

4. **Click OK**
   The PowerPoint window displays a clustered column chart below a worksheet with sample data, as shown in FIGURE C-8. The CHART TOOLS DESIGN tab on the Ribbon contains commands you use in PowerPoint to work with the chart. The worksheet consists of rows and columns. The intersection of a row and a column is called a **cell**. Cells are referred to by their row and column location; for example, the cell at the intersection of column A and row 1 is called cell A1. Each column and row of data in the worksheet is called a **data series**. Cells in column A and row 1 contain **data series labels** that identify the data or values in the column and row. "Category 1" is the data series label for the data in the second row, and "Series 1" is a data series label for the data in the second column. Cells below and to the right of the data series labels, in the shaded blue portion of the worksheet, contain the data values that are represented in the chart. Cells in row 1 appear in the chart **legend** and describe the data in the series. Each data series has corresponding **data series markers** in the chart, which are graphical representations such as bars, columns, or pie wedges. The boxes with the numbers along the left side of the worksheet are **row headings**, and the boxes with the letters along the top of the worksheet are **column headings**.

5. **Move the pointer over the worksheet, then click cell C4**
   The pointer changes to ✚. Cell C4, containing the value 1.8, is the selected cell, which means it is now the **active cell**. The active cell has a thick green border around it.

6. **Click the Close button ✖ on the worksheet title bar, then click the Quick Layout button in the Chart Layouts group**
   The worksheet window closes, and the Quick Layout gallery opens.

7. **Move over all the layouts in the gallery, then click Layout 1**
   This new layout moves the legend to the right side of the chart and increases the size of the data series markers.

8. **Click in a blank area of the slide to deselect the chart, then save your changes**
   The CHART TOOLS DESIGN tab is no longer active.

FIGURE C-7: Insert Chart dialog box

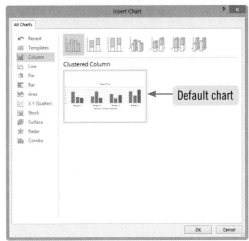

FIGURE C-8: Worksheet open with data for the chart

TABLE C-1: Chart types

chart type	icon looks like	use to
Column		Track values over time or across categories
Line		Track values over time
Pie		Compare individual values to the whole
Bar		Compare values in categories or over time
Area		Show contribution of each data series to the total over time
X Y (Scatter)		Compare pairs of values
Stock		Show stock market information or scientific data
Surface		Show value trends across two dimensions
Radar		Show changes in values in relation to a center point
Combo		Use multiple types of data markers to compare values

PowerPoint 2013

Enter and Edit Chart Data

Learning
Outcomes
• Change chart data
  values
• Format a chart

After you insert a chart into your presentation, you need to replace the sample information with the correct data. If you have data in an Excel worksheet, you can import it from Excel; otherwise, you can type your own data into the worksheet. As you enter data and make other changes in the worksheet, the chart on the slide automatically reflects the new changes. **CASE** *You enter and format survey data you collected that asked people to positively rate four train tours with respect to three factors: suite accommodations, food quality, and overall trip satisfaction.*

STEPS

1. **Click the chart on Slide 10, then click the Edit Data button in the Data group on the CHART TOOLS DESIGN tab on the Ribbon**

   The chart is selected and the worksheet opens in a separate window. The information in the worksheet needs to be replaced with the correct data.

2. **Click the Series 1 cell, type Suite, press [Tab], type Food, press [Tab], then type Overall**

   The data series labels, describing three survey factors, are entered in the worksheet and display in the legend on the chart. Pressing [Tab] moves the active cell from left to right one cell at a time in a row. Pressing [Enter] in the worksheet moves the active cell down one cell at a time in a column.

3. **Click the Category 1 cell, type Atlantic, press [Enter], type Prairie, press [Enter], type Rockies, press [Enter], type Pacific, then press [Enter]**

   The data series labels, describing the tour regions, are entered in the worksheet and appear along the bottom of the chart on the x-axis. The x-axis is the horizontal axis also referred to as the **category axis**, and the y-axis is the vertical axis also referred to as the **value axis**.

4. **Enter the data shown in FIGURE C-9 to complete the worksheet, then press [Enter]**

   Notice that the height of each column in the chart, as well as the values along the y-axis, adjust to reflect the numbers you typed. You have finished entering the data in the Excel worksheet.

5. **Click the Switch Row/Column button in the Data group**

   The data charted on the x-axis switches with the y-axis. Notice the legend now displays the row data series labels for each tour region.

6. **Click the Close button ☒ on the worksheet title bar, then click the Chart Title text box object in the chart**

   The worksheet window closes.

7. **Type Guest Satisfaction, click a blank area of the chart, then click the Chart Styles button ⊿ to the right of the chart to open the Chart Styles gallery**

   The Chart Styles gallery opens on the left side of the chart with STYLE selected.

8. **Scroll down the gallery, click Style 6, click COLOR at the top of the Chart Styles gallery, then click Color 2 in the Colorful section**

   The new chart style and color gives the column data markers a professional look as shown in FIGURE C-10.

9. **Click a blank area on the slide, then save the presentation**

   The Chart Styles gallery closes.

FIGURE C-9: **Worksheet data for the chart**

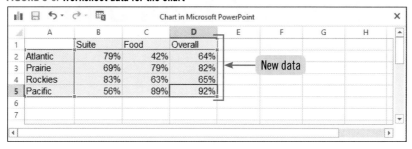

FIGURE C-10: **Formatted chart**

Adding a hyperlink to a chart

You can add a hyperlink to any object in PowerPoint, including a chart. Select that chart, click the INSERT tab on the Ribbon, then click the Hyperlink button in the Links group. If you are linking to another file, click the Existing File or Web Page button, locate the file you want to link to the chart, then click OK. Or, if you want to link to another slide in the presentation, click the Place in This Document button, click the slide in the list, then click OK. Now, during a slide show you can click the chart to open the linked object. To remove the link, click the chart, click the Hyperlink button in the Links group, then click Remove Link.

Insert Slides from Other Presentations

To save time and energy, you can insert one or more slides you already created in other presentations into an existing presentation or one you are currently working on. One way to share slides between presentations is to open an existing presentation, copy the slides you want to the Clipboard, and then paste them into your open presentation. However, PowerPoint offers a simpler way to transfer slides directly between presentations. By using the Reuse Slides pane, you can insert slides from another presentation or a network location called a Slide Library. A **Slide Library** is folder that you and others can access to open, modify, and review presentation slides. Newly inserted slides automatically take on the theme of the open presentation, unless you decide to use slide formatting from the original source presentation. **CASE** ▸ *You decide to insert slides you created for another presentation into the Canadian train tour presentation.*

STEPS

1. **Click the Slide 4 thumbnail in the Thumbnails pane, click the New Slide list arrow in the Slides group, then click Reuse Slides**
   The Reuse Slides pane opens on the right side of the presentation window.

2. **Click the Browse button in the Reuse Slides pane, click Browse File, navigate to the location where you store your Data Files, select the presentation file PPT C-4.pptx, then click Open**
   Six slide thumbnails are displayed in the pane with the first slide thumbnail selected as shown in FIGURE C-11. The slide thumbnails identify the slides in the **source presentation**, PPT C-4.pptx.

3. **Point to each slide in the Reuse Slides pane list to display a preview of the slide, then click the Manitoba Tour slide**
   The new slide appears in the Thumbnails pane and Slide pane in your current presentation as the new Slide 5. Notice the new slide assumes the design style and formatting of your presentation, which is called the **destination presentation**.

4. **Click the Keep source formatting check box at the bottom of the Reuse Slides pane, click the Northern Quebec Tour slide, then click the Keep source formatting check box**
   This new slide keeps the design style and formatting of the source presentation.

5. **Click the Slide 4 thumbnail in the Thumbnails pane, in the Reuse Slides pane click the Trans Canadian Luxury Tour slide, then click the Southern Ontario Tour slide**
   Two more slides are inserted into the presentation with the design style and formatting of the destination presentation. You realize that slides 6 and 8 are not needed for this presentation.

6. **With the Slide 6 thumbnail still selected in the Thumbnails pane, press [Ctrl], click the Slide 8 thumbnail, release [Ctrl], right-click the Slide 8 thumbnail, then click Delete Slide in the shortcut menu**
   Slides 6 and 8 are deleted. Objects on the inserted slides may not be in the correct position on the slide. To ensure objects are positioned correctly on the slide, you can reset the slide defaults.

7. **Click the Slide 6 thumbnail in the Thumbnails pane, press [Shift], click the Slide 5 thumbnail, release [Shift], then click the Reset button in the Slides group**
   The selected slides are set back to the original default settings for this design theme.

8. **Click the Reuse Slides pane Close button ✕, then save the presentation**
   The Reuse Slides pane closes. Compare your screen to FIGURE C-12.

FIGURE C-11: Presentation window with Reuse Slides pane open

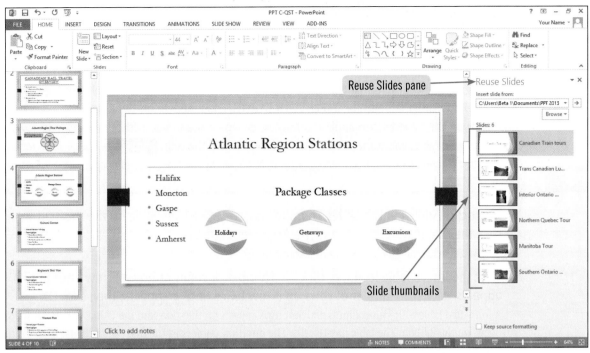

FIGURE C-12: New slides with correct design

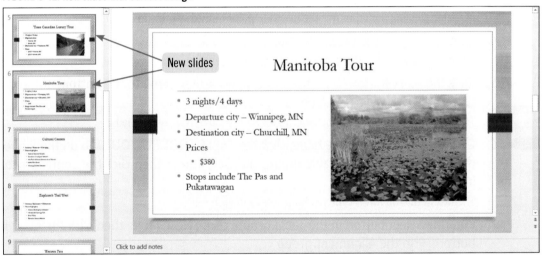

Working with multiple windows

Another way to work with information in multiple presentations is to arrange the presentation windows on your monitor so you see each window side by side. Open each presentation, click the VIEW tab on the Ribbon in any presentation window, then click the Arrange All button in the Window group. Each presentation you have open is placed next to each other so you can easily drag, or transfer, information between the presentations. If you are working with more than two open presentations, you can overlap the presentation windows on top of one another. Open all the presentations you want, then click the Cascade Windows button in the Window group. Now you can to easily jump from one presentation to another by clicking on the presentation title bar or any part of the presentation window.

Insert a Table

Learning
Outcomes
• Insert a table
• Add text to a table
• Change table size
  and layout

As you create your presentation, you may have some information that would look best organized in rows and columns. For example, if you want to compare the basic details of different train accommodations side by side, a table is ideal for this type of information. Once you have created a table, two new tabs, the TABLE TOOLS DESIGN tab and the TABLE TOOLS LAYOUT tab, appear on the Ribbon. You can use the commands on the table tabs to apply color styles, change cell borders, add cell effects, add rows and columns to your table, adjust the size of cells, and align text in the cells. **CASE** ➤ *You decide a table best illustrates the different levels of accommodation services offered by the train tour company.*

STEPS

1. **Right-click** Slide 4 **in the Slides Thumbnails pane, click** New Slide **on the shortcut menu, click the** title placeholder, **then type** Accommodations

   A new slide with the Title and Content layout appears.

2. **Click the** Insert Table icon ⊞, **click the** Number of columns down arrow **once until 4 appears, click the** Number of rows up arrow **twice until 4 appears, then click** OK

   A formatted table with four columns and four rows appears on the slide, and the TABLE TOOLS DESIGN tab opens on the Ribbon. The table has 16 cells. The insertion point is in the first cell of the table and is ready to accept text.

   QUICK TIP
   Press [Tab] when the insertion point is in the last cell of a table to create a new row.

3. **Type** Classic, **press** [Tab], **type** Deluxe, **press** [Tab], **type** Luxury, **press** [Tab], **type** Business, **then press** [Tab]

   The text you typed appears in the top four cells of the table. Pressing [Tab] moves the insertion point to the next cell; pressing [Enter] moves the insertion point to the next line in the same cell.

4. **Enter the rest of the table information shown in** FIGURE C-13

   The table would look better if it were formatted differently.

5. **Click the** More button ⊤ **in the Table Styles group, scroll to the bottom of the gallery, then click** Dark Style 1 – Accent 3

   The background and text color change to reflect the table style you applied.

   QUICK TIP
   Change the height or width of any table cell by dragging its borders.

6. **Click the** Classic cell **in the table, click the** TABLE TOOLS LAYOUT tab **on the Ribbon, click the** Select button **in the Table group, click** Select Row, **then click the** Center button ≡ **in the Alignment group**

   The text in the top row is centered horizontally in each cell.

7. **Click the** Select button **in the Table group, click** Select Table, **then click the** Align Bottom button ▥ **in the Alignment group**

   The text in the entire table is aligned at the bottom within each cell.

   QUICK TIP
   To change the cell color behind text, click the Shading list arrow in the Table Styles group, then choose a color.

8. **Click the** TABLE TOOLS DESIGN tab, **click the** Effects button **in the Table Styles group, point to** Cell Bevel, **then click** Convex (2nd row)

   The 3D effect makes the cells of the table stand out. The table would look better in a different place on the slide.

9. **Place the pointer** ⸙ **over the top edge of the table, drag the table straight down as shown in** FIGURE C-14, **click a blank area of the slide, then save the presentation**

   The slide looks better with more space between the table and the slide title.

FIGURE C-13: Inserted table with data

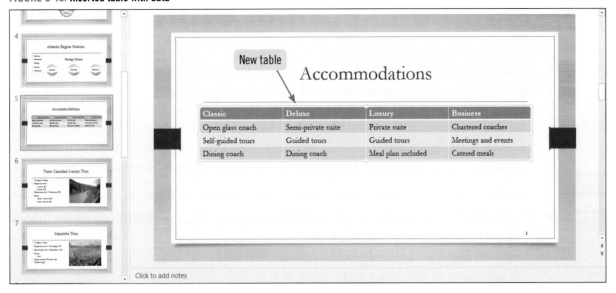

FIGURE C-14: Formatted table

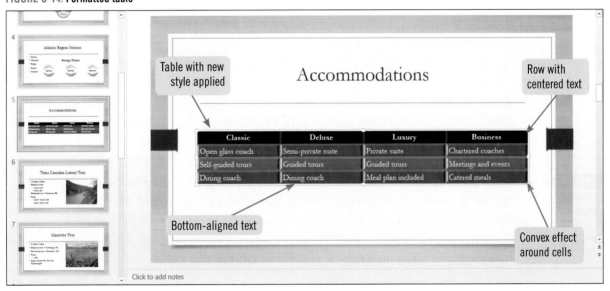

Drawing tables

Choose the slide where you want the table, click the Table button in the Tables group on the Insert tab, then click Draw Table. The pointer changes to ✐. Drag to define the boundaries of the table in the area of the slide where you want the table. A dotted outline appears as you draw . Next, you draw to create the rows and columns of your table. Click the TABLE TOOLS DESIGN tab on the Ribbon, click the Draw Table button in the Draw Borders group, then draw lines for columns and rows. Be sure to draw within the boundary line of the table. You can also create a table by clicking the Table button in the Tables group on the Insert tab, then dragging ⬚ over the table grid to create a table.

Insert and Format WordArt

As you work to create an interesting presentation, your goal should include making your slides visually appealing. Sometimes plain text can come across as dull and unexciting in a presentation. **WordArt** is a set of decorative text styles, or text effects, you can apply to any text object to help direct the attention of your audience to a certain piece of information. You can use WordArt in two different ways: you can apply a WordArt text style to an existing text object that converts the text into WordArt, or you can create a new WordArt object. The WordArt text styles and effects include text shadows, reflections, glows, bevels, 3D rotations, and transformations. **CASE** ▸ *Use WordArt to create a new WordArt text object on Slide 8.*

STEPS

1. **Click the** Slide 8 thumbnail **in the Thumbnails pane, click the** INSERT tab **on the Ribbon, then click the** WordArt button **in the Text group**

   The WordArt gallery appears displaying 20 WordArt text styles.

2. **Click** Gradient Fill – Orange, Accent 1, Reflection **(second row)**

   A text object appears in the middle of the slide displaying sample text with the WordArt style you just selected. Notice the DRAWING TOOLS FORMAT tab is open on the Ribbon.

3. **Click the edge of the** WordArt text object, **then when the pointer changes to** ⬩⬩⬩, **drag the text object to the blank area of the slide**

4. **Click the** More button ⬇ **in the WordArt Styles group, move** ⬚ **over all of the WordArt styles in the gallery, then click** Fill – Orange, Accent 1, Outline – Background 1, Hard Shadow – Accent 1

   The WordArt Styles change the sample text in the WordArt text object. The new WordArt style is applied to the text object.

5. **Drag to select the text** Your text here **in the WordArt text object, click the** Decrease Font Size button A˅ **in the Mini toolbar until** 44 **appears in the Font Size text box, type** Best Value, **press [Enter], then type** Of the Summer

   The text is smaller and appears on two lines.

6. **Click the** Text Effects button **in the WordArt Styles group, point to** Transform, **click** Inflate **in the Warp section (sixth row), then click a blank area of the slide**

   The inflate effect is applied to the text object. Compare your screen to **FIGURE C-15**.

7. **Click the** Reading View button 📖 **on the status bar, click the** Next button ⏵ **until you reach Slide 13, click the** Menu button 🗔, **then click** End Show

8. **Click the** Slide Sorter button ⊞ **on the status bar, then click the** Zoom Out icon ➖ **on the status bar until all 13 slides are visible**

   Compare your screen with **FIGURE C-16**.

9. **Click the** Normal button 🗔 **on the status bar, add your name and the date as a footer to the slides, save your changes, submit your presentation to your instructor, then exit PowerPoint**

FIGURE C-15: WordArt inserted on slide

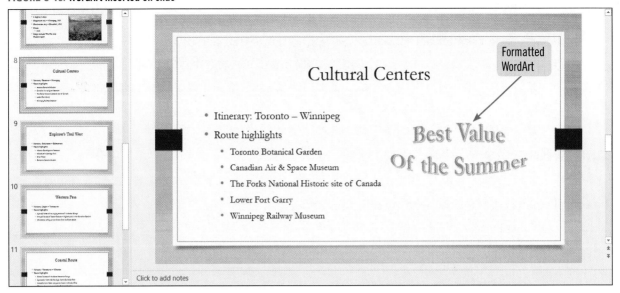

FIGURE C-16: Completed presentation in Slide Sorter view

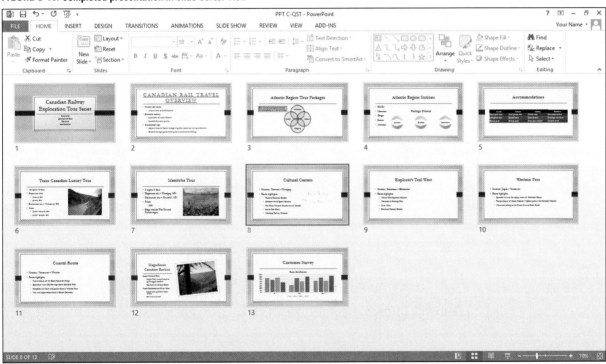

Saving a presentation as a video

You can save your PowerPoint presentation as a full-fidelity video, which incorporates all slide timings, transitions, animations, and narrations. The video can be distributed using a disc, the Web, or email. Depending on how you want to display your video, you have three resolution settings from which to choose: Computer & HD Displays, Internet & DVD, and Portable Devices. The Large setting, Computer & HD Displays (1280 X 720), is used for viewing on a computer monitor, projector, or other high-definition displays. The Medium setting, Internet & DVD (852 X 480), is used for uploading to the Web or copying to a standard DVD. The Small setting, Portable Devices (424 X 240), is used on portable devices including portable media players such as Microsoft Zune. To save your presentation as a video, click the FILE tab, click Export, click Create a Video, choose your settings, then click the Create Video button.

Practice

Concepts Review

Label each element of the PowerPoint window shown in FIGURE C-17.

FIGURE C-17

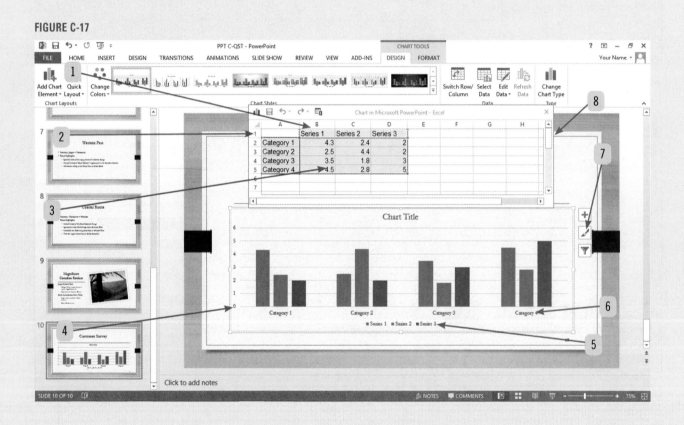

Match each term with the statement that best describes it.

9. Picture
10. Worksheet
11. Data series marker
12. Table
13. Data series

a. Each column or row of data in a worksheet
b. A digital photo or clip art
c. The graphical representation of numerical data in chart
d. Contains the numerical data displayed in a chart
e. PowerPoint object that organizes data in columns and rows

Select the best answer from the list of choices.

14. When you _____ a document into a presentation, PowerPoint creates slides from the outline based on the styles in the document.

    a. link
    b. create
    c. import
    d. package

15. According to this unit, a picture is:

    a. Created in another program.
    b. Defined as an embedded painting.
    c. Created using the Picture Tools Format tab.
    d. Only used to enhance a slide in Slide Show view.

16. A text label is best used for:

    a. WordArt.
    b. A long paragraph.
    c. A content placeholder.
    d. A small text phrase.

17. When you insert slides using the Reuse Slides pane, the current open presentation is also called the _____ presentation.

    a. reused
    b. source
    c. destination
    d. first

18. An object that has its own data source and becomes a part of your presentation after you insert it best describes which of the following?

    a. A Word outline
    b. An embedded object
    c. A WordArt object
    d. A table

19. Use _____ to apply a set of decorative text styles or text effects to text.

    a. a picture
    b. rich text format
    c. a hyperlink
    d. WordArt

20. A simple way to insert slides from another presentation is to use the _____ pane.

    a. Insert Slides
    b. Reuse Slides
    c. Slides Group
    d. Browse

Skills Review

1. **Insert text from Microsoft Word.**

    a. Open the file PPT C-5.pptx from the location where you store your Data Files, then save it as **PPT C-Colcom**. You will work to create the completed presentation as shown in FIGURE C-18.

    b. Click Slide 3 in the Thumbnails pane, then use the Slides from Outline command to insert the file PPT C-6.docx from the location where you store your Data Files.

    c. In the Thumbnails pane, drag Slide 6 above Slide 5 then delete Slide 7, "Expansion Potential".

    d. Select Slides 4, 5, and 6 in the Slides tab, reset the slides to the default theme settings, then save your work.

FIGURE C-18

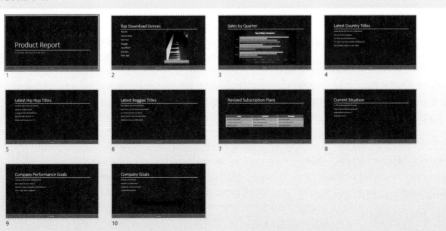

PowerPoint 2013

Skills Review (continued)

2. Insert and style a picture.

   a. Select Slide 2 in the Thumbnails pane, then insert the picture PPT C-7.jpg from the location where you store your Data Files.

   b. Crop the top portion of the picture down to the piano keys, then crop the left side of the picture about 1/4 inch.

   c. Drag the picture up so it is in the center of the blank area of the slide.

   d. Click the Color button, then change the picture color to Tan, Accent color 3 Dark.

   e. Save your changes.

3. Insert a text box.

   a. On Slide 2, insert a text box below the picture.

   b. Type **Public submissions for music up 9%**.

   c. Delete the word **for**, then drag the word **music** after the word **Public**.

   d. Select the text object, then click the More button in the Shape Styles group on the DRAWING TOOLS FORMAT tab.

   e. Click Moderate Effect – Tan, Accent 3, then fit the text box to the text by dragging its sizing handles.

   f. Center the text object under the picture using Smart Guides.

4. Insert a chart.

   a. Go to Slide 3, Sales by Quarter, click the Chart button in the Illustrations group on the INSERT tab, click Bar in the left column, then insert a Clustered Bar chart.

   b. Close the worksheet, drag the top-middle sizing handle of the chart down under the slide title, then apply the Layout 1 quick layout to the chart.

5. Enter and edit chart data.

   a. Show the worksheet, then enter the data shown in TABLE C-2 into the worksheet.

   b. Click the Switch Row/Column button in the Data group, then close the worksheet window.

   c. Type **Top Selling Categories** in the chart title text object.

   d. Click the Chart Styles button next to the chart then change the chart style to Style 7.

   e. Click COLOR in the Charts Styles gallery, then change the color to Color 9 in the Monochromatic section.

   f. Close the Charts Styles gallery, then save your changes.

TABLE C-2

	Hip hop	Reggae	Country
1st Qtr	290,957	208,902	530,457
2nd Qtr	229,840	425,854	490,823
3rd Qtr	485,063	535,927	356,978
4th Qtr	565,113	303,750	637,902

6. Insert slides from other presentations.

   a. Make sure Slide 3 is selected, then open the Reuse Slides pane.

   b. Open the file PPT C-8.pptx from the location where you store your Data Files.

   c. Insert the second slide thumbnail, then insert the first slide thumbnail and the third thumbnail.

   d. Close the Reuse Slides pane, then using [Shift] select Slide 4 in the Thumbnails pane.

   e. Click the Reset button in the Slides group, then save your work.

7. Insert a table.

   a. Add a new slide after Slide 6 with the Title and Content layout.

   b. Add the slide title **Revised Subscription Plans**.

   c. Insert a table with three columns and four rows.

   d. Enter the information shown in TABLE C-3, then change the table style to Medium Style 2 – Accent 2.

   e. In the TABLE TOOLS LAYOUT tab, center the text in the top row.

   f. Select the whole table, open the TABLE TOOLS DESIGN tab, click the Effects button, point to Cell Bevel, then apply the Art Deco effect.

   g. Move the table to the center of the blank area of the slide, then save your changes.

TABLE C-3

Basic	Standard	Premium
$.99 per download	$11.99 per month	$34.99 per year
Unlimited downloads	Max. 100 downloads	Unlimited downloads
Limited access	Limited access	Unlimited access

Skills Review (continued)

8. Insert and format WordArt.

a. Go to Slide 10, then, insert a WordArt text object using the style Fill – White, Text 1, Outline – Background 1, Hard Shadow – Background 1.

b. Type **ColCom Productions Inc.**, then apply the WordArt style Fill – Gold, Accent 1, Outline – Background 1, Hard Shadow – Accent 1.

c. Apply the Deflate Top Transform effect (seventh row) to the text object, then move the text object to the middle of the blank area of the slide.

d. View the presentation in Slide Show view, add your name as a footer to all the slides, then save your changes.

e. Submit your presentation to your instructor, close your presentation, and exit PowerPoint.

Independent Challenge 1

You are a financial management consultant for Chapman & Rowley Investments LLP, located in Nyack, New York. One of your responsibilities is to create standardized presentations on different financial investments for use on the company Web site. As part of the presentation for this meeting, you insert a chart, add a WordArt object, and insert slides from another presentation.

a. Open the file PPT C-9.pptx from the location where you store your Data Files, then save it as **PPT C-C&R**.

b. Add your name as the footer on all of the slides, then apply the Ion Design Theme.

c. Insert a clustered column chart on Slide 2, then enter the data in TABLE C-4 into the worksheet.

d. Close the worksheet, format the chart using Style 11, then move the chart below the slide title text object.

e. Type **Annualized Return** in the chart title text object.

f. Open the Reuse Slides pane, open the file PPT C-10.pptx from the location where you store your Data Files, then insert slides 2, 3, and 4.

g. Close the Reuse Slides pane, move Slide 5 above Slide 4, then select Slide 3.

h. Insert a WordArt object with the Fill – Dark Red, Accent 1, Shadow style, type **Never too early**, press [Enter], type **To**, press [Enter], then type **Start saving**.

i. Click the Text Effects button, point to Transform, then apply the Button text effect from the Follow Path section.

j. Move the WordArt object to a blank area of the slide, click the Text Effects button, point to Shadow, then apply the shadow Offset Top.

k. View the presentation slide show, make any necessary changes, then save your work. See FIGURE C-19.

l. Submit the presentation to your instructor, then close the presentation, and exit PowerPoint.

TABLE C-4

	Stocks	Bonds	Mutual funds
1 Year	1.9%	1.2%	2.8%
3 Year	4.3%	3.4%	4.7%
5 Year	3.9%	2.8%	7.3%
7 Year	2.6%	3.0%	6.2%

FIGURE C-19

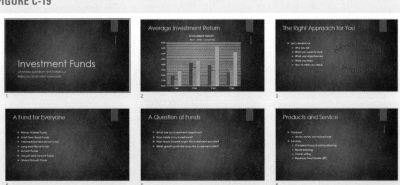

Independent Challenge 2

You work for Prince Rupert Harbor Group, a company in Prince Rupert, British Columbia, that oversees all of the commercial business at the Prince Rupert port. You have been asked to enhance a marketing presentation that is going to promote the port facilities. You work on completing a presentation by inserting two pictures, a text box, and a table.

a. Start PowerPoint, open the file PPT C-11.pptx from the location where you store your Data Files, and save it as **PPT C-PRHG**.

b. Add your name and today's date to Slide 1 in the Subtitle text box.

c. Apply the Wisp theme to the presentation.

d. On Slide 5, click the Pictures icon in the content placeholder, then insert the file PPT C-12.jpg from the location where you store your Data Files.

e. Apply the Double Frame, Black picture style to the picture, click the Color button, then change the color to Temperature: 8800 K (Color Tone section).

f. Insert a text box on the slide below the picture, type **2nd largest fishing fleet in Canada**, then format the text and text box with three formatting commands.

g. Go to Slide 2, select the picture, click the Picture Effects button, point to Soft Edges, then click 10 Point.

h. Open the Artistic Effects gallery, then apply the Blur effect to the picture.

i. Go to Slide 4, create a new table, then enter the data in TABLE C-5. Format the table using at least two formatting commands. Be able to identify which formatting commands you applied to the table.

j. View the final presentation in slide show view. Make any necessary changes (refer to FIGURE C-20).

k. Save the presentation, submit the presentation to your instructor, close the file, and exit PowerPoint.

TABLE C-5

Total	Aug 2016	Aug 2015	Variance
Total containers	47,524.0	43,418.0	9.5%
Loaded containers	35,283.0	34,016.5	3.7%
Empty containers	12,241.0	9,401.5	30.2%
Total tons	475,240.0	434,180.0	9.5%

FIGURE C-20

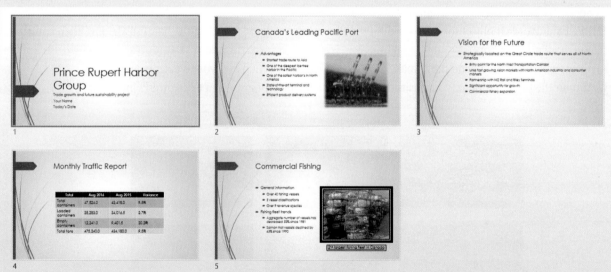

Independent Challenge 3

You work for OneGlobal Inc., a company that produces instructional software to help people learn foreign languages. Once a year, OneGlobal holds a meeting with their biggest client, the United States Department of State, to brief the government on new products and to receive feedback on existing products. Your supervisor has started a presentation and has asked you to look it over and add other elements to make it look better.

a. Start PowerPoint, open the file PPT C-13.pptx from the location where you store your Data Files, and save it as **PPT C-OneGlobal**.

b. Add an appropriate design theme to the presentation.

c. Insert the Word outline PPT C-14.docx after the Product Revisions slide.

d. Insert and format a text object and a WordArt object.

e. Insert an appropriate table on a slide of your choice. Use your own information, or use text from a bulleted list on one of the slides.

f. Insert and format at least two appropriate shapes that emphasize slide content. If appropriate, use the Align, Distribute, and Group commands to organize your shapes.

g. Add your name as footer text on the slides and the notes and handouts, then save the presentation.

h. Submit your presentation to your instructor, close the file, then exit PowerPoint.

Independent Challenge 4: Explore

You are in the Foreign Exchange Club at your college, and one of your assignments is to present information on past foreign student exchanges to different businesses and other organizations off campus. You need to create a pictorial presentation that highlights a trip to a different country. Create a presentation using your own pictures. If you don't have access to any appropriate pictures, use the three pictures provided in the Data Files for this unit: PPT C-15.jpg, PPT C-16.jpg, and PPT C-17.jpg. *(NOTE: To complete steps below, your computer must be connected to the Internet.)*

a. Start PowerPoint, create a new blank presentation, and save it as **PPT C-Club** to the location where you store your Data Files.

b. Locate and insert the pictures you want to use. Place one picture on each slide using the Content with Caption slide layout.

c. Click the Crop list arrow, and use one of the other cropping options to crop a picture.

d. Add information about each picture in the text placeholder, and enter a slide title. If you use the pictures provided, research Truro, England, using the Internet for relevant information to place on the slides.

e. Apply an appropriate design theme, then apply an appropriate title and your name to the title slide.

f. View the final presentation slide show (refer to FIGURE C-21).

g. Add a slide number and your class name as footer text to all of the slides, save your work, then submit your presentation to your instructor.

h. Close the file, and exit PowerPoint.

FIGURE C-21

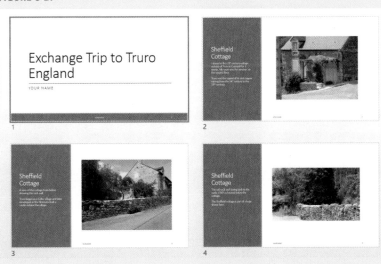

Visual Workshop

Create a one-slide presentation that looks like FIGURE C-22. The slide layout shown in FIGURE C-22 is a specific layout designed for pictures. Insert the picture file PPT C-18.jpg to complete this presentation. Add your name as footer text to the slide, save the presentation as **PPT C-Alaska** to the location where you store your Data Files, then submit your presentation to your instructor.

FIGURE C-22

Finishing a Presentation

CASE You have reviewed your work and are pleased with the slides you created for the Quest Specialty Travel presentation. Now you are ready to add some final touches and effects to the slides to make the PowerPoint presentation interesting to watch.

Unit Objectives

After completing this unit, you will be able to:

- Modify masters
- Customize the background and theme
- Use slide show commands
- Set slide transitions and timings

- Animate objects
- Use proofing and language tools
- Inspect a presentation
- Evaluate a presentation

Files You Will Need

PPT D-1.pptx	PPT D-6.pptx
PPT D-2.jpg	PPT D-7.jpg
PPT D-3.jpg	PPT D-8.pptx
PPT D-4.pptx	PPT D-9.pptx
PPT D-5.jpg	

Modify Masters

Learning
Outcomes
• Navigate Slide
  Master view
• Add and modify
  a picture

Each presentation in PowerPoint has a set of **masters** that store information about the theme and slide layouts. Masters determine the position and size of text and content placeholders, fonts, slide background, color, and effects. There are three Master views: Slide Master view, Notes Master view, and Handout Master view. Changes made in Slide Master view are reflected on the slides in Normal view; changes made in Notes Master view are reflected in Notes Page view, and changes made in Handout Master view appear when you print your presentation using a handout printing option. The primary benefit to modifying a master is that you can make universal changes to your whole presentation instead of making individual repetitive changes to each of your slides. **CASE** *You want to add the QST company logo to every slide in your presentation, so you open your presentation and insert the logo to the slide master.*

STEPS

1. **Start PowerPoint, open the presentation PPT D-1.pptx from the location where you store your Data Files, save the presentation as PPT D-QST, then click the VIEW tab on the Ribbon**

   The title slide for the presentation appears.

   QUICK TIP
   You can press and
   hold [Shift] and click
   the Normal button
   on the status bar to
   display the slide
   master.

2. **Click the Slide Master button in the Master Views group, scroll to the top of the Master Thumbnails pane, then click the Organic Slide Master thumbnail (first thumbnail)**

   The Slide Master view appears with the slide master displayed in the Slide pane as shown in **FIGURE D-1**. A new tab, the SLIDE MASTER tab, appears next to the HOME tab on the Ribbon. The slide master is the Organic theme slide master. Each theme comes with its own slide master. Each master text placeholder on the slide master identifies the font size, style, color, and position of text placeholders on the slides in Normal view. For example, for the Organic theme, the Master title placeholder positioned at the top of the slide uses a black, 44 pt, Garamond font. Slide titles use this font style and formatting. Each slide master comes with associated slide layouts located below the slide master in the Master Thumbnails pane. Slide layouts follow the information on the slide master, and changes you make are reflected in all of the slide layouts.

   QUICK TIP
   When working with
   slide layouts, you
   can right-click the
   thumbnail to open a
   shortcut menu of
   commands.

3. **Point to each of the slide layouts in the Master Thumbnails pane, then click the Title and Content Layout thumbnail**

   As you point to each slide layout, a ScreenTip appears identifying each slide layout by name and lists if any slides in the presentation are using the layout. Slides 2–6, and 13 are using the Title and Content Layout.

4. **Click the Organic Slide Master thumbnail, click the INSERT tab on the Ribbon, then click the Pictures button in the Images group**

   The Insert Picture dialog box opens.

5. **Select the picture file PPT D-2.jpg from the location where you store your Data Files, then click Insert**

   The QST logo picture is placed on the slide master and will now appear on all slides in the presentation. The picture is too large and needs to be repositioned on the slide.

6. **Click 1.61" in the Shape Width text box in the Size group, type .50, press [Enter], drag the QST logo to the upper-left corner of the slide, then click a blank area of the slide**

   The picture snaps into the corner of the slide.

7. **Click the SLIDE MASTER tab on the Ribbon, then click the Preserve button in the Edit Master group**

   Preserving the selected master ensures the Organic slide master remains with this presentation even if you eventually select another master. Compare your screen to **FIGURE D-2**.

8. **Click the Normal button 🖳 on the status bar, then save your changes**

Finishing a Presentation

FIGURE D-1: Slide Master view

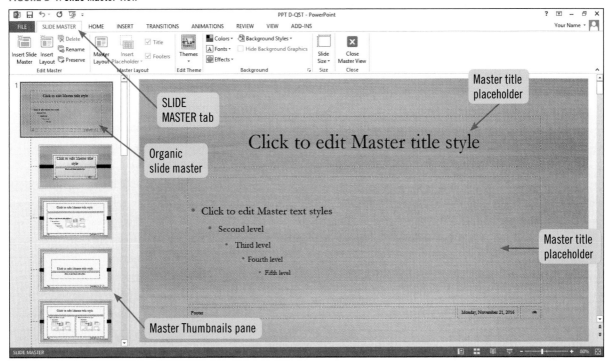

FIGURE D-2: Picture added to slide master

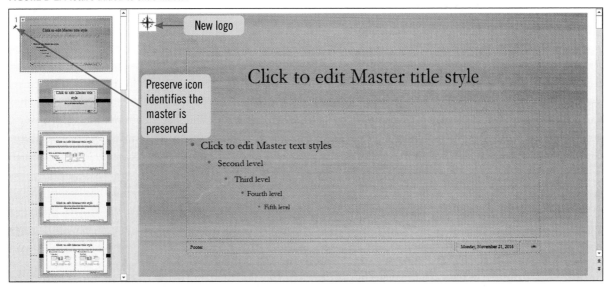

Create custom slide layouts

As you work with PowerPoint, you may find that you need to develop a customized slide layout. For example, you may need to create presentations for a client that has slides that display four pictures with a caption underneath each picture. To make everyone's job easier, you can create a custom slide layout that includes only the placeholders you need. To create a custom slide layout, open Slide Master view, and then click the Insert Layout button in the Edit Master group. A new slide layout appears below the last layout for the selected master in the slide thumbnails pane.

You can choose to add several different placeholders including Content, Text, Picture, Chart, Table, SmartArt, Media, and Picture. Click the Insert Placeholder list arrow in the Master Layout group, click the placeholder you want to add, drag ✛ to create the placeholder, then position the placeholder on the slide. In Slide Master view, you can add or delete placeholders in any of the slide layouts. You can rename a custom slide layout by clicking the Rename button in the Edit Master group and entering a descriptive name to better identify the layout.

Customize the Background and Theme

Learning Outcomes
• Apply a slide background and change the style
• Modify presentation theme

Every slide in a PowerPoint presentation has a **background**, the area behind the text and graphics. You modify the background to enhance the slides using images and color. A **background graphic** is an object placed on the slide master. You can quickly change the background appearance by applying a background style, which is a set of color variations derived from the theme colors. Theme colors determine the colors for all slide elements in your presentation, including slide background, text and lines, shadows, fills, accents, and hyperlinks. Every PowerPoint theme has its own set of theme colors. See **TABLE D-1** for a description of the theme colors. **CASE** ▶ *The QST presentation can be improved with some design enhancements. You decide to modify the background of the slides by changing the theme colors and fonts.*

STEPS

1. **Click the** DESIGN tab **on the Ribbon, then click the** Format Background button **in the Customize group**

   The Format Background pane opens displaying the Fill options. The Picture or texture fill option button is selected indicating the slide has a texture background.

QUICK TIP
To add artistic effects, picture corrections, or picture color changes to a slide background, click the Effects or Picture icons in the Format Background pane, then click one of the options.

2. **Click the** Solid fill option button, **review the slide, click the** Gradient fill option button, **review the slide, click the** Pattern fill option button, **then click the** Diagonal brick pattern (sixth row)

   FIGURE D-3 shows the new background on Slide 1 of the presentation. The new background style does not appear over the whole slide because there are background items on the slide master preventing you from seeing the entire slide background.

3. **Click the** Hide Background Graphics check box **in the Format Background pane**

   All of the background items, which include the QST logo, the white box behind the text objects, and the colored shapes, are hidden from view, and only the text objects and slide number remain visible.

4. **Click the** Hide Background Graphics check box, **then click the** Reset Background button **at the bottom of the Format Background pane**

   All of the background items and the texture slide background appear again as specified by the theme.

QUICK TIP
To create a custom theme, click the VIEW tab, click the Slide Master button in the Master Views group, then click the Colors button, the Fonts button, or the Effects button in the Background group.

5. **Click the** File button **under Insert picture from section in the Format Background pane, select the picture file PPT D-3.jpg from the location where you store your Data Files, then click** Insert

   The new picture fills the slide background behind the background items.

6. **Click the** Slide 3 thumbnail **in the Thumbnails pane, then point to the** dark brown theme variant **in the Variants group**

   Notice how the new theme variant changes the color of the shapes on the slide and the background texture. A **variant** is a custom variation of the applied theme, in this case the Organic theme. Theme variants are similar to the original theme, but they are made up of different complementary colors, slide backgrounds, such as textures and patterns, and background elements, such as shapes and pictures.

7. **Point to the other** variants **in the Variants group, click the** third variant **from the left, click the** Format Background pane Close button **☒, then save your work**

   The new variant is applied to the slide master and to all the slides in the presentation, except Slide 1. The slide background on Slide 1 did not change because you have already applied a picture to the slide background. Compare your screen to **FIGURE D-4**.

FIGURE D-3: New background style applied

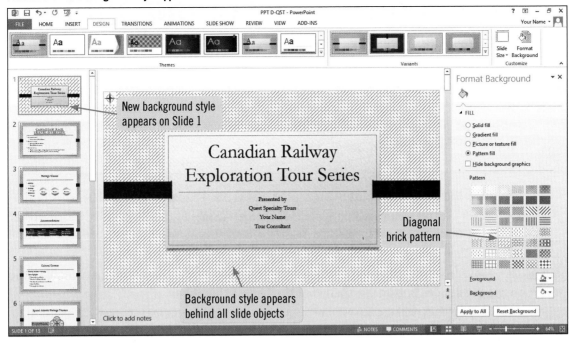

FIGURE D-4: New theme variant

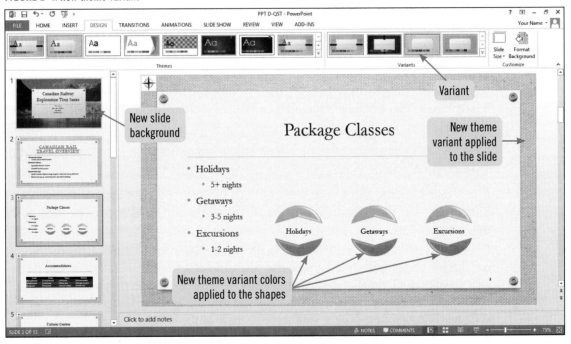

TABLE D-1: Theme colors

color element	description
Text/Background colors	Contrasting colors for typed characters and the slide background
Accent colors	There are six accent colors used for shapes, drawn lines, and text; the shadow color for text and objects and the fill and outline color for shapes are all accent colors; all of these colors contrast appropriately with background and text colors
Hyperlink color	Colors used for hyperlinks you insert
Followed Hyperlink color	Color used for hyperlinks after they have been clicked

PowerPoint 2013

Use Slide Show Commands

With PowerPoint, Slide Show view is used primarily to deliver a presentation to an audience, either over the Internet using your computer or through a projector connected to your computer. As you've seen, Slide Show view fills your computer screen with the slides of the presentation, showing them one at a time. Once the presentation is in Slide Show view, you can draw, or **annotate**, on the slides or jump to other slides in the presentation. **CASE** *You run the slide show of the presentation and practice using some of the custom slide show options.*

STEPS

1. **Click the Slide Show button 🖵 on the status bar, then press [Spacebar]**

   Slide 3 filled the screen first, and then Slide 4 appears. Pressing [Spacebar] or clicking the left mouse button is the easiest way to move through a slide show. See TABLE D-2 for other basic slide show keyboard commands. You can easily navigate to other slides in the presentation during the slide show.

2. **Move ⌖ to the lower-left corner of the screen to display the Slide Show toolbar, click the See all slides button ⊞, then click the Slide 1 thumbnail**

   Slide 1 appears on the screen with the Slide Show toolbar displayed. You can emphasize points in your presentation by annotating the slide during a slide show.

3. **Click the Pen and laser pointer tools button ⊘, on the Slide Show toolbar, then click Highlighter**

   The pointer changes to the highlighter pointer ▌. You can use the highlighter anywhere on the slide.

4. **Drag ▌, to highlight Presented by and Your Name in the subtitle text object, then press [Esc]**

   Two lines of text are highlighted as shown in FIGURE D-5. While the annotation tool is visible, mouse clicks do not advance the slide show; however, you can still move to the next slide by pressing [Spacebar] or [Enter]. Pressing [Esc] or [Ctrl][A] while using an annotation pointer switches the pointer back to ⌖.

5. **Right-click anywhere on the screen, point to Pointer Options, click Eraser, the pointer changes to ⌖, then click the Your Name highlight annotation in the subtitle text object**

   The highlight annotation on the text is erased.

6. **Press [Esc], click the More slide show options button ⊙ on the Slide Show toolbar, click Show Presenter View, then click the Pause the timer button ❚❚ above the slide as shown in FIGURE D-6**

   Presenter view is a special view that you typically use when showing a presentation through two monitors; one that you see as the presenter and one that your audience sees. The current slide appears on the left of your screen (which is the only object your audience sees), the next slide in the presentation appears in the upper-right corner of the screen. Speaker notes, if you have any, appear in the lower-right corner. The timer you paused identifies how long the slide has been viewed by the audience.

7. **Click ⊙, click Hide Presenter View, then click the Advance to the next slide button ⊳ on the Slide Show toolbar**

   The next slide appears.

8. **Press [Enter] to advance through the entire slide show until you see a black slide, then press [Spacebar]**

   If there are annotations on your slides, you have the option of saving them when you quit the slide show. Saved annotations appear as drawn objects in Normal view.

9. **Click Discard, then save the presentation**

   The highlight annotation is deleted on Slide 1, and Slide 3 appears in Normal view.

FIGURE D-5: Slide 1 in Slide Show view with annotations

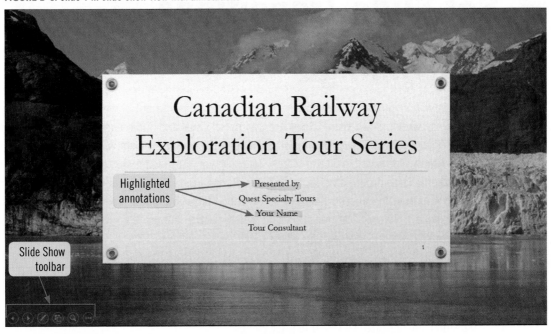

FIGURE D-6: Slide 1 in Presenter view

TABLE D-2: Basic Slide Show view keyboard commands

keyboard commands	description
[Enter], [Spacebar], [PgDn], [N], [down arrow], or [right arrow]	Advances to the next slide
[E]	Erases the annotation drawing
[Home], [End]	Moves to the first or last slide in the slide show
[up arrow], [PgUp], or [left arrow]	Returns to the previous slide
[S]	Pauses the slide show when using automatic timings; press again to continue
[B]	Changes the screen to black; press again to return
[Esc]	Stops the slide show

Set Slide Transitions and Timings

Learning Outcomes
- Apply and modify a transition
- Modify slide timings

In a slide show, you can determine how each slide advances in and out of view and how long each slide appears on the screen. **Slide transitions** are the special visual and audio effects you apply to a slide that determine how each slide moves on and off the screen during the slide show. **Slide timing** refers to the amount of time a slide is visible on the screen. Typically, you set slide timings only if you want the presentation to automatically progress through the slides during a slide show. Setting the correct slide timing, in this case, is important because it determines how much time your audience has to view each slide. Each slide can have a different slide transition and different slide timing. **CASE** ▶ *You decide to set slide transitions and 8-second slide timings for all the slides.*

STEPS

1. **Click the Slide 1 thumbnail in the Thumbnails pane, then click the TRANSITIONS tab on the Ribbon**

   Transitions are organized by type into three groups.

2. **Click the More button ⤓ in the Transition to This Slide group, then click Blinds in the Exciting section**

   The new slide transition plays on the slide, and a transition icon ⭐ appears next to the slide thumbnail in the Thumbnails pane as shown in **FIGURE D-7**. You can customize the slide transition by changing its direction and speed.

   QUICK TIP
   You can add a sound that plays with the transition from the Sound list arrow in the Timing group.

3. **Click the Effect Options button in the Transition to This Slide group, click Horizontal, click the Duration up arrow in the Timing group until 2.00 appears, then click the Preview button in the Preview group**

   The Blinds slide transition now plays horizontal on the slide for 2.00 seconds. You can apply this transition with the custom settings to all of the slides in the presentation.

4. **Click the Apply To All button in the Timing group, then click the Slide Sorter button ▦ on the status bar**

   All of the slides now have the customized Blinds transition applied to them as identified by the transition icons located below each slide. You also have the ability to determine how slides progress during a slide show—either manually by mouse click or automatically by slide timing.

5. **Click the On Mouse Click check box under Advance Slide in the Timing group to clear the check mark**

   When this option is selected, you have to click to manually advance slides during a slide show. Now, with this option disabled, you can set the slides to advance automatically after a specified amount of time.

   QUICK TIP
   Click the transition icon under any slide in Slide Sorter view to see its transition play.

6. **Click the After up arrow in the Timing group, until 00:08.00 appears in the text box, then click the Apply To All button**

   The timing between slides is 8 seconds as indicated by the time under each slide in Slide Sorter view. See **FIGURE D-8**. When you run the slide show, each slide will remain on the screen for 8 seconds. You can override a slide's timing and speed up the slide show by clicking the left mouse button.

7. **Click the Slide Show button 🖵 on the status bar**

   The slide show advances automatically. A new slide appears every 8 seconds using the Blinds transition.

8. **When you see the black slide, press [Spacebar], then save your changes**

   The slide show ends and returns to Slide Sorter view with Slide 1 selected.

FIGURE D-7: Applied slide transition

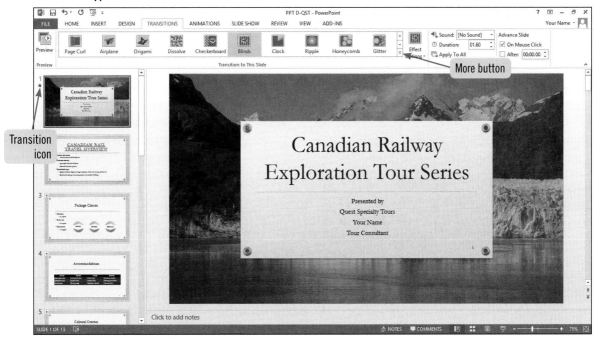

FIGURE D-8: Slide sorter view showing applied transition and timing

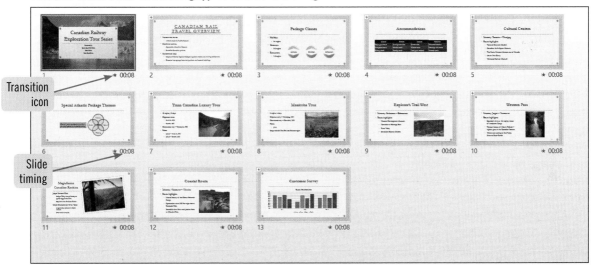

Rehearsing slide show timings

You can set different slide timings for each slide; for example, the title slide can appear for 20 seconds and the second slide for 1 minute. To set timings click the Rehearse Timings button in the Set Up group on the SLIDE SHOW tab. Slide Show view opens and the Recording toolbar shown in **FIGURE D-9** opens. It contains buttons to pause between slides and to advance to the next slide. After opening the Recording toolbar, you can practice giving your presentation by manually advancing each slide in the presentation. When you are finished, PowerPoint displays the total recorded time for the presentation and you have the option to save the recorded timings. The next time you run the slide show, you can use the timings you rehearsed.

FIGURE D-9: Recording toolbar

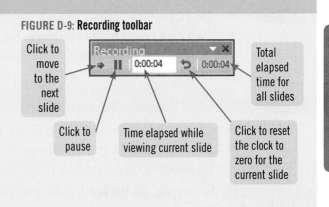

PowerPoint 2013

Animate Objects

Animations let you control how objects and text appear and move on the screen during a slide show and allow you to manage the flow of information and emphasize specific facts. You can animate text, pictures, sounds, hyperlinks, SmartArt diagrams, charts, and individual chart elements. For example, you can apply a Fade animation to bulleted text so each paragraph enters the slide separately from the others. Animations are organized into four categories, Entrance, Emphasis, Exit, and Motion Paths. The Entrance and Exit animations cause an object to enter or exit the slide with an effect. An Emphasis animation causes an object visible on the slide to have an effect and a Motion Path animation causes an object to move on a specified path on the slide. **CASE** *You animate the text and graphics of several slides in the presentation.*

STEPS

1. **Double-click the Slide 3 thumbnail to return to Normal view, click the ANIMATIONS tab on the Ribbon, then click the circle shapes object**

   Text as well as other objects, like a picture, can be animated during a slide show.

2. **Click the More button ▼ in the Animation group, then click Spin in the Emphasis section**

   Animations can be serious and business-like, or humorous, so be sure to choose appropriate effects for your presentation. A small numeral 1, called an animation tag [1], appears at the top corner of the object. **Animation tags** identify the order in which objects are animated during slide show.

3. **Click the Effect Options button in the Animation group, click Two Spins, then click the Duration up arrow in the Timing group until 03.00 appears**

   Effect options are different for every animation, and some animations don't have effect options. Changing the animation timing increases the duration of the animation and gives it a more dramatic effect. Compare your screen to **FIGURE D-10**.

4. **Click the Slide Show button 🖵 on the status bar until you see Slide 4, then press [Esc]**

   After the slide transition finishes, the shapes object spins twice for a total of three seconds.

5. **Click the Slide 2 thumbnail in the Thumbnails pane, click the bulleted list text object, then click Float In in the Animation group**

   The text object is animated with the Float In animation. Each line of text has an animation tag with each paragraph displaying a different number. Accordingly, each paragraph is animated separately.

6. **Click the Effect Options button in the Animation group, click All at Once, click the Duration up arrow in the Timing group until 02.50 appears, then click the Preview button in the Preview group**

   Notice the animation tags for each line of text in the text object now have the same numeral (1), indicating that each line of text animates at the same time.

7. **Click Canadian in the title text object, click ▼ in the Animation group, scroll down, then click Loops in the Motion Paths section**

   A motion path object appears over the shapes object and identifies the direction and shape, or path, of the animation. When needed, you can move, resize, and change the direction of the motion path. Notice the numeral 2 animation tag next to the title text object indicating it is animated *after* the bulleted list text object. Compare your screen to **FIGURE D-11**.

8. **Click the Move Earlier button in the Timing group, click the SLIDE SHOW tab on the Ribbon, then click the From Beginning button in the Start Slide Show group**

   The slide show begins from Slide 1. The animations make the presentation more interesting to view.

9. **When you see the black slide, press [Enter], then save your changes**

FIGURE D-10: Animation applied to shape object

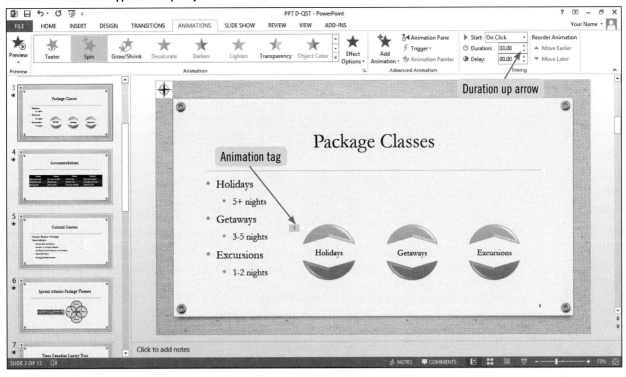

FIGURE D-11: Motion path applied to text object

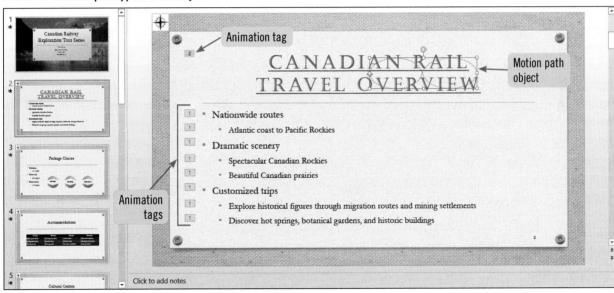

Attaching a sound to an animation

Text or objects that have animation applied can be customized further by attaching a sound for extra emphasis. First, select the animated object, then on the ANIMATIONS tab click the Animation Pane button in the Advanced Animation group. In the Animation Pane, click the animation you want to apply the sound to, click the Animation list arrow, then click Effect Options to open the animation effect's dialog box. In the Enhancements section, click the Sound list arrow, then choose a sound. Click OK when you are finished. Now, when you run the slide show, the sound you applied will play with the animation.

Use Proofing and Language Tools

Learning Outcomes
• Spell check a presentation
• Translate slide text

As your work on the presentation file nears completion, you need to review and proofread your slides thoroughly for errors. You can use the Spell Checker feature in PowerPoint to check for and correct spelling errors. This feature compares the spelling of all the words in your presentation against the words contained in the dictionary. You still must proofread your presentation for punctuation, grammar, and word-usage errors because the Spell Checker recognizes only misspelled and unknown words, not misused words. For example, the spell checker would not identify the word "last" as an error, even if you had intended to type the word "cast." PowerPoint also includes language tools that translate words or phrases from your default language into another language using the Microsoft Translator. **CASE** ▸ *You're finished working on the presentation for now, so it's a good time to check spelling. You then experiment with language translation because the final presentation will be translated into French.*

STEPS

1. **Click the REVIEW tab on the Ribbon, then click the Spelling button in the Proofing group**

   PowerPoint begins to check the spelling in your presentation. When PowerPoint finds a misspelled word or a word that is not in its dictionary, the Spelling pane opens, as shown in **FIGURE D-12**. In this case, PowerPoint identifies the misspelled word in the table on Slide 4 and suggests you replace it with the correctly spelled word "Business."

2. **Click Change in the Spelling pane**

   PowerPoint changes the misspelled word and then continues to check the rest of the presentation for errors. This presentation has several names that are not in the dictionary that you can ignore. If PowerPoint finds any other words it does not recognize, either change or ignore them. When the Spell Checker finishes checking your presentation, the Spelling pane closes, and an alert box opens with a message stating the spelling check is complete.

3. **Click OK in the Alert box, then click the Slide 1 thumbnail in the Thumbnails pane**

   The alert box closes. Now you need to see how the language translation feature works.

4. **Click the Translate button in the Language group, then click Choose Translation Language**

   The Translation Language Options dialog box opens.

5. **Click the Translate to list arrow, click Hebrew, then click OK**

   The Translation Language Options dialog box closes.

6. **Click the Translate button in the Language group, click Mini Translator [Hebrew], click anywhere in the subtitle text object, then select all of the text**

   The Microsoft Translator begins to analyze the selected text, and a semitransparent Microsoft Translator box appears below the text. The Mini toolbar may also appear.

7. **Move the pointer over the Microsoft Translator box**

   A Hebrew translation of the text appears as shown in **FIGURE D-13**. The translation language setting remains in effect until you reset it.

8. **Click the Translate button in the Language group, click Choose Translation Language, click the Translate to list arrow, click Arabic, click OK, click the Translate button again, then click Mini Translator [Arabic]**

   The Mini Translator is turned off, and the translation language is restored to the default setting.

FIGURE D-12: **Spelling pane**

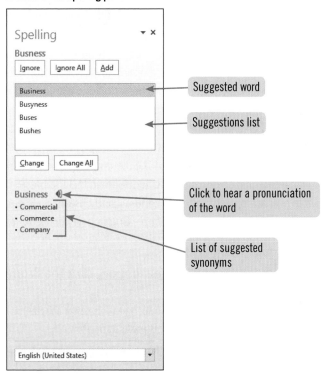

FIGURE D-13: **Translated text in the Microsoft Translator box**

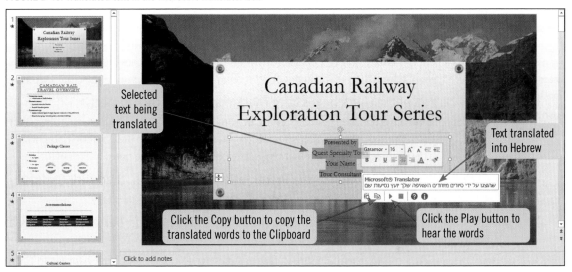

Checking spelling as you type

By default, PowerPoint checks your spelling as you type. If you type a word that is not in the dictionary, a wavy red line appears under it. To correct an error, right-click the misspelled word, then review the suggestions, which appear in the shortcut menu. You can select a suggestion, add the word you typed to your custom dictionary, or ignore it. To turn off automatic spell checking, click the FILE tab, then click Options to open the PowerPoint Options dialog box. Click Proofing in the left column, then click the Check spelling as you type check box to deselect it. To temporarily hide the wavy red lines, click the Hide spelling errors check box to select it. Contextual spelling in PowerPoint identifies common grammatically misused words, for example, if you type the word "their" and the correct word is "there," PowerPoint will identify the mistake and place a wavy red line under the word. To turn contextual spelling on or off, click Proofing in the PowerPoint Options dialog box, then click the Check grammar with spelling check box.

Inspect a Presentation

Learning Outcomes
- Modify document properties
- Inspect and remove unwanted data

Reviewing your presentation can be an important step. You should not only find and fix errors, but also locate and delete confidential company or personal information and document properties you do not want to share with others. If you share presentations with others, especially over the Internet, it is a good idea to inspect the presentation file using the Document Inspector. The **Document Inspector** looks for hidden data and personal information that is stored in the file itself or in the document properties. Document properties, also known as **metadata**, includes specific data about the presentation, such as the author's name, subject matter, title, who saved the file last, and when the file was created. Other types of information the Document Inspector can locate and remove include presentation notes, comments, ink annotations, invisible on-slide content, off-slide content, and custom XML data. **CASE** ▸ *You decide to view and add some document properties, inspect your presentation file, and learn about the Mark as Final command.*

STEPS

1. **Click the FILE tab on the Ribbon, click the Properties button, then click Show Document Panel**

    The Document Properties panel opens showing the file location and the title of the presentation. Now enter some descriptive data for this presentation file.

2. **Enter the data shown in FIGURE D-14, then click the Document Properties panel Close button** ✖

    This data provides detailed information about the presentation file that you can use to identify and organize your file. You can also use this information as search criteria to locate the file at a later time. You now use the Document Inspector to search for information you might want to delete in the presentation.

3. **Click the FILE tab on the Ribbon, click the Check for Issues button, click Inspect Document, then click Yes to save the changes to the document**

    The Document Inspector dialog box opens. The Document Inspector searches the presentation file for seven different types of information that you might want removed from the presentation before sharing it.

4. **Make sure all of the check boxes have check marks, then click Inspect**

    The presentation file is reviewed, and the results are shown in FIGURE D-15. The Document Inspector found items having to do with document properties, which you just entered, and presentation notes, which are on Slide 13. You decide to leave the document properties alone but delete the notes.

5. **Click the Remove All button in the Presentation Notes section, then click Close**

    All notes are removed from the Notes pane for the slides in the presentation.

6. **Click the FILE tab on the Ribbon, click the Protect Presentation button, click Mark as Final, then click OK in the alert box**

    An information alert box opens. Be sure to read the message to understand what happens to the file and how to recognize a marked-as-final presentation. You decide to complete this procedure.

7. **Click OK, click the HOME tab on the Ribbon, then click anywhere in the title text object**

    When you select the title text object, the Ribbon closes automatically and an information alert box at the top of the window notes that the presentation is marked as final, making it a read-only file. Compare your screen to FIGURE D-16. A **read-only** file is one that can't be edited or modified in any way. Anyone who has received a read-only presentation can only edit the presentation by changing its marked-as-final status. You still want to work on the presentation, so you remove the marked-as-final status.

8. **Click the Edit Anyway button in the information alert box, then save your changes**

    The Ribbon and all commands are active again, and the file can now be modified.

FIGURE D-14: Document Properties Panel

FIGURE D-15: Document Inspector dialog box

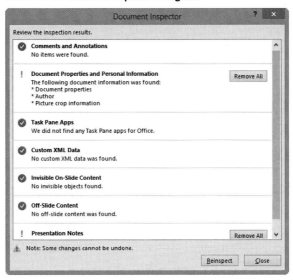

FIGURE D-16: Marked As Final presentation

Digitally sign a presentation

What is a digital signature, and why would you want to use one in PowerPoint? A **digital signature** is similar to a handwritten signature in that it authenticates your document; however, a digital signature, unlike a handwritten signature, is created using computer cryptography and is not visible within the presentation itself. There are three primary reasons you would add a digital signature to a presentation: one, to authenticate the signer of the document; two, to ensure that the content of the presentation has not been changed since it was signed; and three, to assure the reader of the origin of the signed document. To add a digital signature, click the FILE tab on the Ribbon, click the Protect Presentation button, click Add a Digital Signature, then follow the dialog boxes.

Evaluate a Presentation

A well-designed and organized presentation requires thought and preparation. An effective presentation is focused and visually appealing—easy for the speaker to present, and simple for the audience to understand. Visual elements can strongly influence the audience's attention and can influence the success of your presentation. **CASE** ▶ *You know your boss and other colleagues will critique your presentation, so you take the time to evaluate your presentation's organization and effectiveness.*

STEPS

1. **Click the** Reading View button 📖 **on the status bar, then press [Spacebar] when the slide show finishes**

2. **Click the** Slide 5 thumbnail **in the Thumbnails pane, click the** Section button **in the** Slides group, **then click** Add Section

   The presentation is divided into two sections, which appear in the Thumbnails pane. The section you created is the Untitled Section, and the section for all the slides before the new section is the Default Section. Sections help you organize your slides into logical groups.

3. **Right-click** Untitled Section **in the Thumbnails pane, click** Rename Section, **type** Tour Packages, **then click** Rename

4. **Click the** Slide Sorter view button 🎛 **on the status bar, save your work, then compare your screen to** FIGURE D-17

5. **Double-click** Slide 1, **add your name to the notes and handouts footer, evaluate your presentation according to the guidelines below, submit your presentation to your instructor, then close the presentation and exit PowerPoint**

   FIGURE D-18 shows a poorly designed slide. Contrast this slide with the guidelines below and your presentation.

DETAILS

When evaluating a presentation, it is important to:

- **Keep your message focused and your text concise**

  Don't put every word you plan to say on your slides. Your presentation text should only provide highlights of your message. Keep the audience anticipating explanations to the key points in the presentation. Supplement the information on your slides with further explanation and details during your presentation. Try to limit each slide to six words per line and six lines per slide. Use bulleted lists to help prioritize your points visually.

- **Keep the design simple, easy to read, and appropriate for the content**

  A design theme makes the presentation visually consistent. If you design your own layout, use similar design elements and limit the number of design elements, using them sparingly throughout the presentation; otherwise, your audience may get overwhelmed and not understand the message.

- **Choose attractive colors that make the slide easy to read**

  Use contrasting complementary colors for slide background and text to make the text readable.

- **Choose fonts and styles that are easy to read and emphasize important text**

  As a general rule, use no more than two fonts in a presentation and vary the font size. If you are giving an on-screen presentation, use nothing smaller than 24 points. Use bold and italic attributes selectively.

- **Use visuals to help communicate the message of your presentation**

  Commonly used visuals include clip art, photographs, charts, worksheets, tables, and videos. Whenever possible, replace text with a visual, but be careful not to overcrowd your slides. White space on your slides enhances the presentation.

FIGURE D-17: Final presentation in Slide Sorter view

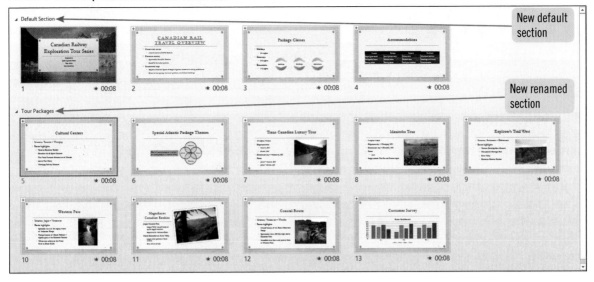

New default section

New renamed section

FIGURE D-18: A poorly designed slide

Fill color does not match theme

Too many fonts and font styles used

Too many words used

Too many font colors

Shapes serves no purpose

Too much text on the slide

Setting permissions

In PowerPoint, you can set specific access permissions for people who review or edit your work so you have better control over your content. For example, you may want to give a user permission to edit or change your presentation but not allow them to print it. You can also restrict a user by permitting them to view the presentation without the ability to edit or print the presentation, or you can give the user full access or control of the presentation. To use this feature, you first must have access to an information rights management service from Microsoft or another rights management company. Then, to set user access permissions, click the FILE tab, click the Protect Presentation button, point to Restrict Access, then click an appropriate option.

Practice

Concepts Review

Label each element of the PowerPoint window shown in FIGURE D-19.

FIGURE D-19

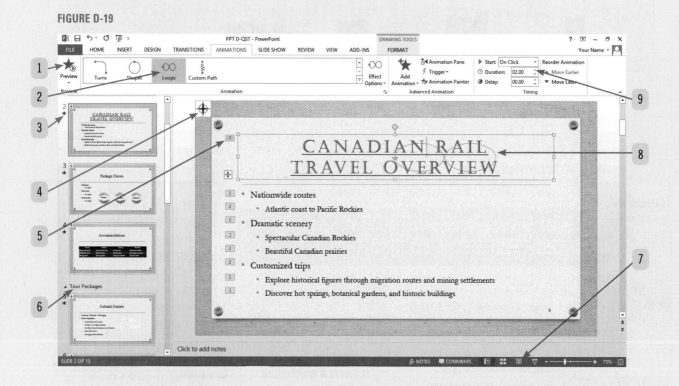

Match each term with the statement that best describes it.

10. Transitions
11. Exception
12. Background graphic
13. Annotate
14. Masters
15. Animations

a. An object placed on the slide master
b. Slides that store theme and placeholder information
c. Visual effects that determine how objects appears on the slide
d. Visual effects that determine how a slide moves in and out of view during a slide show
e. A change you make to a slide that does not follow the theme
f. To draw on a slide during a slide show

Select the best answer from the list of choices.

16. The Document Inspector looks for _____ and personal information that is stored in the presentation file.
    - **a.** Themes
    - **b.** Hidden data
    - **c.** Animation tags
    - **d.** Video settings

17. Apply a(n) _____ to your presentation to quickly modify the applied theme.
    - **a.** Variant
    - **b.** Exception
    - **c.** Theme
    - **d.** Animation

18. Which PowerPoint file *can't* be edited or modified?
    - **a.** Inspected file
    - **b.** File saved in another file format
    - **c.** Read-only file
    - **d.** Template file

19. Use _____ view to show your presentation through two monitors.
    - **a.** Reading
    - **b.** Presenter
    - **c.** Slide Show
    - **d.** Projector

20. Set slide _____ to make your presentation automatically progress through the slides during a slide show.
    - **a.** Animations
    - **b.** Autoplay effects
    - **c.** Variants
    - **d.** Timings

21. According to the book, which guidelines should you follow when you create a presentation?
    - **a.** Slides should include most of the information you wish to present.
    - **b.** Use many different design elements to keep your audience from getting bored.
    - **c.** Slides should outline the message in a concise way.
    - **d.** Use text rather than visuals as often as possible.

22. Which of the following statements about masters is *not* true?
    - **a.** Changes made to the slide master are reflected in the handout and notes masters as well.
    - **b.** Masters store information.
    - **c.** Each slide layout in the presentation has a corresponding slide layout in Slide Master view.
    - **d.** The design theme is placed on the slide master.

Skills Review

1. **Modify masters.**
   - **a.** Open the presentation PPT D-4.pptx from the location where you store your Data Files, then save the presentation as **PPT D-DataSource**.
   - **b.** Open Slide Master view using the VIEW tab, then click the Integral Slide Master thumbnail.
   - **c.** Insert the picture PPT D-5.jpg, then resize the picture so it is 1.0" wide.
   - **d.** Drag the picture to the upper-right corner of the slide within the design frame of the slide, then deselect the picture.
   - **e.** Preserve the Integral master, switch to Normal view, then save your changes.

2. **Customize the background and theme.**
   - **a.** Click the DESIGN tab, click the More button in the Variants group, then click the first variant in the second row.
   - **b.** Go to Slide 4, then open the Format Background pane.
   - **c.** Click the Color button, then click Tan, Accent 2 in the top row.
   - **d.** Set the Transparency to 50%, close the Format Background pane then save your changes.

Skills Review (continued)

3. **Use slide show commands.**
   a. Open Slide Show view, then go to Slide 1 using the See all slides button on the Slide Show toolbar.
   b. Use the Pen annotation tool to circle the slide title.
   c. Go to Slide 2, then use the Highlighter to highlight four points in the bulleted text on the slide.
   d. Erase two highlight annotations on the bulleted text, then press [Esc].
   e. Open Presenter view, then stop the timer.
   f. Advance the slides to Slide 5, then click the Zoom into the slide button (now called the Zoom out button) on the Slide Show toolbar, then click in the center of the graph.
   g. Click the Zoom into the slide button, then return to Slide 1.
   h. Hide Presenter view, advance through the slide show, don't save any ink annotations, then save your work.

4. **Set slide transitions and timings.**
   a. Go to Slide Sorter view, click the Slide 1 thumbnail, then apply the Ripple transition to the slide.
   b. Change the effect option to From Bottom-Right, change the duration speed to 2.50, then apply to all the slides.
   c. Change the slide timing to 5 seconds, then apply to all of the slides.
   d. Switch to Normal view, view the slide show, then save your work.

5. **Animate objects.**
   a. Go to Slide 3, click the ANIMATIONS tab, then select the double-headed arrow on the slide.
   b. Apply the Split effect to the object, click the Pricing shape, apply the Shape effect, then preview the animations.
   c. Click the COG shape, apply the Shape effect, then preview the animations.
   d. Select the Pricing shape and the COG shape, click the Effect Options button, then click Box.
   e. Click the double-headed arrow, click the Effect Options button, click Horizontal Out, then preview the animations.

6. **Use proofing and language tools.**
   a. Check the spelling of the document, and change any misspelled words. Ignore any words that are correctly spelled but that the spell checker doesn't recognize. There is one misspelled word in the presentation.
   b. Go to Slide 3, then set the Mini Translator language to Ukrainian.
   c. View the Ukrainian translation of text on Slide 3.
   d. Choose one other language (or as many as you want), translate words or phrases on the slide, reset the default language to Arabic, turn off the Mini Translator, then save your changes.

7. **Inspect a presentation.**
   a. Open the Document Properties pane, type your name in the Author text box, type **Internet Product** in the Subject text box, then type **Review** in the Status text box.
   b. Close the Document Properties pane, then open the Document Inspector dialog box.
   c. Make sure the Off-Slide Content check box is selected, then inspect the presentation.
   d. Delete the off-slide content, then close the dialog box. Save your changes.

8. **Evaluate a presentation.**
   a. Go to Slide 4, add a section, then rename it **Pricing and Sales**.
   b. Select the Default section at the top of the Thumbnails pane, then rename it **Intro**.
   c. Go to Slide 1, then run a slide show.
   d. Evaluate the presentation using the points described in the lesson as criteria, then submit a written evaluation to your instructor.
   e. Add the slide number and your name to the slide footer on all the slides, then save your changes.

Skills Review (continued)

f. Switch to Slide Sorter view, then compare your presentation to FIGURE D-20.

g. Submit your presentation to your instructor, then close the presentation.

FIGURE D-20

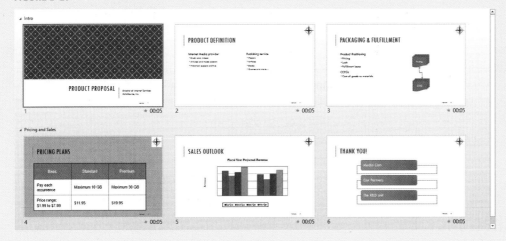

Independent Challenge 1

You are a travel consultant for Pacific Tour Enterprises, located in Houston, Texas. You have been working on a sales presentation that is going to be accessed by customers on the company Web site. You need to finish up what you have been working on by adding transitions, timings, and animation effects to the sales presentation.

a. Open the file PPT D-6.pptx from the location where you store your Data Files, and save the presentation as **PPT D-Pacific**.

b. Add the slide number and your name as the footer on all slides, except the title slide.

c. Open Slide Master View, click the Facet Slide Master thumbnail, insert the picture PPT D-7.jpg, then resize the picture so it is 1.0" wide.

d. Right-click a blank area of the master slide, point to Grid and Guides, click Add Vertical Guide, then make sure the guide is in the center of the master slide.

e. Move the picture to the top of the slide centered over the vertical guide, remove the vertical guide, then close Slide Master view.

f. Apply the Wipe animation to the title text on each slide.

g. Apply the Underline animation to the bulleted text objects on each slide.

h. Apply the Shape animation to the table on Slide 5, then change the effect option to Box.

i. Apply the Comb slide transition, apply a 7-second slide timing, then apply to all of the slides.

j. Check the spelling of the presentation, then save your changes.

k. View the slide show, and evaluate your presentation. Make changes if necessary.

l. Submit your presentation to your instructor, close the presentation, then exit PowerPoint.

Independent Challenge 2

You are a development engineer at Advanced Performance Sports, Inc., an international sports product design company located in Phoenix, Arizona. Advanced Performance designs and manufactures items such as bike helmets, bike racks, and kayak paddles, and markets these items primarily to countries in North America and Western Europe. You need to finish the work on a quarterly presentation that outlines the progress of the company's newest technologies by adding animations, customizing the background, and using the Document Inspector.

a. Open the file PPT D-8.pptx from the location where you store your Data Files, and save the presentation as **PPT D-Sports**.

Independent Challenge 2 (continued)

b. Apply an appropriate design theme, then apply a gradient fill slide background to the title slide using the Format Background pane.

c. Apply the Glitter slide transition to all slides, then animate the following objects: the bulleted text on Slide 2 and the table on Slide 4. View the slide show to evaluate the effects you added and make adjustments as necessary.

d. Use the Microsoft Translator to translate the bulleted text on Slide 2 using two different languages.

e. Run the Document Inspector with all options selected, identify what items the Document Inspector finds, close the Document Inspector dialog box, then review the slides to find the items.

f. Add a slide at the end of the presentation that identifies the items the Document Inspector found.

g. Run the Document Inspector again, and remove all items except the document properties.

h. View the slide show, and make annotations to the slides. Save the annotations at the end of the slide show.

i. Add your name as a footer to all slides, run the spell checker, save your work, then run the slide show to evaluate your presentation.

j. Submit your presentation to your instructor, then close the presentation and exit PowerPoint.

Independent Challenge 3

You work for Thomas Lincoln & Associates, a full-service investment and pension firm. Your manager wants you to create a presentation on small business pension plan options. You have completed adding the information to the presentation, now you need to add a design theme, format information to highlight certain facts, add animation effects, and add slide timings.

a. Open the file PPT D-9.pptx from the location where you store your Data Files, and save the presentation as **PPT D-Thomas**.

b. Apply an appropriate design theme, then apply a theme variant.

c. Apply animation effects to the following objects: the shapes on Slide 3 and the bulleted text on Slide 5. View the slide show to evaluate the effects you added, and make adjustments as necessary.

d. Convert the text on Slide 4 to a Radial Cycle SmartArt graphic (found in the Cycle category).

e. Apply the Polished Effect style to the SmartArt graphic.

f. Go to Slide 3, align the Sector and Quality arrow shapes to their bottoms, then align the Allocation and Maturity arrow shapes to their right edges.

g. On Slides 6 and 7 change the table style format to Light Style2 - Accent 4, and adjust the position of the tables on the slides, if necessary.

h. Apply a 10-second timing to Slides 3–7 and a 5-second timing to Slides 1 and 2.

i. Add a section between Slide 5 and Slide 6, then rename the section **Plans**.

j. Rename the Default section in the Slides tab to **Intro**.

k. Add your name as a footer to the slides, run the Spell Checker, save your work, then run the slide show to evaluate your presentation. An example of a finished presentation is shown in FIGURE D-21.

FIGURE D-21

l. Submit your presentation to your instructor, then close the presentation and exit PowerPoint.

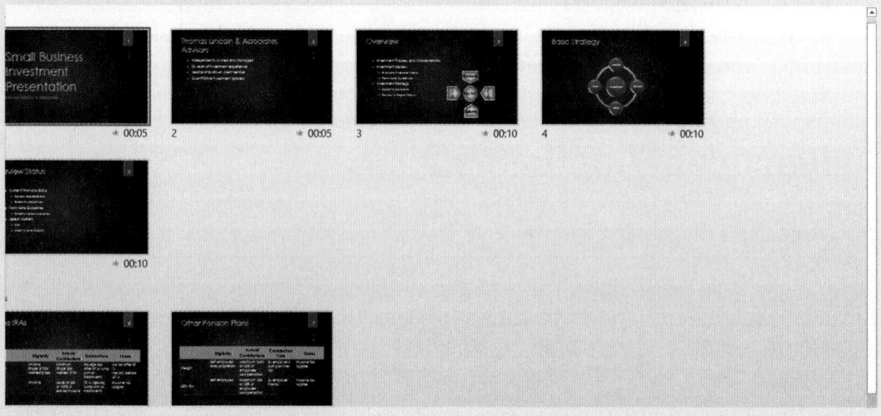

Independent Challenge 4: Explore

You work for the operations supervisor at the Southern Alabama State University student union. Create a presentation that you can eventually publish to the college Web site that describes all of the services offered at the student union. (*Note: To complete this Independent Challenge, you may need to be connected to the Internet.*)

a. Plan and create the slide presentation that describes the services and events offered at the student union. To help create content, use the student union at your school or use the Internet to locate information on college student unions. The presentation should contain at least six slides.

b. Use an appropriate design theme.

c. Add at least one photograph to the presentation, then style and customize one photo.

d. Save the presentation as **PPT D-SASU** to the location where you store your Data Files. View the slide show, and evaluate the contents of your presentation. Make any necessary adjustments.

e. Add slide transitions and animation effects to the presentation. View the slide show again to evaluate the effects you added.

f. To help you to complete this step, use the information on rehearsing slide timings found in the Set Slide Transition and Timings lesson in this unit. Click the Slide Show tab, click the Rehearse Timings button in the Set Up group, then click the Next button on the Recording toolbar to advance each slide in the presentation.

g. Click Yes to save slides timings at the end of the slide show.

h. Go to Slide 2, translate the bottom text box into Korean, then click the Copy button on the Microsoft Translator box.

i. Insert a new text box on Slide 2, paste the Korean text into the text box, then move the Korean text box below the translated English text box.

j. Change the language in the Microsoft translator back to Arabic, then turn off the Microsoft Translator.

k. Add the slide number and your name as a footer to the slides, check the spelling, inspect, then save the presentation.

l. Submit your presentation to your instructor, then exit PowerPoint. An example of a finished presentation is shown in FIGURE D-22.

FIGURE D-22

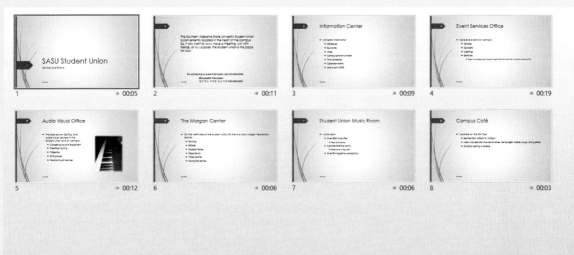

Visual Workshop

Create a one-slide presentation that looks like FIGURE D-23, which shows a slide with a specific slide layout, slide background, theme, and theme variant. Add your name as footer text to the slide, save the presentation as **PPT D-Glacier** to the location where you store your Data Files, then submit your presentation to your instructor.

FIGURE D-23

Working with Advanced Tools and Masters

CASE As a sales associate for Quest Specialty Travel, you have been working on a train tour presentation that details the specifics of Canadian train tours. After receiving some initial feedback, you revise the presentation by enhancing shapes, customizing animations, and customizing the master views.

Unit Objectives

After completing this unit, you will be able to:

- Draw and format connectors
- Use advanced formatting tools
- Customize animation effects
- Create custom slide layouts
- Format master text
- Change master text indents
- Adjust text objects
- Use templates and add comments

Files You Will Need

PPT E-1.pptx	PPT E-4.pptx
PPT E-2.pptx	PPT E-5.pptx
PPT E-3.pptx	PPT E-6.pptx

Draw and Format Connectors

PowerPoint has a number of connector tools that enable you to create three different types of connector lines or arrows—straight, elbow (bent), or curved. For example, you would use the connector tools to connect shapes with a line or arrow. Use the Curve tool to create a free-form curved line. Once you have drawn a line or connector, you can format it using Quick Styles, outline color, or effects. **CASE** ▶ *Drawing and formatting connecting lines between the shapes on Slide 3 will enhance the look of the shapes.*

STEPS

1. **Start PowerPoint, open the presentation** PPT E-1.pptx **from the location where you store your Data Files, save the presentation as** PPT E-QST, **click the** Slide 8 thumbnail **in the Thumbnails pane, then click the** More button ⬇ **in the Drawing group**

   Slide 8 of the presentation appears in Normal view, and the Shapes gallery is open.

2. **Right-click the** Elbow Connector button ⌐ **in the Lines section, click** Lock Drawing Mode **on the shortcut menu, then position** ╋ **on the top connection site** ▣ **on the** Vancouver red triangle shape

   Notice the shape has six possible connection sites to anchor a line or arrow. Locking the drawing mode allows you to draw the same shape multiple times without having to reselect the tool in the Shapes Gallery. See **FIGURE E-1**.

3. **Press and hold the** left mouse button on the ▣, **then drag to the right to connect to the** bottom left ▣ **on the** Jasper red triangle shape

   Green handles (circles) appear at each end of the elbow connector line, indicating that it is attached to the two shapes. The line has one adjustment handle (yellow square) in the middle of the elbow connector that allows you to alter the path of the line.

4. **Position** ╋ **on the top** ▣ **on the** Jasper red triangle shape, **drag** ╋ **to the top** ▣ **on the** Edmonton red triangle shape, **then press [Esc]**

   A second connector line now flows from the top of the Jasper red triangle shape to the top of the Edmonton red triangle shape. Pressing [Esc] unlocks the drawing mode.

5. **Click the** Jasper to Edmonton connector line, **position** ⤢ **over the** green handle **on the** Edmonton red triangle shape, **then drag the** green handle **to the bottom left** ▣ **on the** Edmonton red triangle shape

   The right connector line now flows from the top of the Jasper red triangle shape to the bottom left of the Edmonton red triangle shape as shown in **FIGURE E-2**.

6. **Click the** Vancouver to Jasper connector line, **click the** DRAWING TOOLS FORMAT tab **on the Ribbon, click** ⬇ **in the Shape Styles group, then click** Moderate Line – Dark 1 (second row)

   The style of the line becomes more distinct.

7. **Click the** Shape Outline list arrow **in the Shape Styles group, point to** Weight, **then click** 1½pt

   The line is wider and easier to see.

8. **Right-click the** Vancouver to Jasper connector line, **point to** Connector Types **on the shortcut menu, click** Curved Connector, **click a blank area of the slide, then save your presentation**

   The connector line is now curved. Compare your screen to **FIGURE E-3**.

FIGURE E-1: Shape with connection sites

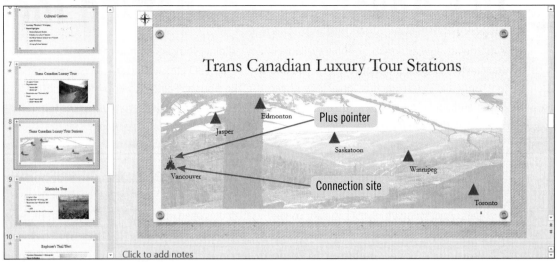

FIGURE E-2: Moved connector line

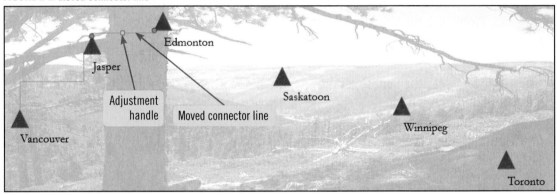

FIGURE E-3: Formatted connector line

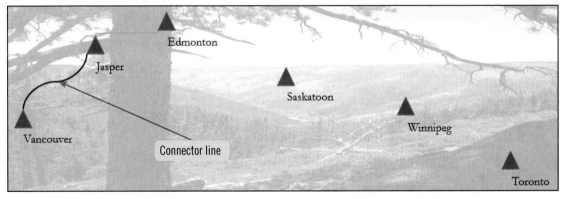

Changing page setup and slide orientation

When you need to customize the size and orientation of the slides in your presentation, you can do so using the Slide Size command in the Customize group on the DESIGN tab. Click the Slide Size button to change the slide size to Widescreen (16:9) or Standard (4:3), or click Custom Slide Size to open the Slide Size dialog box. In the Slide Size dialog box, you can change the width and height of the slides to 13 different settings, including On-screen Show, Letter Paper, 35mm Slides, and Banner. You can also set a custom slide size by specifying the height and width of the slides. If the presentation would work better in Portrait rather than Landscape mode, you can set the slide orientation by clicking either the Portrait or Landscape option button in the Slides section. The orientation setting for the slides is separate from the orientation setting for the notes, handouts, and outline.

Use Advanced Formatting Tools

With the advanced formatting tools available in PowerPoint, you can change the attributes of any object. You can format text and shapes using solid and texture fills, 3D effects, and shadows. To create a cohesive look on a slide with multiple objects, you can use the Format Painter to copy the attributes from one object and apply them to other objects. **CASE** ▶ *In this lesson, you finish formatting the connector lines on Slide 8 and then use the advanced formatting tools to enhance the red triangle shapes.*

STEPS

1. **Click the Vancouver to Jasper connector line, click the HOME tab on the Ribbon, then click the Format Painter button in the Clipboard group**

   The Format Painter tool "picks up" or copies the attributes of an object and pastes them on the next object you select.

2. **Position ⬚ 🖌 over the Jasper to Edmonton connector line, click the Jasper to Edmonton connector line, then click a blank area of the slide**

   Both connector lines are formatted using the same line width and color, as shown in **FIGURE E-4**.

QUICK TIP
To fill a shape with a picture, right-click the shape, click the Fill button, then click Picture to open the Insert Pictures dialog box.

3. **Right-click the Vancouver red triangle shape, click the Fill button on the shortcut menu, point to Texture, then click Denim (top row)**

   The blue denim texture fills the shape.

4. **Right-click the Vancouver red triangle shape, then click Format Picture on the shortcut menu**

   The Format Picture pane opens.

5. **Click 3-D FORMAT, click the Top bevel button, click the Slope icon, scroll down the Format Picture pane, click the Lighting button, then click the Flood icon in the Neutral section**

   The lighting effect defines the bevel effect better.

6. **Click 3-D ROTATION, scroll down the Format Picture pane, then click the X Rotation Right button ⟳ three times until 15° appears in the X Rotation text box**

   The shape changes perspective, and you can see the effect and the depth of the effect.

7. **Click ARTISTIC EFFECTS, scroll down the Format Picture pane, click the Artistic Effects button ▦▾, click Crisscross Etching (4th row), then click the Close button ✕ in the Format Picture pane**

   Changing the artistic effect slightly enhances the 3D effect already applied to the shape.

QUICK TIP
You can also press [Esc] to turn off the Format Painter.

8. **Double-click the Format Painter button in the Clipboard group, click each of the five remaining red triangle shapes, then click Format Painter button again to turn off the Format Painter**

   Double-clicking the Format Painter button locks the Format Painter allowing you to apply the same formatting to multiple objects on the slide without having to reselect the tool. Now the six triangle shapes on the slide have the same fill and 3D effects.

9. **Click a blank area of the slide, then save your changes**

   Compare your screen with **FIGURE E-5**.

FIGURE E-4: Formatted connector lines

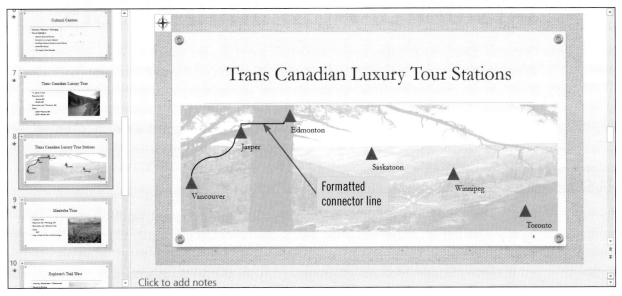

FIGURE E-5: Formatted shapes

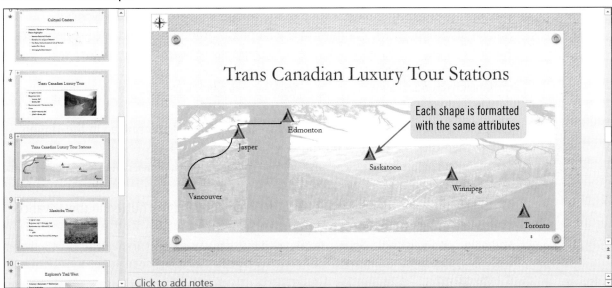

Creating columns in a text box

When the information you are working with fits better in a column format, you have the ability to create columns within text objects. Select the text object, click the Add or Remove Columns button in the Paragraph group on the HOME tab, then click either One Column, Two Columns, Three Columns, or More Columns. The More Columns option allows you to set up to 16 columns and customize the spacing between columns. You can display the ruler to set specific widths for the columns and further customize the columns.

PowerPoint 2013

Working with Advanced Tools and Masters

Customize Animation Effects

Learning Outcomes
- Apply multiple animations to an object
- Change animation order

Animating objects allows you to control how information flows and objects move on the slide during a slide show. The simplest way to animate an object is to apply a standard animation effect from the Animation group on the ANIMATIONS tab. There are additional entrance, emphasis, exit, and motion path animation effects available through the menu at the bottom of the Animation gallery that you can apply to objects. You can customize effect options including starting time, direction, and speed. And when you want to apply animation settings from one object to another, you can use the Animation Painter. **CASE** *You decide to animate the triangle shapes and connector lines you created on Slide 8.*

STEPS

1. **Click the ANIMATIONS tab on the Ribbon, click the** Vancouver triangle shape, **click the More button** ▼ **in the Animation group, then click** More Entrance Effects **at the bottom of the gallery**

   The Change Entrance Effect dialog box opens. Effects are grouped by categories: Basic, Subtle, Moderate, and Exciting.

QUICK TIP
To delete all animation effects from an object, select the object on the slide, then click None in the Animation group.

2. **Click** Spinner **in the Moderate section, click** OK, **click the** Duration up arrow **in the Timing group until** 01.00 **appears in the text box, then click the** Preview button **in the Preview group**

   An animation tag [1] appears next to the triangle shape.

3. **Click the** Vancouver to Jasper connector line, **click** Wipe **in the Animation group, click the** Vancouver triangle shape, **click the** Add Animation button **in the Advanced Animation group, click** Color Pulse **in the Emphasis group, then click the** Preview button

   The Add Animation feature allows you to apply multiple animations to the same object. Notice another animation tag appears behind Animation tag 1 next to the Vancouver triangle shape, which indicates the shape now has two animations applied to it. You want both animations on the Vancouver triangle shape to run consecutively.

4. **Click the** Animation tag 2 [2] **on the slide, click the** Move Later button **in the Timing group, then click the** Preview button

   The animations for the triangle shape now run consecutively before the animation for the connector line. Compare your screen to **FIGURE E-6**.

5. **Click the** Vancouver triangle shape, **click the** Animation Painter button **in the Advanced Animation group, then click the** Jasper triangle shape

   Notice that when you use the Animation Painter all the animations and animation settings from the first shape are applied to the second shape. The Vancouver to Jasper connector line animation would look better if it was delayed.

QUICK TIP
To set an animation to run after you click another object, click the Trigger button in the Advanced Animation group, point to On Click of, then select an object.

6. **Click the** Vancouver to Jasper connector line, **click the** Delay up arrow **in the Timing group until** 00.50 **appears, then click the** Preview button

   The delay between the triangle shape and the connector line animations defines each animation effect.

7. **Click the** Animation Painter button **in the Advanced Animation group, click the** Jasper to Edmonton connector line, **then click the** Preview button

   Now both connector lines have the same animation and animation settings. The Jasper to Edmonton connector line would look a little better if animated from the left.

8. **Click the** Effect Options button **in the Animation group, click** From Left, **click the** Preview button, **then save your changes**

   Compare your screen to **FIGURE E-7**.

FIGURE E-6: Animation effects applied to the objects

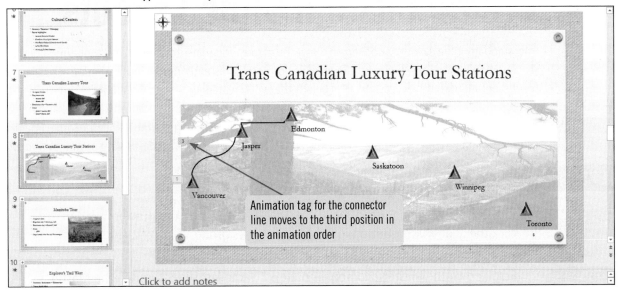

FIGURE E-7: Completed animation effects

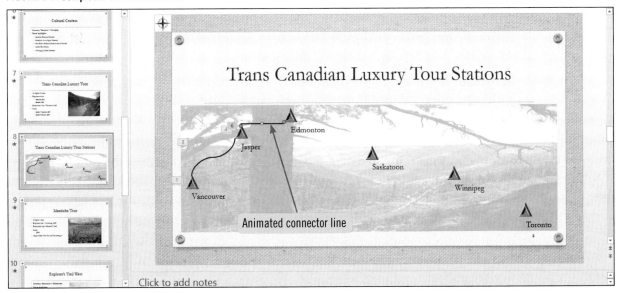

Understanding animation timings

Each animated object on a slide has a starting time in relation to the other animated objects. There are three different starting time options: Start On Click, Start With Previous, and Start After Previous. The Start On Click timing option starts the animation effect when you click the mouse. The Start With Previous timing option begins the animation effect at the same time as the previous effect in the animation list, so two or more animation effects play at once. The Start After Previous timing option begins the animation immediately after the previous animation without clicking the mouse.

Create Custom Slide Layouts

Learning
Outcomes
• Add a new slide
  master layout
• Create master
  placeholders

The standard slide layouts supplied in PowerPoint are adequate to design most of the slides for presentations that you will create. However, if you are consistently modifying a standard slide layout for presentations, having a custom slide layout that you created and saved would be helpful. To create a custom slide layout, you choose from eight different placeholders, including text, chart, and media placeholders. You draw the placeholder on the slide in Slide Master view; these then become a part of the presentation. **CASE** ▶ *You decide to create a custom slide layout that displays picture thumbnails on the slide that you can use as navigation buttons during a slide show.*

STEPS

1. **Click the VIEW tab on the Ribbon, click the Ruler check box in the Show group, then click the Slide Master button in the Master Views group**

   Slide Master view opens, and the ruler is displayed.

   QUICK TIP
   To insert an additional slide master to use in your presentation, click the Insert Slide Master button in the Edit Master group.

2. **Scroll down the Master Thumbnails pane, click the last slide layout in the Master Thumbnails pane, then click the Insert Layout button in the Edit Master group**

   A new slide layout is added to the presentation and appears in the Master Thumbnails pane with a title text placeholder and footer placeholders as shown in FIGURE E-8. The new slide layout contains all of the slide background elements associated with the current theme.

3. **Click the Insert Placeholder list arrow in the Master Layout group, then click Picture**

   The pointer changes to ┼ when moved over the slide.

4. **Position the pointer on the slide so ┼ is lined up on the 5" mark on the left side of the horizontal ruler and the 1" mark on the top of the vertical ruler**

   As you move the pointer on the slide its position is identified on the rulers by red dotted lines.

5. **Drag a box down and to the right until ┼ is lined up with the 2 ½" mark on the horizontal ruler and the ½" mark below 0 on the vertical ruler**

   You drew a 2 ½" x 1 ½" square picture placeholder on the slide. You can duplicate the placeholder.

6. **Click the HOME tab on the Ribbon, click the Copy button list arrow in the Clipboard group, click Duplicate, then duplicate the picture placeholder four more times**

   There are six picture placeholders on the slide.

   QUICK TIP
   To help position placeholders precisely on the slide as shown in FIGURE E-9, you can also display the guides and use the Align and Distribute commands.

7. **Drag each picture placeholder using Smart Guides to a position on the slide as shown in FIGURE E-9, then click the SLIDE MASTER tab on the Ribbon**

   The placeholders are arranged on the slide layout.

8. **Click the Rename button in the Edit Master group, select the default name, type Picture, click Rename, then position the pointer ⇖ over the last slide layout in the Master Thumbnails pane**

   The new name of the custom slide layout appears in the ScreenTip. The new Picture layout now appears when you click the Layout button or the New Slide list button in the Slides group on the HOME tab.

9. **Right-click a blank area of the slide, click Ruler, click the Close Master View button in the Close group, then save your changes**

   The rulers close, and Slide 8 appears in Normal view.

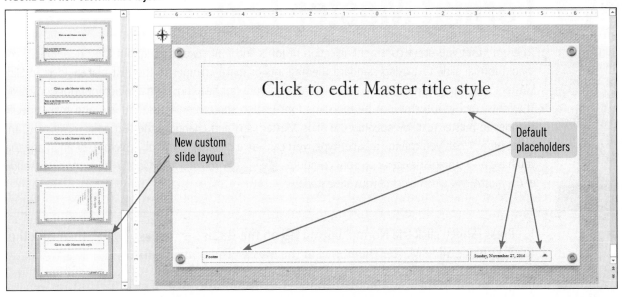

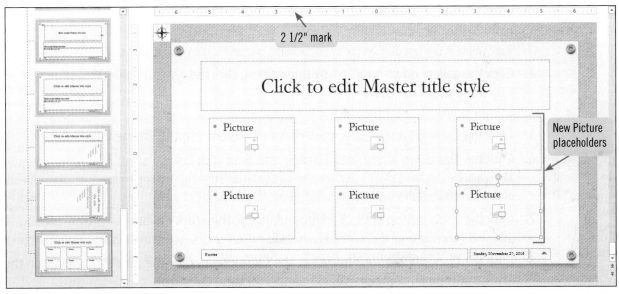

Restoring the slide master layout

If the slide master is missing a placeholder, open Slide Master view, then click the Master Layout button in the Master Layout group to reapply the placeholder. Clicking the Master Layout button opens the Master Layout dialog box, as shown in FIGURE E-10. Click the placeholder check box to reapply the placeholder. To quickly apply or remove the title or footer placeholders on a slide master, click the Title or Footers check boxes in the Master Layout group.

FIGURE E-10: Master Layout dialog box

PowerPoint 2013

Format Master Text

To ensure that you use a consistent selection of fonts and font styles throughout the presentation, you should format slide text using standard theme fonts or make changes to the text placeholders in Slide Master view. A font theme defines two fonts—a major font (for headings) and a minor font (for body text). The fonts used in a theme can be the same font or two contrasting fonts. You can also make specific changes to master text, by opening the Slide Master view and changing the text color, style, size, and bullet type. When you change a bullet type, you can use a character symbol, a picture, or an image that you have on a storage device or on your computer. **CASE** *You decide to make a few formatting changes to the master text placeholder of your presentation.*

STEPS

1. **Press [Shift], click the Normal button ▣ on the status bar, release [Shift], then click the 1_Organic Slide Master thumbnail in the Master Thumbnails pane**

   Slide Master view appears with the slide master displayed in the Slide pane.

2. **Right-click Click to edit Master text styles in the master text placeholder, point to Bullets on the shortcut menu, then click Bullets and Numbering**

   The Bullets and Numbering dialog box opens. The Bulleted tab is selected; the Numbered tab in this dialog box is used to create sequentially numbered or lettered bullets.

3. **Click Customize, click the Font list arrow in the Symbol dialog box, scroll down the alphabetical list, then click Webdings**

   The Symbol dialog box displays the available bullet choices for the Webdings font.

4. **Click the gallery down scroll arrow three times, click the symbol (code 116) shown in FIGURE E-11, then click OK**

   The new symbol appears in the Bullets and Numbering dialog box.

5. **Click the Color list arrow ▣▾, then click Red, Accent 3 in the Theme Colors section**

6. **Click the Size down arrow until 100 appears, then click OK**

   The symbol and color of the new bullet in the second level of the master text placeholder changes. The size of the bullet is decreased to 100% of the size of the second-level text.

7. **Click the Fonts button in the Background group, then click Calibri**

   All of the fonts change for the presentation including all of the slide layouts in the Master Thumbnail pane.

8. **Click the Close Master View button in the Close group, click the Slide 7 thumbnail in the Thumbnails pane, then save your changes**

   You see how the changes affect the body text bullets in Normal view. Compare your screen to FIGURE E-12.

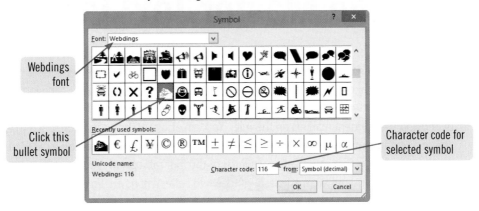

Webdings font

Click this bullet symbol

Character code for selected symbol

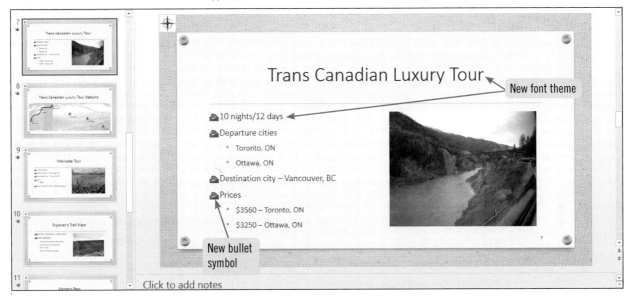

Trans Canadian Luxury Tour

New font theme

🏠 10 nights/12 days
🏠 Departure cities
    • Toronto, ON
    • Ottawa, ON
🏠 Destination city – Vancouver, BC
🏠 Prices
    • $3560 – Toronto, ON
    • $3250 – Ottawa, ON

New bullet symbol

Click to add notes

Understanding exceptions to the slide master

If you change the format of text on a slide and then apply a different theme to the presentation, the slide that you formatted retains the text-formatting changes you made rather than taking the new theme formats. These format changes that differ from the slide master are known as exceptions. Exceptions can only be changed on the individual slides where they occur. For example, you might change the font and size of a particular text object on a slide to make it stand out and then decide later to add a different theme to your presentation. The text you formatted before you applied the theme is an exception, and it is unaffected by the new theme. Another way to override the slide master is to remove the background graphics on one or more slides. You might want to do this to get a clearer view of your slide text. Click the DESIGN tab, click Format Background in the Customize group, then click the Hide Background Graphics check box in the Background group to select it.

Change Master Text Indents

Master text and content placeholders have five levels of text, called **indent levels**. You can modify indent levels using PowerPoint's ruler. For example, you can change the space between a bullet and text of an indent level or change the position of the whole indent level. The position of each indent level on the ruler is represented by two small triangles and a square called **indent markers**. You can modify an indent level by moving these indent markers on the ruler. You can also set tabs on the horizontal ruler, which identifies where a text indent or a column of text begins. By clicking the **tab selector** located at the far left of the horizontal ruler, you are able to choose which of the four tab options you want to use. TABLE E-1 describes PowerPoint's indent and tab markers. **CASE** *To better emphasize the text in the master text placeholder, you change the first two indent levels.*

STEPS

1. **Press [Shift], click the Normal button 🔲 on the status bar, release [Shift], then click the 1_Organic Slide Master thumbnail in the Master Thumbnails pane**
   Slide Master view opens.

2. **Click Click to edit Master text styles in the master text placeholder, click the VIEW tab on the Ribbon, then click the Ruler check box in the Show group**
   The horizontal and vertical rulers for the master text placeholder appear. The indent markers, on the horizontal ruler, are set so the first line of text—in this case, the bullet—begins to the left of subsequent lines of text. This is called a **hanging indent**.

TROUBLE
If you accidentally drag an indent marker past the mark, click the Undo button on the Quick Access toolbar and try again.

3. **Position ▷ over the Hanging Indent marker △, then drag to the ½" mark on the ruler**
   The space between the first indent-level bullet and text increases. Compare your screen to FIGURE E-13.

4. **Click Second level in the master text placeholder, then drag the Left indent marker ☐ to the 1" mark shown in FIGURE E-14**
   The whole indent level moves to the right.

5. **Click 🔲 on the status bar, click the Slide 12 thumbnail in the Thumbnails pane, then click to the left of the word Experience in the text object**
   Slide Master view closes, and Slide 12 appears in Normal view, showing the Master text indent changes in the text object. A left tab stop on the ruler allows you to move a line of text in one tab stop.

6. **Click on the ⅝" mark on the ruler, then press [Tab], as shown in FIGURE E-15**
   A left-aligned tab ⌊ appears on the ruler. When you press [Tab] the text moves to the right and is aligned with the text above it. Every text object in PowerPoint has default tab stops identified by small boxes at every ½" mark under the ruler. You can drag one default tab stop to reposition all the tab stops as a group.

7. **Click to the left of the word Over in the text object, click on the ⅝" mark on the ruler, then press [Tab]**
   The text moves to the right one tab stop.

8. **Right-click a blank area of the slide, click Ruler in the shortcut menu, then save your changes**
   The rulers close.

FIGURE E-13: Master level text with moved hanging indent marker

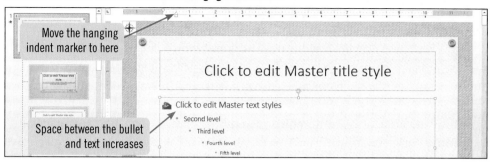

FIGURE E-14: Second-level indent moved

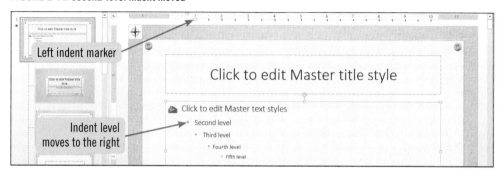

FIGURE E-15: Left tab stop added to ruler

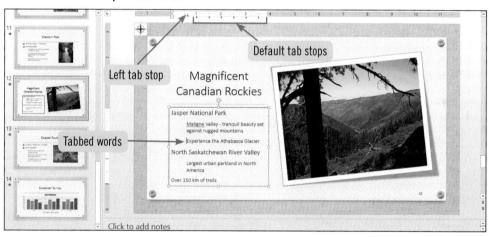

TABLE E-1: Indent and tab markers

symbol	name	function
▽	First line indent marker	Controls the position of the first line of text in an indent level
⌂	Hanging indent marker	Controls the position of the hanging indent
□	Left indent marker	Controls the position of subsequent lines of text in an indent level
∟	Left-aligned tab	Aligns tab text on the left
⊥	Center-aligned tab	Aligns tab text in the center
⌐	Right-aligned tab	Aligns tab text on the right
⊥	Decimal-aligned tab	Aligns tab text on a decimal point

PowerPoint 2013

Adjust Text Objects

You have complete control over the placement of text on slides in PowerPoint, whether the text is in a shape or in a text object. All text in PowerPoint is created within a text box, which has **margins** that determine the distance between the edge of the text and all four edges of the text box. You can also modify the space between lines of text (or bullets) between paragraphs, and the space between lines of text within a paragraph. **Paragraph spacing** is the space before and after paragraphs (bullet levels). **Leading**, (rhymes with "wedding") refers to the amount of space between lines of text within the same paragraph (bullet level). Using the text-alignment feature, you can move text within text boxes or shapes. **CASE** *You decide to move the text margin in the text object on Slide 3, change the alignment of text on Slide 2, and then change paragraph spacing of the text object on Slide 12.*

STEPS

1. **Click the Slide 3 thumbnail in the Thumbnails pane, click the HOME tab on the Ribbon, right-click a blank area of the slide, then click Ruler on the shortcut menu**
   Slide 3 appears in the slide pane with the rulers showing.

2. **Right-click Holidays in the text object, click Format Shape on the shortcut menu, click the Size & Properties icon 🔳 in the Format Shape pane, then click TEXT BOX in the Format Shape pane**
   The Format Shape pane opens.

3. **Click the Left margin up arrow until 0.4" appears, click the Top margin up arrow until 0.1" appears, then click the bottom margin up arrow until 0.1" appears**
   This adjusts the left, top, and bottom text margins and centers the text left to right within the shape as shown in **FIGURE E-16**.

4. **Click the Slide 2 thumbnail in the Thumbnails pane, click Nationwide in the text object, then click 🔳 in the Format Shape pane**
   Notice the text overflows the bottom border of the text object shape.

5. **Click the Resize shape to fit text option button in the Format Shape pane, click the Vertical alignment list arrow, click Middle Centered, then close the Format Shape pane**
   The text in the text object is aligned in the middle center of the shape. The Format Shape pane closes.

6. **Click the Slide 12 thumbnail in the Thumbnails pane, press [Shift], click the text object, release [Shift], click the Line Spacing button 📑▾ in the Paragraph group, then click Line Spacing Options**
   The Paragraph dialog box opens.

7. **In the Spacing section, click the Before up arrow until 6 pt appears, click the After down arrow until 0 pt appears, then click OK**
   The spacing before and after each bullet on Slide 12 changes. Compare your screen to **FIGURE E-17**.

8. **Right-click a blank area of the slide, click Ruler, then save your changes**
   The Ruler closes.

9. **Submit your work to your instructor, click the FILE tab, then click Close to close the presentation but do not exit PowerPoint**

Working with Advanced Tools and Masters

FIGURE E-16: Changed text margin

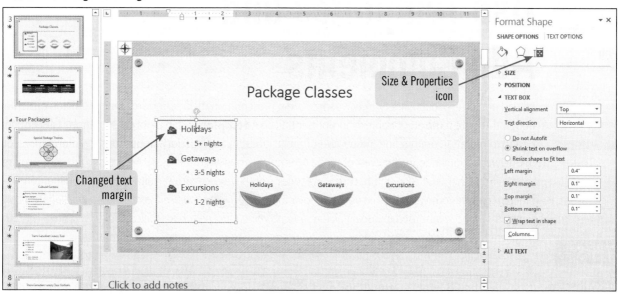

FIGURE E-17: Changed line spacing

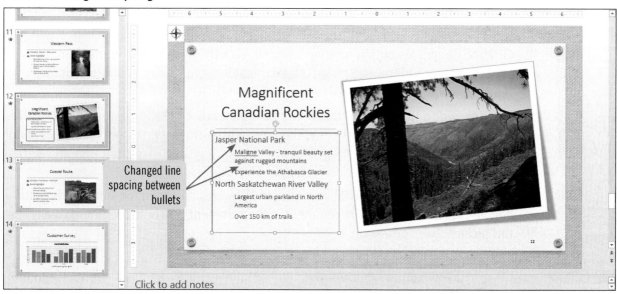

Changing text direction

Using the Text Direction button in the Paragraph group on the HOME tab, you can change the direction of text in a text object or shape. There are four text direction options available: Horizontal, Rotate all text 90°, Rotate all text 270°, and Stacked. The Horizontal option is the standard default text direction for all text in PowerPoint.

The Rotate all text 90° text direction rotates text so it faces the right margin of a text object or shape. The Rotate all text 270° text direction rotates text so it faces the left margin of a text object or shape. The Stacked text direction stacks letters vertically on top of one another.

Use Templates and Add Comments

PowerPoint offers you a variety of ways to create a presentation including starting with a blank presentation, a theme, a template, or an existing presentation. A **template** is a type of presentation that contains design information on the slide master and often includes text and design suggestions for information you might want to include in the presentation. A template usually contains a cohesive set of theme colors, theme fonts, theme effects, and background styles. You have access to sample templates online from the office.microsoft.com Web site that you can download. **CASE** *You need to review available photo album templates that could be used to display pictures of upcoming tour specials for the company Web site. NOTE: To complete the steps below, your computer must be connected to the Internet.*

STEPS

1. **Click the FILE tab on the Ribbon, click New, then click Photo Albums in the Suggested searches section**
   The New PowerPoint start screen opens, and PowerPoint searches office.com for available photo album templates. See **FIGURE E-18**.

2. **Click Classic Photo Album, wait for the template to load, then click the Create button**
   A new presentation with seven slides appears.

3. **Click the Save button 🔲 on the Quick Access toolbar, then save the file as PPT E-Classic Photo Album to the location where you store your Data Files**

4. **Click the Comments button on the status bar, click the New button in the Comments pane, then type This sample photo album might work for our next photo proposal**
   The Comments pane opens, and a comment icon appears on the slide, as shown in **FIGURE E-19**.

5. **Click the Slide 5 thumbnail in the Thumbnails pane, click the left photograph, click the New button in the Comments pane, then type This picture style would look great in our upcoming album**
   A new comment icon appears on Slide 5 next to the left photograph.

6. **Click the REVIEW tab on the Ribbon, click the Previous button in the Comments group, double-click at the end of the comment in the comment text box, then type I really like this picture style**
   The comment text box opens. To add or edit comment text, you need to open the comment text box.

7. **Click the Show Comments list arrow in the Comments group, then click Show Markup**
   The comment icon on Slide 1 and the Comment pane are hidden. The Show Markup button is a toggle button, which alternates between showing and hiding comments.

8. **Click the Next button in the Comments group, then add your name to the slide footer**
   When you move to the next comment, the comment icon and the Comment pane are visible again.

9. **Click the Comments button on the status bar, save your work, submit your presentation to your instructor, close the presentation, then exit PowerPoint**

FIGURE E-18: Sample templates available from office.com

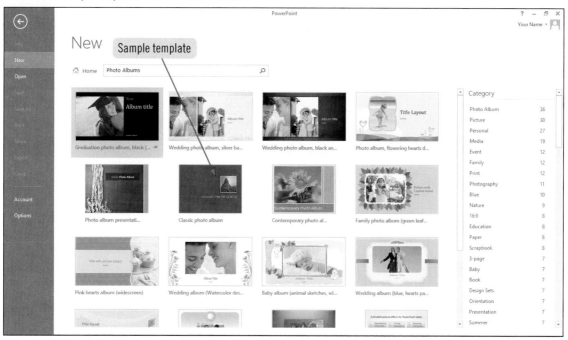

FIGURE E-19: Classic Photo Album template applied and new comment

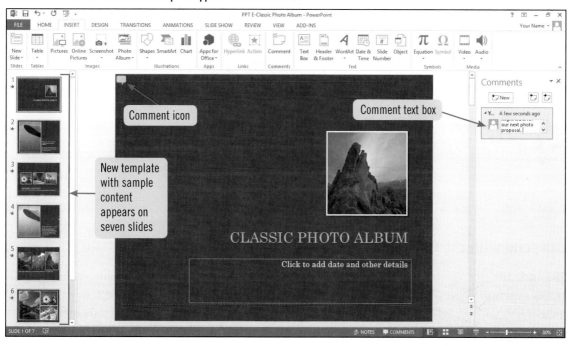

Understanding PowerPoint templates and themes

So what exactly is the difference between a PowerPoint template and a PowerPoint theme? A theme is a coordinated set of colors, fonts, and effects (such as shadows and reflections) that is used to modify the slide design of your presentation. For example, a theme is like the various colors a painter uses to paint the inside of a house where the walls are one color, the ceilings are a second color, and the window and door trim is a third color. A template, on the other hand, is a presentation that contains a theme and includes sample text about a specific subject matter, such as health and fitness. The sample text in a template provides you with the basic information that you can then use to modify the presentation with your own information.

Working with Advanced Tools and Masters

PowerPoint 2013

Practice

Concepts Review

Label each element of the PowerPoint window shown in FIGURE E-20.

FIGURE E-20

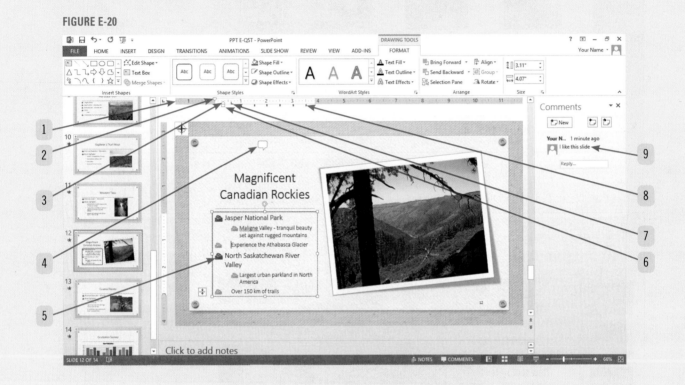

Match each term with the statement that best describes it.

10. Hanging indent
11. Paragraph spacing
12. Template
13. Indent level
14. Leading
15. Tab

a. A text level in a text object, usually started with a bullet
b. Identifies where the text indent or column of text begins
c. The first line of text begins to the left of subsequent lines of text
d. A presentation with a theme and includes sample text about a specific subject matter
e. The space between lines of text
f. The space after a paragraph or bullet level

Select the best answer from the list of choices.

16. A _____ is a type of presentation that contains custom design information and includes suggestions for sample text.
   a. Master
   b. Template
   c. Master layout
   d. Theme

17. **The small triangles and square on the ruler that represent the position of each level in a text placeholder are:**
   a. Indent levels.
   b. Tabs.
   c. Ruler marks.
   d. Indent markers.

18. **To apply the same formatting characteristics to multiple objects, double-click the _____ button.**
   a. Copy
   b. Format Picture
   c. Format Painter
   d. Multiple Format

19. **The Start _____ animation timing option allows you to play more than one animation at the same time.**
   a. After Previous
   b. On Click
   c. With Previous
   d. Before Previous

20. **Which of the following statements about connectors is *not* true?**
   a. The line connector has an adjustment handle in the middle of it to draw a new line.
   b. A connector has green handles that attach to connection sites on shapes.
   c. You can attach a connector to different points on a shape.
   d. A connection line can be rerouted to a closer connection point.

21. **Locking the _____ of a shape allows you to draw the same shape multiple times.**
   a. Quick Styles
   b. Connector site
   c. Drawing mode
   d. Format painter

Skills Review

1. **Draw and format connectors.**
   a. Start PowerPoint and open the presentation PPT E-2.pptx, then save it as **PPT E-Report** to the location where you store your Data Files.
   b. Go to Slide 4, click the More button in the Drawing group, right-click the Elbow Arrow Connector shape icon, then click Lock Drawing Mode.
   c. Position the pointer over the left connection site on the Plant shape, then drag to the top connection site on the Regional Warehouse shape.
   d. Position the pointer over the right connection site on the Plant shape, drag to the top connection site on the Individual Stores shape, then press [Esc].
   e. Click the Line button (top row) in the Drawing group, position the pointer over the right connection site on the Regional Warehouse shape, then drag to the left connection site on the Individual Stores shape.
   f. Click the Select button in the Editing group, click Selection Pane, press [Ctrl], click each elbow connector, then release [Ctrl] to select the three connectors.
   g. Right-click one of the connectors, click the Outline button, make the line style for the connectors $2\frac{1}{4}$ point wide and change the line color to a black solid line, then deselect the objects.
   h. Right-click the connector between the Regional Warehouse shape and the Individual Stores shape, click the Outline button, point to Dashes, click Dash Dot, then deselect the object.
   i. Click the Selection pane Close button, then save the presentation.

Skills Review (continued)

2. Use advanced formatting tools.

a. Go to Slide 1, right-click the 2016 Fiscal Year shape in the middle of the slide, then click Format Shape.

b. In the Format Shape pane, click FILL, click the Gradient fill option button, click the Preset gradients list arrow, then click the Bottom Spotlight - Accent 4 icon.

c. Scroll down the Format Shape pane, click LINE, then set the Width to 3 pt.

d. Click the Color button, click White, Text 1, then click TEXT OPTIONS at the top of the Format Shape pane.

e. Click the Color button, click Black, Background 1, then close the Format Shape pane.

f. On the HOME tab, double-click the Format Painter button in the Clipboard group, go to Slide 4, apply the picked up styles to each of the diamond objects, press [Esc], then save your changes.

3. Customize animation effects.

a. Click the ANIMATIONS tab, click the Plant shape, click the More button in the Animation group, then click Shape in the Entrance section.

b. Click the Effect Options button in the Animation group, then click Diamond.

c. Select the left elbow arrow connector, click the More button in the Animation group, click More Entrance Effects, apply the Strips animation, click OK, then click the Duration up arrow until 1.00 appears.

d. Click the left elbow arrow connector, click the Animation Painter button, then click the right elbow arrow connector.

e. Click Effects Options button, click Right Down, then click the Preview button.

f. Select the Regional Warehouse shape, apply the Shape animation, then change the Effect Options to Diamond.

g. Click the Move Earlier button in the Timing group, then click the Preview button.

h. Use the Animation Painter to apply the Regional Warehouse shape animation to the Individual Stores shape, then click the Preview button.

i. Select the dotted line, click Wipe in the Animation group, then change the Effect Options to From Right.

j. Click the Add Animation button, click Wipe, change the Effect Options to From Left, then click the Preview button.

k. Save your changes.

4. Create custom slide layouts.

a. Switch to Slide Master view, then click the last slide layout in the Master Thumbnails pane.

b. Insert a new custom slide layout, then display the ruler and the guides.

c. Add a 3" square Media placeholder, move the vertical guide left to 4.13, move the horizontal guide up to .75, then move the Media placeholder to the intersection of the guides.

d. Move the vertical guide right to 0.00, add a 4" x 3" Table placeholder, then move the table placeholder to the intersection of the guides.

e. Name the custom slide layout **Media Table**, turn off guides, then save your changes.

5. Format master text.

a. Click the Savon Slide Master thumbnail in the Master Thumbnails pane, then format the first-level bulleted item in the master text placeholder as bold.

b. Change the bullet symbol of the first-level bullet to the Wingdings font flag character bullet (code 79).

c. Use the Bullets and Numbering dialog box to set the size of the bullet to 90% of the text.

d. Change the bullet color to White, Text 1.

e. Set the size of the second-level bullet symbol to 125% of the text, change the color to Red, then save your changes.

Skills Review (continued)

6. Change master text indents.

  a. Move the hanging indent marker of the first-level bullet to the ³/₈" mark on the ruler and left indent marker of the second-level bullet as shown in **FIGURE E-21**.

  b. Hide the rulers, switch to Normal view, go to Slide 5, then save the presentation.

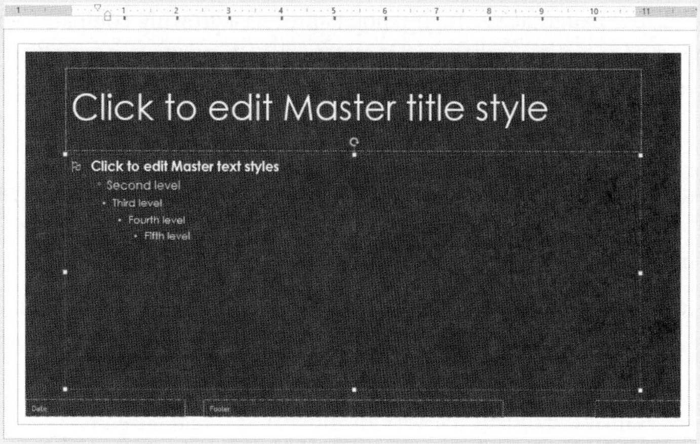

7. Adjust text objects.

  a. Press [Shift], right-click anywhere in the text object on Slide 5, release [Shift], then click Format Shape on the shortcut menu.

  b. Click the Size and Properties icon in the Format Shape pane, then click TEXT BOX.

  c. Change the vertical alignment of the text to Top Centered.

  d. Click the Resize shape to fit text option button, then close the Format Shape pane. **FIGURE E-22** shows the completed presentation in Slide Sorter view.

  e. Add your name to the slide footer, save your work, then close the presentation but do not exit PowerPoint.

FIGURE E-21

FIGURE E-22

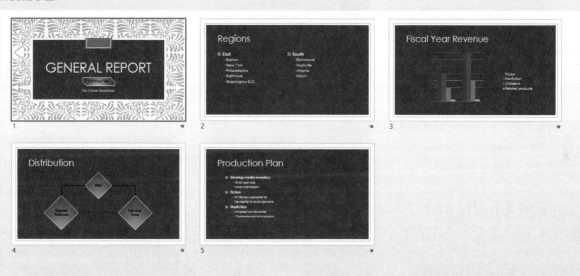

8. Use templates and add comments.

  a. Click the FILE tab, click New, click Education in the Suggested searches section, click State history report presentation, then click Create.

  b. Save the presentation as **PPT E-State History** to the location where you store your Data Files.

  c. Click the REVIEW tab on the Ribbon, click the New Comment button, type **What do you think of this template for our project?**, then go to Slide 3.

  d. Add a new comment, type **Do you have a picture of our flag?**, click the Previous button, then click the New button on the Comments pane.

  e. Type **I like this template.**, close the Comments pane, add your name to the slide footer, then save your work.

  f. Submit your presentation to your instructor, close the presentation, then exit PowerPoint.

Independent Challenge 1

You work in marketing at Pierson James Agency in Los Angeles, California. Pierson James represents all types of artists and specializes in alternative and hip hop bands. As a growing company, your business is looking for investment capital to expand its business markets and increase sales. It is your responsibility to develop a presentation the owners can present to potential investors. You have been working on the content of the presentation, and now you are ready to add custom animations and customize slide master text.

a. Open the presentation PPT E-3.pptx from the location where you store your Data Files, then save it as **PPT E-Pierson**.

b. Preview the presentation in Reading View.

c. Open Slide Master view, click the Parallax Slide Master thumbnail, then bold the text in the first-level indent.

d. Apply the Webdings font character code 37 at 125% the size of text in the first-level indent, then change the bullet color to Lavender, Accent 6.

e. Adjust the indent markers for the first indent level as shown in **FIGURE E-23**.

f. Convert the text on Slide 4 to a SmartArt graphic using the Vertical Bullet List SmartArt graphic layout, then apply the Subtle Effect SmartArt Style to the graphic.

g. Go to Slide 5, create at least two shapes connected by connectors, then format all of the objects using advanced formatting techniques you learned in the lesson.

h. Apply animation effects to objects and text on at least three slides, then preview the presentation in Slide Show view.

FIGURE E-23

i. Add comments to two slides, then add your name and slide number to the slides (except the title slide).

j. Check spelling, save the presentation, then submit your presentation to your instructor.

k. Close the presentation and exit PowerPoint.

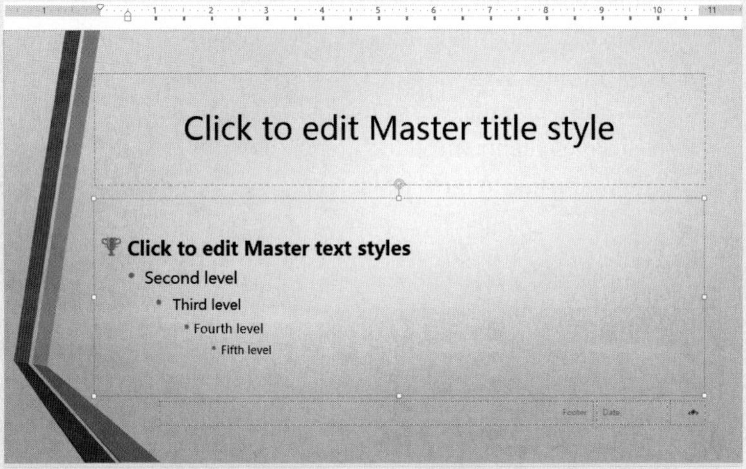

Independent Challenge 2

You are the owner of Gourmet To U, a catering company in Vancouver, British Columbia. You have built your business on private parties, wedding receptions, and special events over the last five years. To expand your business, you decide to pursue the business and formal events markets. Use PowerPoint to develop a presentation that you can use to gain corporate catering accounts.

a. Open the presentation PPT E-4.pptx from the location where you store your Data Files, then save it as **PPT E-Gourmet**.

b. Open Slide Master view, click the Banded Slide Master thumbnail, then change the Font theme to Constantia-Franklin Gothic Book.

c. Change the bullet in the first-level indent level to an arrow bullet 90% of text size, then change the bullet in the second-level indent level to a small filled square, 110% of text size.

d. Adjust the indent marker for the first indent level so there is $1/8$" of space between the arrow bullet and the text.

e. Connect the two shapes on Slide 4 using an arrow connector. Draw an elbow double-arrow connector between the shapes formatted with a 3 pt Square Dot dash line.

f. Change the left margin of each shape on Slide 4 to 0".

Independent Challenge 2 (continued)

g. On Slide 2 change the line spacing to 6 pt Before and 12 pt After in the text object.

h. Create a new custom slide layout using at least two different placeholders, then save the new layout as **Custom1**.

i. View the presentation in Reading view, then add your name and slide number to the slides footer (except the title slide).

j. Check spelling, save the presentation, then submit your presentation to your instructor.

k. Close the presentation and exit PowerPoint.

Independent Challenge 3

You are a computer game designer for Cyborg Games, an Internet interactive game developer. One of your responsibilities is to develop new interactive game concepts and present the information at a company meeting. Complete the presentation provided, which promotes two new interactive Internet game concepts you've developed. Use the following game ideas in your presentation or create two game ideas of your own.

- *Special Forces* is an interactive war game where you play a member of a U.S. special forces team during the Gulf War in Iraq. You have the option to play with and against others online to achieve one of 10 different objectives.
- *Revolution* is an interactive action/adventure game where you play a U.S. soldier during the Revolutionary War.

a. Open the presentation PPT E-5.pptx from the location where you store your Data Files, then save it as **PPT E-Cyborg**. If you develop your own material, open a new presentation, storyboard the ideas for the presentation, then create at least six slides. What do you want your audience to know about the product idea?

b. Apply a theme, and then change the theme variant. Modify the theme as necessary, such as changing background objects, font theme, color theme, or effect theme.

c. Edit existing text, and add additional information you think is appropriate to create a professional presentation.

d. Format the master text and title placeholders on the slide master to fit the subject matter.

e. Change the bullet for the first and second indent levels in the master text placeholder, then format the bullets.

f. Create a custom slide layout, name it **Concept**, then apply it to at least one slide in the presentation.

g. Add your name to the slides footer, then save the presentation.

h. View the presentation in Slide Show view, check spelling, save the presentation, then submit your presentation to your instructor.

i. Close the presentation, and exit PowerPoint.

Independent Challenge 4: Explore

You work for the operations manager at the Western University Student Activities Center. You have been working on a presentation that you eventually will publish to the college Web site that describes all of the services offered at the Student Activities Center. Complete work on the presentation by working with masters and animation effects.

a. Open the presentation PPT E-6.pptx from the location where you store your Data Files, save it as **PPT E-Western**, then apply a theme.

b. Apply animation effects to at least four objects in the presentation. Customize the animation settings as necessary.

c. Create a custom slide layout, and apply it to a slide.

d. Format the bullet and text in the master text and title placeholders on the slide master to fit the subject matter.

e. Modify master text indents on the slide master, then create shapes and connector lines on at least one slide.

f. Adjust the alignment, line spacing, and margins of at least one text object.

g. On Slide 8, change the title object text direction to Stacked.

h. Add your name to the slides footer, check spelling, view the final slide show, then submit your presentation to your instructor.

i. Close the presentation and exit PowerPoint.

Visual Workshop

Create a slide that looks like the example in FIGURE E-24. Be sure to use connector lines. Use the features on the DRAWING TOOLS FORMAT tab and specifically the Shape Outline button to customize the connector lines. The Design shape is a merged shape of two shapes. Add your name to the slide footer, then save the presentation as **PPT E-Process**. Submit your presentation to your instructor, then exit PowerPoint.

FIGURE E-24

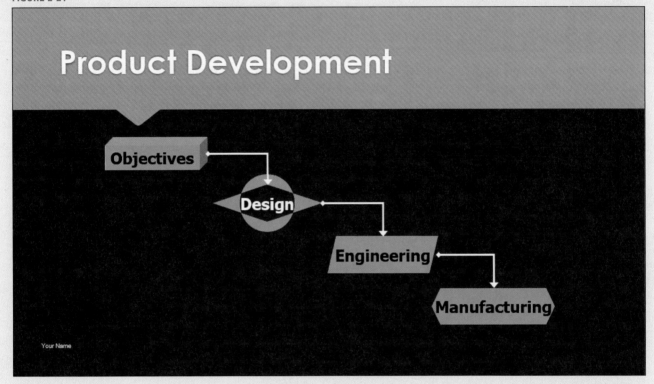

Enhancing Charts

CASE In this unit, you continue to work on the Quest Specialty Travel (QST) presentation that includes charts. You customize the chart layout, format chart elements, and animate the chart. Finally, you embed an Excel chart, and then you link an Excel worksheet to the presentation.

Unit Objectives

After completing this unit, you will be able to:

- Work with charts in PowerPoint
- Change chart design and style
- Customize a chart
- Format chart elements
- Animate a chart
- Embed an Excel chart
- Link an Excel worksheet
- Update a linked Excel worksheet

Files You Will Need

PPT F-1.pptx	PPT F-8.pptx
PPT F-2.xlsx	PPT F-9.pptx
PPT F-3.xlsx	PPT F-10.xlsx
PPT F-4.pptx	PPT F-11.xlsx
PPT F-5.xlsx	PPT F-12.pptx
PPT F-6.xlsx	PPT F-13.xlsx
PPT F-7.pptx	PPT F-14.xlsx

Work with Charts in PowerPoint

One of the best ways to enhance a presentation is to insert graphic elements such as a chart. When you have numerical data that you want to compare, a chart helps the audience visualize and understand the information. Because Excel is integrated with PowerPoint, you can easily create fantastic-looking charts on any slides in your presentation. **CASE** ▶ *As you continue to develop the QST presentation, you plan to include charts on several slides. You review the features, benefits, and methods of charting in PowerPoint.*

DETAILS

- ### Create PowerPoint charts
  If you have Microsoft Office 2013 installed on your computer, PowerPoint integrates with Excel to create charts. When you create a chart in PowerPoint using the Chart button on the INSERT tab or the Insert Chart icon in a content placeholder, a chart is placed on the slide and a separate worksheet window opens displaying the chart's data. See **FIGURE F-1**. Using the worksheet window you can perform basic functions such as adding or editing chart data. If you want to manipulate the data in the worksheet using advanced commands, filters, or formulas, you can open the worksheet directly in Excel without exiting PowerPoint.

- ### Embed or link a chart
  You have two options when inserting an Excel chart to your presentation: you can embed it or link it. Embedded and linked charts are objects created in another program, such as Excel, and inserted in a slide. An embedded chart becomes a part of the presentation like a picture or a piece of clip art. The embedded chart's data is stored in the worksheet that is included with the presentation file. You can embed a chart in PowerPoint using the Object button on the INSERT tab or by copying a chart from Excel and pasting it on a slide. A linked chart displays a picture of the chart on the slide that is linked or a connected to the original file in Excel. The chart is saved in a separate file, not with the presentation. If you want to make changes to a linked Excel chart, you must open the saved Excel file that contains the chart. You can open embedded or linked charts through PowerPoint or Excel.

- ### Modify charts using styles and layouts
  Because themes and theme effects are alike for all Office programs, you can apply a specific theme or effect to a chart in Excel, and PowerPoint will recognize the theme or effect. Using themes gives your chart a consistent look with other objects in your presentation; in addition, there are a number of chart layouts that you can apply to your chart. A chart layout specifies where chart elements, such as axes titles, data labels, and the legend, are displayed within the chart area. To easily format a chart you can select one of the three formatting buttons on the right side of the chart as shown in **FIGURE F-2**: the Chart Elements button ➕, the Chart Styles button 🖌, and the Chart Filters button ▼. The Chart Elements button allows you to show, hide, or format specific elements such as axis, labels, and gridlines. The Chart Styles button provides chart styles and color themes you can apply to a chart. The Chart Filters button allows you to show or hide specific data in a chart, such as a data series or category.

- ### Apply advanced formatting to charts
  If the basic predefined chart styles do not provide you with the formatting options you want, you can choose to modify individual elements. For example, you may want to alter the way data labels look or how axes are displayed. You can specify the axes scales and adjust the interval between the values or categories. You can fine-tune individual elements, such as the data series or legend of your chart. You can also add trendlines and error bars to a chart to provide more information about the data. A **trendline** is a graphical representation of an upward or downward trend in a data series, also used to predict future trends. **Error bars** identify potential error amounts relative to each data marker in a data series.

FIGURE F-1: Embedded chart and worksheet

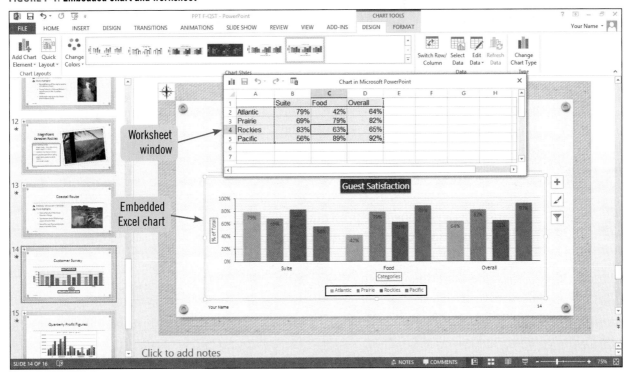

FIGURE F-2: Formatted chart

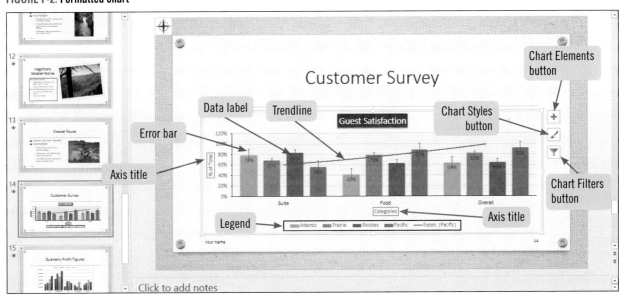

Using Paste Special

Paste Special is used to paste text or objects into PowerPoint using a specific format. For example, you may want to paste some text as a picture or as plain text without formatting. Copy the text, or object, then in PowerPoint click the HOME tab, click the Paste list arrow, click Paste Special, then select the appropriate format option. You can keep source formatting or apply the destination theme. You can also choose whether to embed or link an object

or selected information from another program to PowerPoint using the Paste Special command. This technique is useful when you want to link part of an Excel worksheet or a chart from a workbook that contains both a worksheet and a chart. To link just the chart, open the Microsoft Excel worksheet, then copy the chart. Leaving Excel and the source file open, click the Paste list arrow, click Paste Special, click one of the Paste link options, then click OK.

Change Chart Design and Style

Learning Outcomes
• Modify a chart layout
• Change the chart type

Being able to use Excel to create and modify charts in PowerPoint offers you many advantages, including the ability to use Excel Chart tools to customize chart design, layout, and formatting. After you create a chart, you can immediately alter the way it looks by changing individual chart elements or by applying a predefined chart layout or style. For example, you can select a chart layout that adds a chart title and moves the legend to the bottom of the chart. You can also easily change the color and effects of chart elements by applying one of the styles found in the Chart Styles gallery. **CASE** *The chart that includes survey results needs some work. You change the chart layout, style, and type of the chart on Slide 14.*

STEPS

1. **Start PowerPoint, open the presentation PPT F-1.pptx from the location where you store your Data Files, save the presentation as PPT F-QST, then press [End]**
   Slide 14 appears in the Slide pane.

2. **Click the chart, then click the CHART TOOLS DESIGN tab on the Ribbon**
   The chart is selected and ready to edit.

3. **Click the Quick Layout button in the Chart Layouts group, then click Layout 8 in the Layout gallery**
   This particular layout option adds value and category axis titles to the chart and moves the legend to the right side of the chart, as shown in FIGURE F-3.

4. **Click the Vertical Axis Title, type Categories, click the Horizontal Axis Title, type % of Total, then click in a blank area of the chart**
   The new chart labels help identify aspects of the chart.

5. **Click the Change Chart Type button in the Type group**
   The Change Chart Type dialog box opens.

6. **Click Column in the left pane, make sure that Clustered Column is selected, then click OK**
   The data series markers change from bars to columns and rotate 90 degrees. Notice also that the vertical and horizontal axis have switched places with this new chart type.

7. **Click the Chart Styles button ⬘ next to the chart, scroll to the bottom of the gallery, then click Style 14**
   The Style 14 option removes the bold text formatting and the black border around the data markers in the chart.

8. **Click Color at the top of the Chart Styles gallery, click Color 1 in the Colorful section, then click ⬘**
   The data marker colors change to reflect the new color scheme. Compare your screen to FIGURE F-4.

9. **Click a blank area of the slide, then save your presentation**

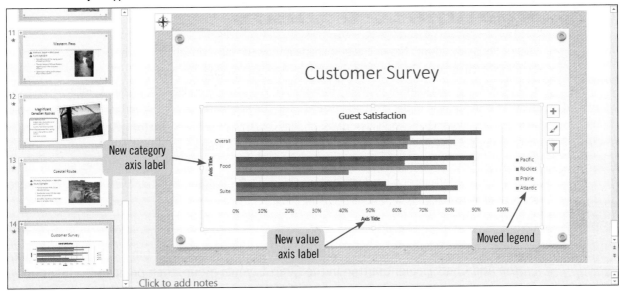

FIGURE F-4: **Chart with new chart type and colors applied**

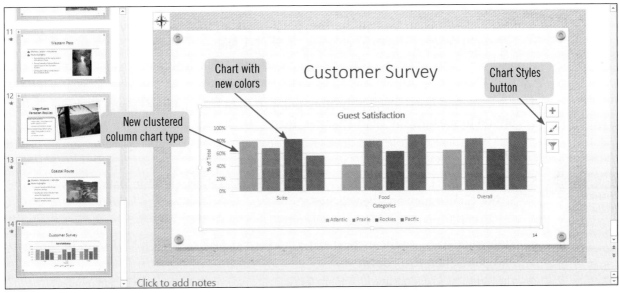

Using AutoFit Options to divide and fit body text

If the AutoFit Options button ⬚ appears while you are entering text in a body text object on a slide with either the Title and Content or the Content with Caption layout, you can click the button and choose from one of three options for dividing up the text in the object. The first option is to split text between two slides. If you choose this option, PowerPoint creates a second slide with the same title and then automatically divides the text between the two slides. The second option is to continue the text on a new slide. Here again, PowerPoint creates a second slide with the same title, but instead of splitting the text between the slides, you are given a blank body text object on the new slide to insert more text. The final option on the AutoFit Options button for splitting text in a body text object is to change the body text object from one column to two columns.

Customize a Chart

Learning Outcomes
• Add gridlines to a chart
• Add data labels to data markers
• Apply tick marks

One of the many advantages of creating charts in PowerPoint is the ability you have to customize chart elements, such as labels, axes, gridlines, and the chart background. For example, you can change the plot area color so the data markers are distinctly set off, or you can add gridlines to a chart. Gridlines help make the data easier to read in the chart and extend from the horizontal axis or the vertical axis across the plot area. There are two types of gridlines: major gridlines and minor gridlines. **Major gridlines** identify major units on the axis and are usually identified by a tick mark. **Tick marks** are small lines of measurement that intersect an axis and identify the categories, values, or series in a chart. **Minor gridlines** identify minor units on the axis and can also be identified by a tick mark. **CASE** ▶ *You decide to improve the appearance of the chart by customizing some elements of the chart.*

STEPS

1. **Click a blank area of the chart, click the CHART TOOLS DESIGN tab on the Ribbon, click the Add Chart Element button in the Chart Layouts group, then point to Gridlines**

   The Gridlines gallery opens. Notice that Primary Major Horizontal is already selected indicating the chart already has major gridlines on the horizontal axis.

2. **Move ▷ over each gridline option to see how the gridlines change on the chart, then click Primary Minor Horizontal**

   Minor horizontal gridlines appear on the chart as shown in FIGURE F-5. Notice that the major gridlines are darker in color than the minor gridlines.

3. **Click the Add Chart Element button, point to Data Table, move ▷ over each data table option to see how the chart changes, then click None**

   You like seeing the data displayed in the chart because it helps define the data markers. However, using the data table takes up too much room on the slide and significantly decreases the size of the chart, making it unreadable.

4. **Click the Add Chart Element button, point to Data Labels, move ▷ over each data label option to see how the chart changes, then click Outside End**

   Data labels, the actual value for each data series marker, appear on top of each data marker. You like the data labels, but you want to move them on top of the data markers.

5. **Click the Chart Elements button ⊞, point to Data Labels, click the Data Labels list arrow, click Inside End, then click ⊞**

   The data labels move inside the data series markers.

6. **Right-click 100% on the vertical axis, click Format Axis, click TICK MARKS in the Format Axis pane, then scroll down**

   The Format Axis pane opens with options for changing the axes, tick marks, labels, and numbers.

7. **Click the Major type list arrow, click Outside, click the Fill & Line icon ◇ at the top of the pane, click LINE, click the Color button list arrow ▲▾, then click Black, Text 1**

   The tick marks on the chart's vertical axis change to black and are easier to see. The value axis title would also look good with a border around it.

8. **Click % of Total in the chart, click the Solid line option button in the BORDER section of the Format Axis Title pane, click the Color button list arrow ▲▾, then click Red, Accent 3**

   A dark red border appears around the value axis title. The category axis title would also look good with a border around it.

9. **Click Categories in the chart, press [F4], close the Format Axis Title pane, click a blank area of the slide, then save your presentation**

   Pressing [F4] repeats the last formatting action. Compare your screen to FIGURE F-6.

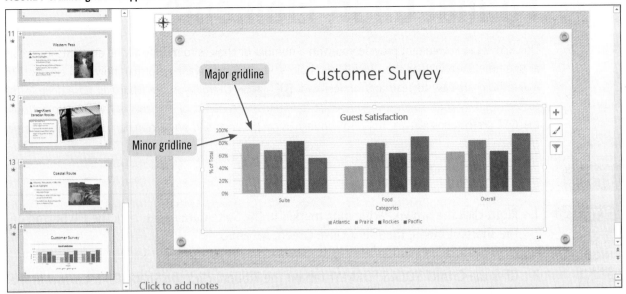

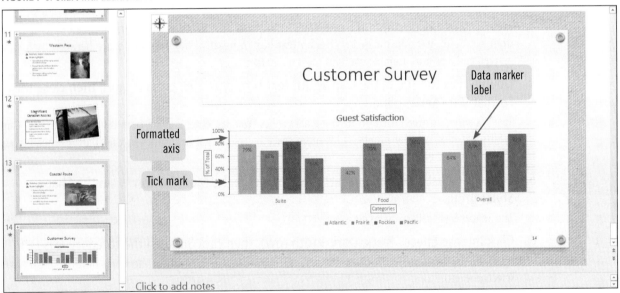

Using the Research task pane

Sometimes when you are developing a presentation, you need help formulating your ideas or researching a subject. PowerPoint has an extensive set of online tools found in the Research task pane that gives you immediate access to many different kinds of information. The Research task pane provides the following research tools: an English dictionary; an English, French, and Spanish thesaurus; a word and phrase translator; and three research Web sites. To open the Research task pane, click the Research button in the Proofing group on the REVIEW tab. The Research options link at the bottom of the Research task pane provides additional research books and research sites that you can add to the Research task pane.

PowerPoint 2013

Format Chart Elements

Learning Outcomes
- Add gradient fill to data markers
- Modify data markers overlap
- Format chart title and axis labels

Quick Styles in PowerPoint provide you with a number of choices to modify all the elements in a chart at one time. Even with all the Quick Style choices, you still may want to format individual elements to make the chart easy to read and understand. **CASE** ▶ *Overall, you like what you have done to the customer survey chart so far, but you decide to format some individual elements of the chart to better fit the QST presentation design. You also consider using the copy and paste commands for inserting other charts on a slide.*

STEPS

1. **Right-click the brown Pacific data marker in the Suite data series, click the Fill button on the shortcut menu, then click Olive Green, Accent 6**
   All of the Pacific data markers are selected and now have an olive green fill color.

2. **Click the CHART TOOLS FORMAT tab on the Ribbon, click the Shape Fill list arrow in the Shape Styles group, point to Gradient, then click Linear Up in the Dark Variations section (bottom row)**
   A gradient effect is added to the Pacific data series markers.

3. **Click the Format Selection button in the Current Selection group to open the Format Data Series pane, make sure SERIES OPTIONS is selected, then click the Series Overlap down arrow until –40% appears in the Series Overlap text box**
   More space is added between the data markers for each data series in the chart. You can enter a value from –100% to 100% in the Series Overlap text box. A negative number adds space between each data marker, and a positive number overlaps the data markers.

4. **Double-click the 100 in the Gap Width text box, type 300, press [Enter], then close the Format Data Series pane**
   Space is added between each of the three data series. You can enter a value from 0% to 500% in the Gap Width text box. A larger number adds more space between each data series in the chart. Compare your screen to **FIGURE F-7**.

5. **Click the Guest Satisfaction chart title, then click the More button ⏷ in the Shape Styles group**
   The Shapes Style gallery opens.

6. **Click Intense Effect - Black, Dark 1 (6th row), then click Suite on the category axis**
   Applying the new style to the chart title makes it stand out. Clicking any of the words on the category axis selects the entire axis.

7. **Click ⏷ in the Shape Styles group, then click Moderate Line - Dark 1 (2nd row)**
   The new style applies a black color to the category axis and better defines the plot area.

8. **Right-click the chart legend, then click Format Legend in the shortcut menu**
   The Format Legend pane opens.

9. **Click the Fill & Line icon ◇ in the Format Legend pane, click the Solid line option button in the BORDER section, click the Color button ▲▾, click Black, Text 1, then click the Width up arrow in the BORDER section until 2 pt appears**
   A solid black border line appears around the legend.

10. **Close the Format Legend pane, click a blank area of the slide, then save the presentation**
    Compare your screen to **FIGURE F-8**.

FIGURE F-7: Modified data markers

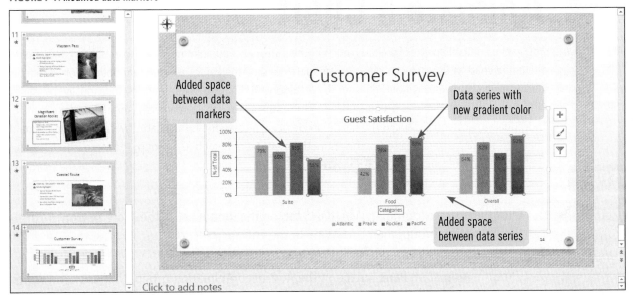

FIGURE F-8: Completed chart

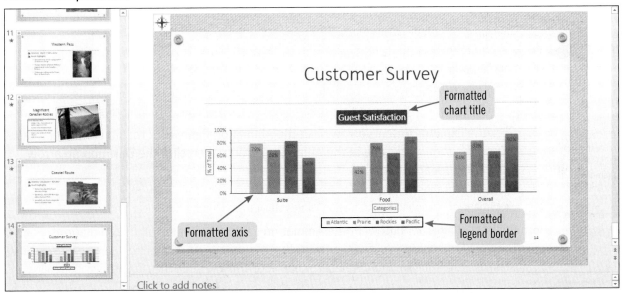

Changing PowerPoint options

You can customize your installation of PowerPoint by changing various settings and preferences. To change PowerPoint settings, click the FILE tab on the Ribbon, then click Options to open the PowerPoint Options dialog box. In the dialog box there are nine sections identified in the left pane, which offer you ways to customize PowerPoint. For example, the General area includes options for viewing the Mini toolbar, enabling Live Preview, and personalizing your copy of Office. You can also set Language options for editing and proofing as well as which language appears on buttons and ScreenTips.

Animate a Chart

Learning
Outcomes
• Animate chart
  data markers
• Set animation
  effects

You can animate elements of a chart, much in the same way you animate other objects. You can animate the entire chart as one object, or you can animate the data markers. There are two options for animating data markers individually: by series or by category. Animating data markers individually by series displays data markers of each data series (or the same-colored data markers.) Animating data markers individually by category displays the data markers of each category in the chart. If you choose to animate the chart's data markers as a series, the entire data series is animated as a group; the same is true for animating data markers by category. **CASE** ▶ *You decide to animate the data series markers of the chart.*

STEPS

QUICK TIP
Exit animation effects cause an object to leave the slide. Exit animation effects are in the Exit section of the Animation gallery.

1. **Click the chart, click the ANIMATIONS tab on the Ribbon, click the More button ⃞ in the Animation group, then click Wipe in the Entrance section**

   The Wipe entrance animation is applied to the entire chart, and PowerPoint plays the animation.

2. **Click the Animation Pane button in the Advanced Animation group, then click the Wipe: Content Placeholder list arrow**

   The Animation Pane opens and displays specific information, such as the type of animation (Entrance, Exit, Emphasis, or Motion Path), the sequence and timeline of the animation, and the name of the animated object. Clicking an animation's list arrow provides access to other custom options. Compare your screen to **FIGURE F-9**.

3. **Click Fly In in the Animation group, then click the Duration up arrow in the Timing group until 1.00 appears**

   The Fly In entrance animation replaces the Wipe entrance animation. A longer duration, or animation timing, slows down the animation.

QUICK TIP
If you don't want to animate the chart background, click the animation list arrow in the Animation Pane, click Effect Options, click the CHART ANIMATION tab, then remove the check in the check box.

4. **Click the Effect Options button in the Animation group, then click By Element in Series in the Sequence section**

   Each data series marker, by series, flies in from the bottom of the slide beginning with the Atlantic data series. There are now 13 animation tags, one for the chart background and one for each data series marker.

5. **Click the Expand contents arrow ⃟ in the Animation Pane, click the first animation tag ⃞ on the slide, click Fade in the Animation group, then click the Duration up arrow until 1.50 appears**

   The Fade animation is now applied to the chart background. Notice the timeline icon for the chart background animation in the Animation Pane is wider to account for the longer duration.

6. **Click the Play From button in the Animation Pane, then watch all the animations**

   The chart background fades into view, then data series markers fly in from the bottom one after another. Notice the advancing timeline (vertical line) as it moves over each animation in the Animation Pane.

QUICK TIP
Due to the large number of animation options available with charts and other objects, be careful how many objects you animate on one slide.

7. **Click the Hide contents arrow ⃟ in the Animation Pane, click the Delay up arrow until 00.50 appears, then click the Play Selected button in the Animation Pane**

   A half-second delay is applied between each animation. Watch closely at how the changed settings affect the progression of the animated data series markers.

8. **Click the Start list arrow in the Timing group, click After Previous, click the Trigger button in the Advanced Animation group, point to On Click of, then click Title 7**

   Now when Slide 14 appears in Slide Show view, you can click the slide title to play the chart animations. The animation tags combine into one lightning bolt tag indicating the animation has a trigger.

9. **Click the Slide Show button ⃞ on the status bar, click the slide title, watch the animation, press [Esc], close the Animation Pane, then save the presentation**

   Compare your screen to **FIGURE F-10**.

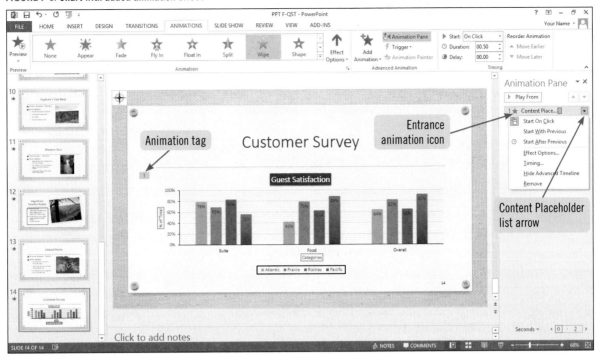

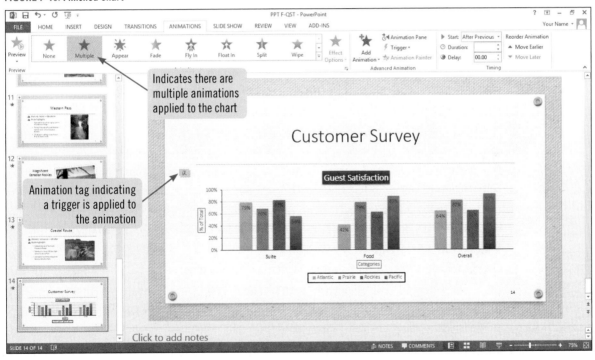

Insert a picture as a slide background

As you have seen, using digital pictures in a presentation can really enhance the look of the presentation and make it more appealing. Most often pictures are inserted as objects on slides, but you can also use a picture as the slide background for one or more slides. To insert a picture as the slide background on an individual slide, click the slide in the Thumbnails pane in Normal view, click the DESIGN tab on the Ribbon, then click the Format Background button in the Customize group. Click the Picture or texture fill option button, click the File button to locate a picture stored on your computer or click the Online button to locate a picture on the Internet, then click Insert. To insert a picture as the slide background for multiple slides, open Slide Master view, then use the same procedure to insert a picture on the slide master.

Embed an Excel Chart

When a chart is the best way to present information on a slide, you can create one within PowerPoint or you can embed an existing Excel chart directly to the slide. When you use another program to create an object, the program, Excel in this case, is known as the **source program**. The object you create with the source program is saved to a file called the **source file**. When you embed a chart into a presentation, the presentation file in which the chart is embedded becomes the **destination file**. **CASE** *You want to include other supporting data from last year's sales numbers in your presentation, so you embed an Excel chart on a new slide.*

STEPS

QUICK TIP
You can also press [Ctrl][D] to duplicate a slide in the Thumbnails pane.

1. **Click the Slide 14 thumbnail in the Thumbnails pane, click the HOME tab on the Ribbon, click the New Slide list arrow in the Slides group, then click Title Only**
   A new slide with the Title Only layout is added to the presentation.

2. **Click the slide title placeholder, type Quarterly Profit Figures, click the INSERT tab on the Ribbon, then click the Object button in the Text group**
   The Insert Object dialog box opens. Using this dialog box, you can create a new chart or locate an existing one to insert on a slide.

QUICK TIP
Another way to embed a chart is to open the chart in Excel, copy it, then paste it into your slide.

3. **Click the Create from file option button, click Browse, navigate to the location where you store your Data Files, click the file PPT F-2.xlsx, click OK, then click OK in the Insert Object dialog box**
   The chart from the Excel data file containing the quarterly profit figures is embedded on the slide. You can open the chart and use the commands in Excel to make any changes to it.

4. **Drag the chart's lower-right sizing handle down and to the right to enlarge the chart, then using Smart Guides drag the chart to the middle of the blank area of the slide**
   The chart is now easier to read and is centered on the slide.

5. **Double-click the chart to open it in Microsoft Office Excel**
   The chart appears inside an Excel worksheet on the slide of the open PowerPoint presentation. Both PowerPoint and Excel are open together, and Excel commands and tabs appear on the Ribbon under the PowerPoint title bar as shown in **FIGURE F-11**.

6. **Click the Sheet 2 tab at the bottom of the Excel worksheet to view the chart data, click cell B8, type 15280.11, press [Enter], click the Next Sheet arrow ▶, then click the Sheet 3 tab**
   The changed number is reflected for the Quarter 1 South America data series in the chart.

QUICK TIP
If the chart you want to embed is in another presentation, open both presentations then copy and paste the chart from one presentation to the other.

7. **Click the chart in Excel, click the CHART TOOLS DESIGN tab on the Excel Ribbon, click the More button ▼ in the Chart Styles group, then click Style 14 (bottom row)**
   The chart style changes with new data marker effects and legend position in the chart.

8. **Right-click the Vertical (Value) Axis, click Font on the shortcut menu, click the Font Style list arrow, click Bold, click OK, click the Horizontal (Category) Axis, then press [F4]**
   Both the value and category axes labels are bold and now easier to read.

9. **Right-click the legend, click Format Legend on the shortcut menu, click the Top option button, then click OK**
   The legend moves to the top of the chart.

10. **Click outside the chart to exit Excel, click a blank area of the slide, then save the presentation**
    Compare your screen to **FIGURE F-12**.

FIGURE F-11: Embedded Excel chart

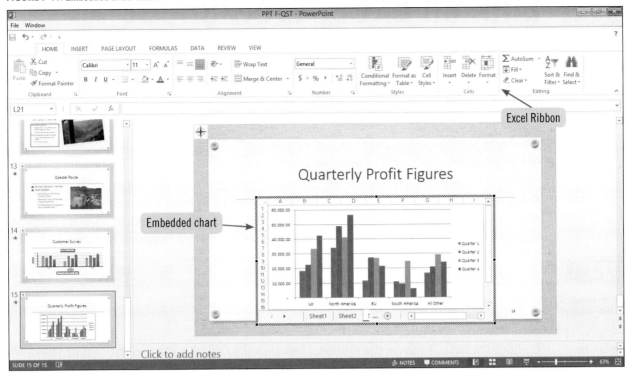

FIGURE F-12: Formatted Excel chart

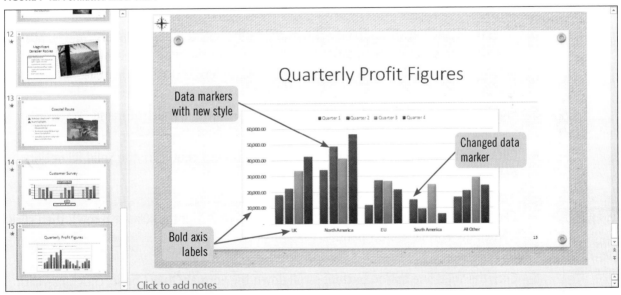

Embedding a worksheet

You can embed all or part of an Excel worksheet in a PowerPoint slide. To embed an entire worksheet, go to the slide where you want to place the worksheet. Click the INSERT tab on the Ribbon, then click the Object button in the Text group. The Insert Object dialog box opens. Click the Create from file option button, click

Browse, locate and double-click the worksheet filename, then click OK. The worksheet is embedded in the slide. Double-click it to edit it using Excel commands as needed to work with the worksheet. To insert only a portion of a worksheet, open the Excel workbook and copy the cells you want to include in your presentation.

Link an Excel Worksheet

Learning
Outcomes
• Link an Excel
  worksheet
• Format a linked
  worksheet

Another way to insert objects to your presentation is to establish a **link**, or connection, between the source file and the destination file. Unlike embedded objects, a linked object is stored in its source file, not on the slide or in the presentation file. So when you link an object to a PowerPoint slide, a representation (picture) of the object, not the object itself, appears on the slide. Any changes made to the source file of a linked object are automatically reflected in the linked representation in your PowerPoint presentation. You can change the contents in a source file of a linked object directly in the source program or from the PowerPoint presentation. Some of the objects that you can link to PowerPoint include bitmap images, Microsoft Excel worksheets, and PowerPoint slides from other presentations. Use linking when you want to be sure your presentation contains the latest information and when you want to include an object, such as an accounting spreadsheet, that may change over time. See **TABLE F-1** for suggestions on when to embed an object and when to link an object. **CASE** *You need to link and format an Excel worksheet to the presentation. The worksheet was created by the QST Accounting Department earlier in the year.*

STEPS

1. **Click the HOME tab on the Ribbon, click the New Slide button, then type QST Revenue**
   A new slide, Slide 16, is created with the slide title QST Revenue.

2. **Click the INSERT tab on the Ribbon, then click the Object button in the Text group**
   The Insert Object dialog box opens.

3. **Click the Create from file option button, click Browse, navigate to the location where you store your Data Files, click the file PPT F-3.xlsx, click OK, click the Link check box, then click OK**
   The Excel worksheet appears on the slide. The worksheet would be easier to see if it were larger.

4. **Drag the lower-left sizing handle down and to the left, then using Smart Guides, position the worksheet in the middle of the blank area of the slide as shown in FIGURE F-13**
   If the worksheet had a background fill color, it would help to emphasize the data and direct the audience's attention.

5. **Right-click the worksheet, then click Format Object on the shortcut menu**
   The Format Object pane opens.

6. **Click the Fill & Line icon ◇ in the Format Object pane, then click the Solid fill option button**
   A gold color is applied behind the worksheet.

7. **Click the Color list arrow 🏷▾, click Orange, Accent 2, Lighter 40% (4th row), then click LINE in the Format Object pane**
   The background color changes to a 40% transparent orange.

8. **Click the Solid line option button, scroll down the Format Object pane, click 🏷▾, click Black, Text 1, click the Width up arrow until 2 pt appears in the Width text box, then click a blank area of the slide**
   The worksheet appears with a new border color and width.

9. **Close the Format Background pane, then save the presentation**
   Compare your screen to **FIGURE F-14**.

FIGURE F-13: Linked Excel worksheet

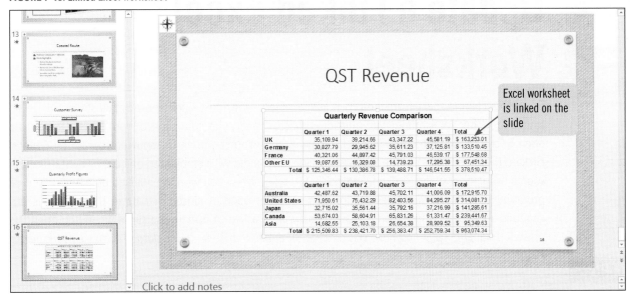

FIGURE F-14: Formatted linked worksheet

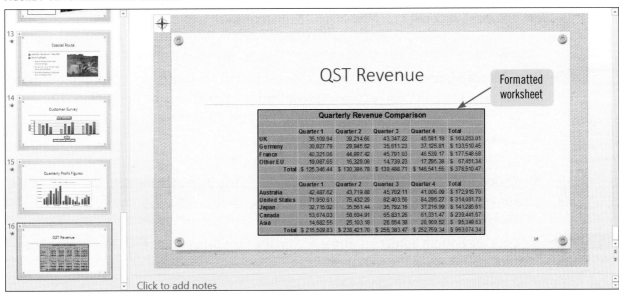

TABLE F-1: Embedding vs. linking

situation	action
When you are the only user of an object and you want the object to be a part of your presentation	Embed
When you want to access the object in its source program, even if the original file is not available	Embed
When you want to update the object manually while working in PowerPoint	Embed
When you always want the latest information in your object	Link
When the object's source file is shared on a network or when other users have access to the file and can change it	Link
When you want to keep your presentation file size small	Link

Learning
Outcomes
• Edit and update a
linked worksheet

Update a Linked Excel Worksheet

To edit or change the information in a linked object, you must open the object's source file in its source program. For example, you must open Microsoft Word to edit a linked Word table, or you must open Microsoft Excel to edit a linked Excel worksheet. You can open the source program by double-clicking the linked object in the PowerPoint slide, as you did with embedded objects, or by starting the source program directly using any method you prefer. When you work on a linked object in its source program, your PowerPoint presentation can be either open or closed. If data in the linked file has changed while the presentation is closed, you will be asked to update the slides when you open the presentation. **CASE** *You have just received an e-mail that some of the data in the Excel worksheet is incorrect, so you update the data in the linked worksheet.*

STEPS

QUICK TIP
You can also double-click the linked worksheet to open it in Excel.

1. **Right-click the Excel worksheet on Slide 16, point to Linked Worksheet Object, then click Edit**

   The worksheet PPT F-3.xlsx opens in the Microsoft Excel window.

2. **Drag the edge of the Excel window to see all the data if necessary, click cell C5, type 30628.67, click cell E13, type 40266.18, then click cell G10**

   The Quarter 2 value for Germany and the Quarter 4 value for Japan change. All totals that include these values in the Total cells are updated accordingly. Compare your screen to **FIGURE F-15**.

QUICK TIP
To edit or open a linked object in your presentation, the object's source program and source file must be available on your computer or network.

3. **Click cell B4, press and hold [Shift], click cell E7, release [Shift], right-click in the selected cell area, then click the Accounting Number Format button $ on the Mini toolbar**

   All of the selected cells now have the accounting format and display the dollar symbol.

4. **Click cell B11, drag to cell E15, then press [F4]**

   The same accounting number format is applied to these cells.

5. **Click cell F8, press [Ctrl], click cell F16, release [Ctrl], then click the Bold button B in the Font group**

   The bold font attribute is added to cells F8 and F16.

QUICK TIP
If your presentation is closed when you update a linked object, a security dialog box opens the next time you open your presentation. Click Update Links in the dialog box to update the linked object.

6. **Click the Bottom Border list arrow ▦ ▾ in the Font group, click Thick Box Border, then click a blank cell in the worksheet**

   A black border is added to cells F8 and F16 to highlight the overall totals.

7. **Click the Excel window Close button ☒, click Save to save your changes, then click a blank area of the slide**

   The Excel window closes. The Excel worksheet in the PPT F-QST.pptx presentation file is now updated with the new data and shows the formatting changes you made. PowerPoint automatically makes all of the changes to the linked object. Compare your screen to **FIGURE F-16**.

8. **Check the spelling, add your name as the footer to the slides and to the handouts, save the presentation, then submit your presentation to your instructor**

   If your instructor requires you to print your presentation, then use the print layout setting 6 Slides Horizontal.

9. **Close the presentation, then exit PowerPoint**

FIGURE F-15: Modified Excel worksheet

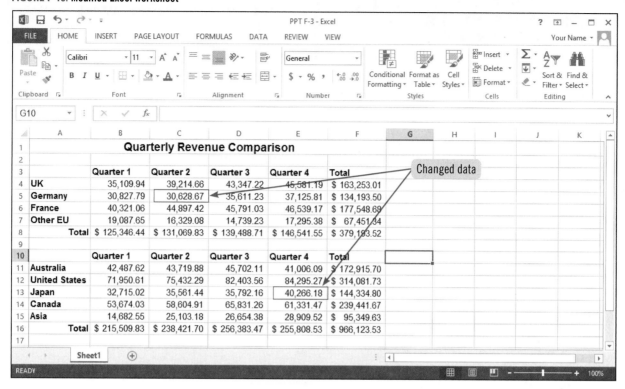

FIGURE F-16: Updated Excel worksheet

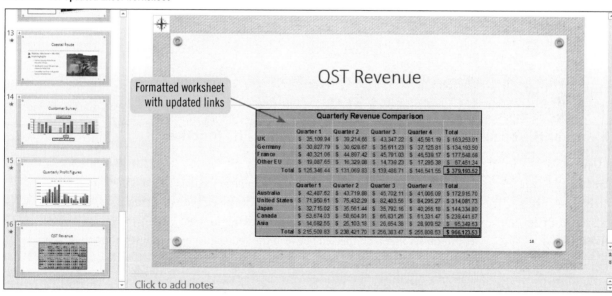

Editing links

Once you link an object to your presentation, you have the ability to edit its link. Using the Links dialog box, you can update a link, open or change a linked object's source file, break a link, and determine if a linked object is updated manually or automatically. The Links dialog box is the only place where you can change a linked object's source file, break a link, and change the link updating method. To open the Links dialog box, click the FILE tab on the Ribbon, then click Edit Links to Files button under Related Documents in the pane.

Practice

Concepts Review

Label each of the elements of the PowerPoint window shown in FIGURE F-17.

FIGURE F-17

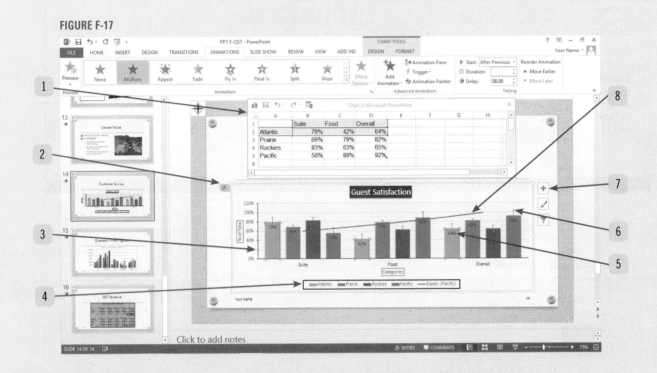

Match each of the terms with the statement that describes its function.

9. Tick mark
10. Overlap
11. Source file
12. Destination file
13. Linked file

a. The space between data series markers
b. An object saved in a separate file that can be embedded into a presentation
c. Small lines that intersect an axis and identify a category or value
d. The file that an embedded object is inserted into
e. An object that is connected between the source file and the destination file

Select the best answer from the list of choices.

14. How do you insert text as plain text without formatting in PowerPoint?
 a. Link the text.
 b. Embed the text.
 c. Paste the destination file.
 d. Use Paste Special.

15. What is used to predict future tendencies in a chart?
 a. Trendlines
 b. Gridlines
 c. Data series
 d. Tick marks

16. Major _____ identify units on the axis and are usually identified by a tick mark.
 a. Guides
 b. Labels
 c. Gridlines
 d. Bars

17. What does a negative number in the Overlap text box do?
 a. Removes space between data markers
 b. Overlaps data markers
 c. Adjusts the space between gridlines
 d. Adds space between data markers

18. What does an animation tag with the lightning bolt represent?
 a. The animation is very fast.
 b. A trigger is applied to the animation.
 c. There are multiple animations.
 d. The animation has a delay.

19. The program used to create the object that has been embedded into a presentation is called the _____ program.
 a. Support
 b. Destination
 c. Source
 d. Linked

20. Which animation method would you use to display data markers independently with the same color?
 a. Individually by series
 b. By series
 c. Individually by category
 d. By category

Skills Review

1. Change chart design and style.
 a. Start PowerPoint, open the presentation PPT F-4.pptx, then save it as **PPT F-Candela** to the location where you store your Data Files.
 b. Click Slide 3 in the Thumbnails pane, then select the chart.
 c. Open the CHART TOOLS DESIGN tab, click the Quick Layout button, then apply Layout 9.
 d. Change the label on the Vertical (Value) Axis to **Millions**, then change the Horizontal (Category) Axis label to **Divisions**.
 e. Apply Style 14 from the Chart Styles group, then change the chart type to 100% Stacked Column.
 f. Type **Fiscal Year** as the chart title, then save your changes.

2. Customize a chart.
 a. Click the Add Chart Elements button, then add primary major vertical gridlines, primary minor horizontal gridlines, and center data labels.
 b. Click the Add Chart Elements button, point to Error Bars, then click Standard Error.
 c. Right-click the value axis label, click the Outline button on the shortcut menu, then click Black, Text 1.
 d. Select the category axis title, then press [F4].
 e. Right-click 100% on the vertical axis, click Format Axis, click TICK MARKS in the Format Axis pane, click the Major type list arrow, then click Cross.

Skills Review (continued)

    f. Click the Minor type list arrow, click Outside, then close the Format Axis pane.

    g. Click a blank area of the chart, then save your changes.

3. Format chart elements.

    a. Open the CHART TOOLS FORMAT tab, click the Chart Elements list arrow in the Current Selection group, then click Series "1st Qtr."

    b. Click the Format Selection button in the Current Selection group, then click the Gap Width up arrow until 125% appears.

    c. Set the Series Overlap to 80%.

    d. Click the Fill & Line icon at the top of the pane, then change the fill to a gradient fill, click the Preset gradients list arrow, then click Bottom Spotlight - Accent 5.

    e. Click the 90 data marker in the chart, click the Effects icon at the top of the pane, then click GLOW.

    f. Click the Presets list arrow, click Orange, 11 pt glow, Accent color 1, then close the pane.

    g. Right-click the legend, click Format Legend, then click the Right option button.

    h. Click the Fill & Line icon, click FILL, click the Solid fill option button, set the Transparency to 50%, then close the pane.

4. Animate a chart.

    a. Select the ANIMATIONS tab, then apply the Float In Entrance animation to the chart.

    b. Click the Effect Options button, then change the animation to By Element in Category.

    c. Click the Animation Pane button, click the Object 4 list arrow in the Animation Pane, click Effect Options, then click the Chart Animation tab in the Float Up dialog box.

    d. Click the Start animation by drawing the chart background check box to deselect it, then click OK.

    e. Change the duration to 1.50 and the delay to .75 for all the animations, then click the Play Selected button in the Animation Pane.

    f. Close the Animation Pane, then save your changes.

5. Embed an Excel chart.

    a. Go to Slide 4, click the INSERT tab, then click the Object button in the Text group.

    b. Click the Create from file option button, click Browse, then locate and embed the file PPT F-5.xlsx from the location where you store your Data Files.

    c. Drag the lower-right sizing handle to increase the size of the chart to fill the blank area of the slide.

    d. Double-click the chart, click the Sheet1 tab in the worksheet that opens, change cell C7 to **54,780.88**, change cell E5 to **67,429.00**, then click the Sheet2 tab.

    e. Right-click the value axis, click the Outline button on the Mini toolbar, click Automatic, click the category axis, then press [F4].

    f. Right-click the legend, click the Outline list arrow on the Mini toolbar, click Orange, Accent 6, then click the CHART TOOLS FORMAT tab.

    g. Click the Shape Outline list arrow in the Shape Styles group, then change the legend outline to a 2 ¼pt square dot dash.

    h. Click a blank area of the slide, then save your changes.

6. Link an Excel worksheet.

    a. Insert a new slide after slide 4 with the Title Only layout.

    b. Type **Candela & Co.**, click the INSERT tab, then click the Object button in the Text group.

    c. Click the Create from file option button, click Browse, locate the file PPT F-6.xlsx from the location where you store your Data Files, then link it to the slide.

    d. Resize the worksheet object by dragging its sizing handles, then center it in the blank area of the slide.

    e. Right-click the worksheet, click Format Object, click the Solid fill option button, click the Color list arrow, then click Brown, Accent 4.

    f. Change the fill transparency to 20%, close the pane, then save your changes.

Skills Review (continued)

7. Update a linked Excel worksheet.

  a. Double-click the worksheet.

  b. Select cells B5 to F9, click the Accounting Number Format list arrow in the Number group, then click Euro.

  c. Click cell F9, then click the Bold button in the Font group.

  d. Click cell C7, type **61727.90**, click cell C6, then type **32757.90**.

  e. Close the Excel window, then click Save to save your changes. The changes appear in the linked worksheet. FIGURE F-18 shows the completed presentation.

  f. Add your name to the handout footer, save your work, submit your presentation to your instructor, close the presentation, and exit PowerPoint.

FIGURE F-18

Independent Challenge 1

You work for Intek Systems, a business consulting company that helps businesses organize or restructure themselves to be more efficient and profitable. You are one of four consultants who work directly with clients. To prepare for an upcoming meeting with executives at a local Internet communications company, you create a brief presentation outlining typical investigative and reporting techniques, past results versus the competition's, and the company's business philosophy. Use PowerPoint to customize a chart on Slide 5 of the presentation.

  a. Start PowerPoint, open the presentation PPT F-7.pptx from the location where you store your Data Files, then save it as **PPT F-Intek**.

  b. Select the chart on Slide 5, then apply Layout 3 from the Quick Layout gallery.

  c. Apply Style 1 from the Chart Styles gallery, then type **AMPI Rating** in the chart title text box.

  d. Change the chart type to Clustered Bar, then add primary minor vertical gridlines to the chart.

  e. Right-click the value axis, click Format Axis, click TICK MARKS, add cross major tick marks, then close the pane.

  f. Click the Chart Elements button, add Inside Base data labels, then add an Exponential trendline.

  g. Add your name as a footer to the slides, check the spelling of the presentation, then view the presentation in Reading View.

  h. Save the presentation, submit your presentation to your instructor, close the presentation, then exit PowerPoint.

Independent Challenge 2

One of your responsibilities working in the Wyoming State schools system is to provide program performance data for educational programs designed for disabled children in the state. You need to develop and give a presentation describing the program's results at a national education forum held this year in Dallas, Texas. You have been working on the presentation, and now you need to use PowerPoint to put the finishing touches on a chart.

a. Start PowerPoint, open the presentation PPT F-8.pptx from the location where you store your Data Files, then save it as **PPT F-Wyoming**.

b. Select the chart on Slide 7, then change the chart type to Clustered Column.

c. Add primary major vertical gridlines, then move the legend to the top of the chart.

d. Open the CHART TOOLS FORMAT tab, click the Math data series, then change the shape fill to a From Center gradient.

e. Change the Reading data series shape fill to the Water droplets texture, then change the Writing data series shape outline to a red 3 pt weight.

f. Apply the Wipe Entrance animation to the chart, then change the Effect options to By Category.

g. Check the spelling in the presentation, add your name as a footer to the slides, then save the presentation.

h. View the presentation in Slide Show view, submit your presentation to your instructor, close the presentation, then exit PowerPoint.

Independent Challenge 3

Genic Industries is a large company that develops and produces medical equipment and technical machines for operating and emergency rooms throughout the United States. You are one of the client representatives in the company, and one of your assignments is to prepare a presentation for the division management meetings on the profitability and efficiency of each division in the company. Use PowerPoint to develop the presentation.

a. Open the file PPT F-9.pptx from the location where you store your Data Files, then save it as **PPT F-Genic**.

b. Apply the Retrospect theme, then apply a variant to the presentation.

c. Add a new slide after the title slide titled **Company Divisions**, then create a SmartArt graphic that identifies the company's six divisions: **Administration**, **Accounting**, **Sales and Marketing**, **Research and Development**, **Product Testing**, and **Manufacturing**.

d. Format the new SmartArt graphic using SmartArt Styles and colors.

e. Go to the Division Performance slide, then embed the chart in the Excel file PPT F-10.xlsx from the location where you store your Data Files.

f. Drag the corner sizing handles of the chart so it fills the blank area of the slide, double-click the chart, click the chart in Excel, then click the CHART TOOLS DESIGN tab.

g. Apply the Style 14 chart style to the chart, right-click Last Yr. in the chart, click Format Axis, scroll down, click LABELS, click the Label Position list arrow, click Low, click OK, then click a blank area of the slide.

h. Go to the Division Budgets slide, then link the worksheet in the Excel file PPT F-11.xlsx from the location where you store your Data Files.

i. Open the linked worksheet in Excel, select cells B5 through F12, click the Accounting Number Format button in the Number group, save the changes to the worksheet, then close Excel.

j. Right-click the linked chart, click Format Object, click the Solid fill option button, change the fill color to an accent color at 35% transparency.

k. Close the pane, resize the worksheet to fill the slide, add your name as a footer to the slides and handouts, check the spelling, then view your presentation in Slide Show view.

l. Submit your presentation to your instructor, close the presentation, then exit PowerPoint.

Independent Challenge 4: Explore

You are on staff at your college newspaper. One of your jobs is to review computer games and post a presentation on the paper's Web site. The presentation identifies the top computer games based on student testing and other reviews. Use PowerPoint to create a presentation that includes research and your own information. Use the basic presentation provided as a basis to develop this presentation. *NOTE: To complete the Independent Challenge, your computer must be connected to the Internet.*

As you create this presentation, follow these guidelines:
- Include three computer games in your presentation.
- Each game has at least one defined mission or task.
- There are three categories of games: Adventure, Action, and Strategy.

If you have access to the Web, you can research the following topics to help you develop information for your presentation:
- Consumer or industry reviews of computer games
- Computer game descriptions and pricing
- **a.** Connect to the Internet, then use a search engine to locate Web sites that have information on PC computer games. Review at least two Web sites that contain information about computer games. Print the home pages of the Web sites you use to gather data for your presentation.
- **b.** Open the presentation PPT F-12.pptx from the location where you store your Data Files, then save it as **PPT F-Games**.
- **c.** Add your name as the footer on all slides and handouts, then apply the Wood Type design theme.
- **d.** (Before you complete this step make a copy of the Data File PPT F-13.xlsx.) Go to the Game Reviews slide, locate and link the Excel chart PPT F-13.xlsx from the location where you store your Data Files.
- **e.** Resize the chart on the slide, then open the linked chart in Excel.
- **f.** Click the Sheet 1 tab at the bottom of the Excel window, provide a name for each game, click the Sheet 2 tab, then save your changes.
- **g.** Right-click the chart legend, click Delete on the shortcut menu, click the Chart Styles button, click COLOR, then click Color 4.
- **h.** Save your changes, then exit Excel.
- **i.** Click the FILE tab, click Edit Links to Files under Related Documents to open the Links dialog box, then click the Automatic Update check box to deselect it.
- **j.** Click the Open Source button, click Sheet1 at the bottom of the Excel window, click cell B4, type **7.6**, click Sheet2 tab, save your work, then exit Excel.
- **k.** Click the Back button to return to your presentation, right-click the Excel chart, then click Update Link in the shortcut menu.
- **l.** Check the spelling in the presentation, save the presentation, then view the presentation in Slide Show view.
- **m.** Submit your presentation to your instructor, close the presentation, then exit PowerPoint.

Visual Workshop

Create a slide that looks like the example in FIGURE F-19. Start a new presentation, then embed the Excel worksheet PPT F-14.xlsx from the location where you store your Data Files. (*Hint*: The worksheet is formatted with a 35% transparent plum fill.) Save the presentation as **PPT F-General**. Add your name and the slide number as a footer to the slide, then submit your presentation to your instructor.

FIGURE F-19

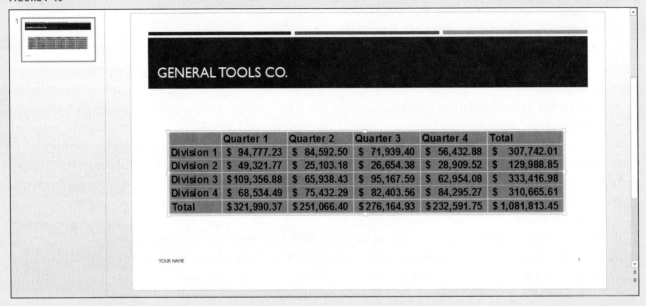

Inserting Graphics, Media, and Objects

| CASE | In this unit, you work on a short presentation that describes other Quest Specialty Travel tour opportunities. You then link it to your primary Train Tour presentation. You use the advanced features in PowerPoint to customize a table, a picture, and a SmartArt graphic. You also insert a video and sound that complements the information as well as action buttons for better navigation. |

Unit Objectives

After completing this unit, you will be able to:

- Create a custom table
- Design a SmartArt graphic
- Enhance a SmartArt graphic
- Insert and edit digital video

- Insert and trim audio
- Edit and adjust a picture
- Add action buttons
- Insert hyperlinks

Files You Will Need

PPT G-1.pptx	PPT G-12.jpg
PPT G-2.jpg	PPT G-13.mp4
PPT G-3.jpg	PPT G-14.wma
PPT G-4.jpg	PPT G-15.jpg
PPT G-5.jpg	PPT G-16.docx
PPT G-6.wmv	PPT G-17.pptx
PPT G-7.wma	PPT G-18.pptx
PPT G-8.jpg	PPT G-19.pptx
PPT G-9.pptx	PPT G-20.pptx
PPT G-10.docx	PPT G-21.jpg
PPT G-11.pptx	

Create a Custom Table

In PowerPoint, you have the ability to create dynamic-looking tables. Tables you create in PowerPoint automatically display the style as determined by the theme assigned to the slide, including color combinations and shading, line styles and colors, and other effects. It is easy to customize the layout of a table or change how data is organized. You can delete and insert rows or columns, merge two or more cells together, or split one cell into more cells. **CASE** > *You open a short presentation on Canadian Train Add-On Tours that you have been working on and finish customizing a table.*

STEPS

1. **Start PowerPoint, open the presentation PPT G-1.pptx from the location where you store your Data Files, save the presentation as PPT G-QST, click the Slide 2 thumbnail in the Thumbnails pane, then click the table**
   Slide 2 appears in the Slide pane with the table selected.

2. **Click the TABLE TOOLS DESIGN tab on the Ribbon, click the Pen Style button in the Draw Borders group, click the dash-dot style (4th style), click the Pen Weight button in the Draw Borders group, click 2 ¼ pt, click the Pen Color button in the Draw Borders group, then click Dark Red in the Standard Colors section**
   The pointer changes to ∅, which indicates that you are in drawing mode.

3. **Click the white vertical column line that divides the Pricing and Includes columns in the first row in the table, then click the vertical column line for each row in that column**
   Compare your screen to **FIGURE G-1**.

4. **Click the Draw Table button in the Draw Borders group, click the TABLE TOOLS LAYOUT tab on the Ribbon, click the Backpack cell in the table, click the Insert Below button in the Rows & Columns group, then enter the information below in the new row**

Snowshoe backpack	Walking	$45/day - 4 days	2 Meals/day

   Clicking the Draw Table button turns the drawing mode off. A new row is added to the table.

5. **Click the Walking Bicycle cell, then click the Split Cells button in the Merge group**
   The Split Cells dialog box opens. The default table is 2 columns and 1 row.

6. **Click the Number of columns down arrow once, click the Number of rows up arrow once, then click OK**
   You split the cell to create a new row in that cell.

7. **Double-click the word Bicycle, right-click Bicycle, click Cut on the shortcut menu, press [Backspace], right-click the new row, then click the Keep Source Formatting Paste Options button 📋 on the shortcut menu**
   The words "Walking" and "Bicycle" are now in two separate rows in the Transportation column. See **TABLE G-1** for Paste button options.

8. **Repeat Steps 5–7 to split the Bicycle pricing data in the Pricing column into two rows, then click the Distribute Rows button in the Cell Size group**
   Now the Bicycle information is separate from the Walking information, and all the rows are the same height as shown in **FIGURE G-2**.

9. **Click outside the table, then save your presentation**

FIGURE G-1: Table with new column line style

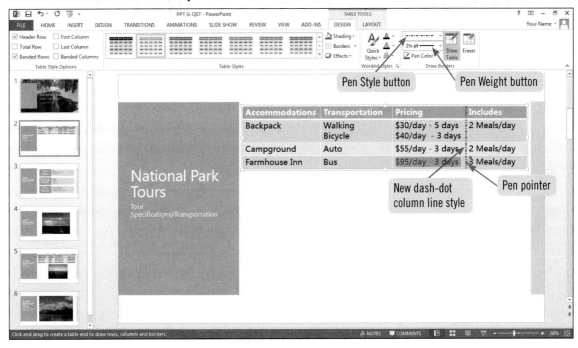

FIGURE G-2: Modified table

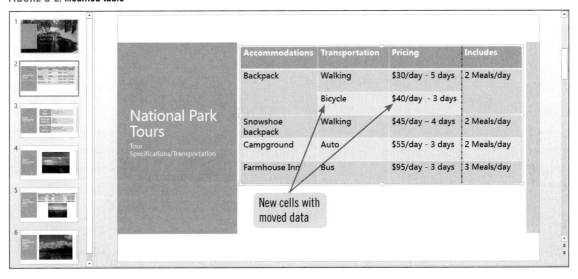

TABLE G-1: Understanding common Paste button options

button	button name	result
	Use Destination Theme	Use the current theme of the presentation
	Keep Source Formatting	Use the formatting characteristics from the object's source file
	Picture	Insert the object as a picture
	Keep Text Only	Insert the object as text only with no formatting
	Embed	Insert the object as an embedded object

Inserting Graphics, Media, and Objects

Design a SmartArt Graphic

Learning
Outcomes
• Add a SmartArt
  bullet
• Modify SmartArt
  graphics

Using SmartArt graphics in a presentation dramatically improves your ability to create vibrant content on slides. SmartArt allows you to easily combine your content with an illustrative diagram, improving the overall quality of your presentation. Better presentations lead to improved understanding and retention by your audience. In a matter of minutes, and with little training, you can create a SmartArt graphic using slide content that would otherwise have been placed in a simple bulleted list. **CASE** ▶ *You continue working on the Canadian Train Add-On tours presentation by changing the graphic layout, adding a shape and text to the SmartArt graphic, and then changing its color and style.*

STEPS

1. **Click the** Slide 3 thumbnail **in the Thumbnails pane, click the** Tour Sites shape **in the SmartArt graphic, then click the** SMARTART TOOLS DESIGN tab **on the Ribbon**

   The Tour Sites shape is selected and displays sizing handles and a rotate handle. Each shape in the SmartArt graphic is separate and distinct from the other shapes and can be individually edited, formatted, or moved within the boundaries of the SmartArt graphic.

2. **If necessary, click the** Text Pane control button ▣ **to open the Text pane, click the** Add Bullet button **in the Create Graphic group, then type** Maligne Valley **in the Text pane**

   A new bullet appears in the Text pane and in the upper-right shape of the graphic. Compare your screen with **FIGURE G-3**.

3. **Click the** More button ▽ **in the Layouts group, click** Horizontal Picture List **(4th row), then click the** Package Details shape

   Live Preview shows you how each of the layouts change the SmartArt graphic. The SmartArt graphic layout changes to Horizontal Picture List.

4. **Click the** Add Shape list arrow **in the Create Graphic group, click** Add Shape After, **then click the** Move Down button **once in the Create Graphic group**

   A new shape in the same style appears with a new bullet in the Text pane and then is moved to the end of the Text pane.

5. **Type** Upgrades, **press [Enter], press [Tab], type** Add trip to Victoria BC, **press [Enter], type** Shopping in Banff, **press [Enter], then type** Personal guide

6. **Click** ▽ **in the SmartArt Styles group, then click** Subtle Effect **in the Best Match for Document section**

   The style of the SmartArt graphic changes.

7. **Click the** Change Colors button **in the SmartArt Styles group, then click** Colorful - Accent Colors **in the Colorful section**

   Each shape now has a different color that follows the Theme colors of the presentation.

8. **Click the** Text Pane button **in the Create Graphic group to close the Text pane, then click the** Right to Left button **in the Create Graphic group**

   The graphic flips and appears as a mirror image. You prefer the original view of the graphic.

9. **Click the** Right to Left button, **click a blank area of the slide, then save your changes**

   Compare your screen to **FIGURE G-4**.

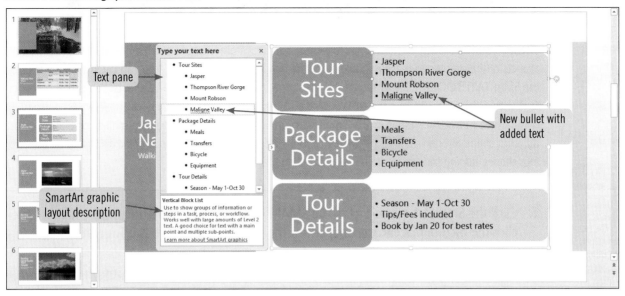

FIGURE G-4: SmartArt graphic with new design

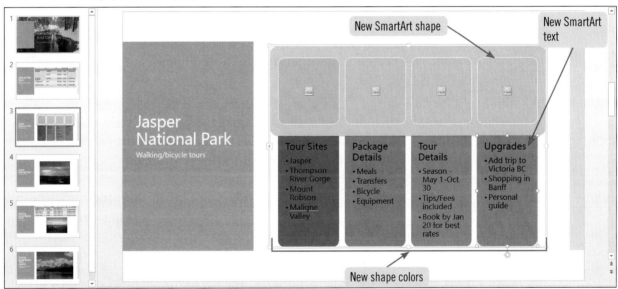

Creating mathematical equations

You can insert or create mathematical equations using the Equation button in the Symbols group on the INSERT tab. Click the Equation button list arrow to access nine common equations, which include the area of a circle, the Pythagorean Theorem (my personal favorite), and the Quadratic Formula (my editor's favorite).

To create your own equations click the Equation button to open the EQUATION TOOLS DESIGN tab. To help you create equations, you have access to eight types of symbols including basic math, geometry, operators, and scripts. You also have the ability to create mathematical structures such as integrals and functions.

Enhance a SmartArt Graphic

Though you can use styles and themes to format a SmartArt graphic, you still may need to refine individual aspects of the graphic to make it look exactly the way you want it to look. You can use the commands on the SMARTART TOOLS FORMAT tab to change shape styles, fills, outlines, and effects. You can also convert text within the SmartArt graphic to WordArt and format the text using any of the WordArt formatting commands. Individual shapes in the SmartArt graphic can be made larger or smaller, or altered into a different shape altogether. **CASE** *You continue working on the SmartArt graphic on Slide 3 by adjusting four shapes, adding pictures to shapes, and adjusting text in the graphic.*

STEPS

1. **Click the** SmartArt graphic, **click the** SMARTART TOOLS FORMAT tab **on the Ribbon, then click the** picture placeholder shape (not the picture icon) **above the Tour Sites shape**
   The shape behind the picture icon is selected.

2. **Click the** Change Shape button **in the Shapes group, then click** Round Same Side Corner Rectangle **in the Rectangles section**
   The form of the shape changes.

3. **Click the** picture placeholder shape **above the Package Details shape, press and hold** [Ctrl], **click the remaining** two picture placeholder shapes, **release** [Ctrl], **press** [F4], **then click in a blank area of the SmartArt graphic**
   All four picture placeholder shapes now have a new shape as shown in FIGURE G-5.

4. **Click the** picture icon ⊡ **in the picture placeholder shape above the Tour Sites shape**
   The Insert Picture dialog box opens.

5. **Click the** From a file Browse button, **navigate to the location where you store your Data Files, click** PPT G-2.jpg, **then click** Insert
   The picture is placed in the picture placeholder shape. Notice the picture fills the contour of the shape.

6. **Following the instructions in Step 5, click** ⊡ **above the Package Details shape, insert the file** PPT G-3.jpg, **click** ⊡ **above the Tour Details shape, insert the file** PPT G-4.jpg, **click** ⊡ **above the Upgrades shape, then insert the file** PPT G-5.jpg
   All four shapes in the SmartArt graphic have pictures in them.

7. **Click the** picture above the Tour Sites shape, **click the** Larger button **in the Shapes group, click the** picture above the Package Details shape, **press and hold** [Ctrl], **click the remaining** two pictures, **release** [Ctrl], **then press** [F4]
   All of the pictures are a little larger now.

8. **Click a blank area inside the SmartArt graphic, then drag the SmartArt graphic's** sizing handles **to enlarge the graphic as shown in** FIGURE G-6
   The SmartArt graphic fills the white area on the slide.

9. **Click a blank area of the slide, then save your work**

FIGURE G-5: New shapes in SmartArt graphic

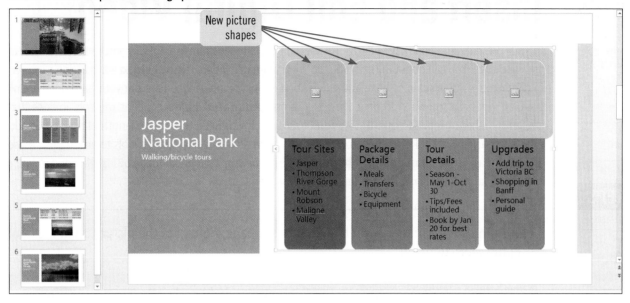

FIGURE G-6: Completed SmartArt graphic

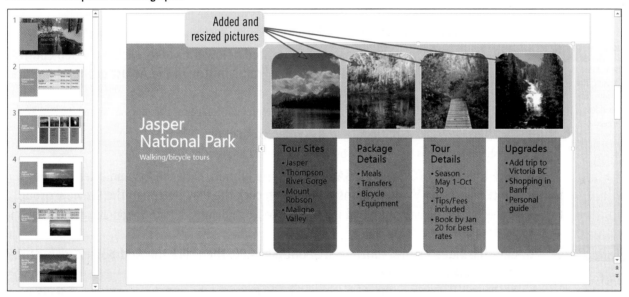

Saving a presentation in PDF, XPS, or other fixed file formats

In certain situations, such as when sharing sensitive or legal materials with others, you may find it necessary to save your presentation file in a fixed layout format. A **fixed layout format** is a specific file format that "locks" the file from future change and allows others only the ability to view or print the presentation. To save a presentation in one of these fixed formats, click the FILE tab on the Ribbon, click Export, click Create PDF/XPS Document, then click the Create a PDF/XPS button. The Publish as PDF or XPS dialog box opens. Select the appropriate file type in the Save as type list box, choose other options (optimization), then publish your presentation in a fixed layout format. To view a fixed layout format presentation, you need appropriate viewer software that you can download from the Internet. Other common file formats supported in PowerPoint 2013 include PowerPoint Template (.potx), PowerPoint Show (.ppsx), OpenDocument Presentation (.odp), and PowerPoint Picture Presentation (.pptx). On the FILE tab click Export, then click Change File Type to save a file in another file format and to view descriptions of these and other supported file formats.

Insert and Edit Digital Video

In your presentation, you may want to use special effects to illustrate a point or capture the attention of your audience. You can do this by inserting digital or animated video. **Digital video** is live action captured in digital format by a video camera. You can embed or link a digital video file from your hard drive or link a digital video file from a Web page on the Internet. **Animated video** contains multiple images that stream together or move to give the illusion of motion. If you need to edit the length of a video or add effects or background color to a video, you can use PowerPoint's video-editing tools to accomplish those and other basic editing tasks. **CASE** ▶ *You continue to develop your presentation by inserting and editing a video clip you shot while on a walking tour during your train trip.*

STEPS

1. **Click the** Slide 4 thumbnail **in the Thumbnails pane, right-click the** picture, **then click** Cut **in the shortcut menu**

   The picture is deleted from the slide leaving an empty Content placeholder.

2. **Click the** Insert Video icon 🖳 **in the Content placeholder, click the** From a file Browse **button, navigate to the location where you store your Data Files, click** PPT G-6.wmv, **click the** Insert list arrow, **then click** Link to File

   The PPT G-6.wmv video clip displaying a black preview image is linked to the slide. By linking the digital video to the presentation, you do not increase the file size of the presentation, but remember, you need direct access to the location where the video file is stored in order to play it.

3. **Move** ▷ **over the** video control timeline **located below the video, click the** video control timeline **at about 00:10.00, click the** Poster Frame button **in the Adjust group, then click** Current Frame

   The video frame at about 00:10.00 is now set as the preview image for the video as shown in **FIGURE G-7**.

4. **Click the** Play/Pause button ▷ **in the video control bar**

   The short video plays through once but does not rewind to the beginning.

5. **Click the** VIDEO TOOLS PLAYBACK tab **on the Ribbon, click the** Rewind after Playing **check box in the Video Options group, then click the** Play button **in the Preview group**

   The video plays through once, and this time the video rewinds back to the beginning and displays the preview image.

6. **Click the** video control timeline **at about 00:24.00, then click the** Add Bookmark button **in the Bookmarks group**

   A yellow circle appears in the video control timeline indicating the video has a bookmark. A **bookmark** can indicate a point of interest in a video; it can also be used to jump to a specific point in a video.

7. **Click the** Slide Show button 🖳 **on the status bar, move** ▷ **over the video, the pointer changes to** 🖑, **then click the bookmark as shown in** FIGURE G-8

   The video moves to the bookmarked frame.

8. **Click the** Play/Pause button ▶ **on the video**

   The video plays from the bookmarked frame to the end of the video and then rewinds to the beginning.

9. **Press [Esc], click the** video, **click the** VIDEO TOOLS FORMAT tab **on the Ribbon, click the** More button 🔻 **in the Video Styles group, then click** Beveled Rounded Rectangle **in the Moderate section**

   A rounded bevel effect is added to the video.

10. **Click a blank area of the slide, then save your work**

Inserting Graphics, Media, and Objects

Trimming a video

After you watch a video clip, you may determine certain portions of the video are not relevant to your slide show. From PowerPoint, a video clip can be trimmed only from the beginning or the end of the clip; you can't use PowerPoint to trim out the middle of a clip. To trim a video clip, select the video, click the VIDEO TOOLS PLAYBACK tab, then click the Trim Video button in the Editing group. The Trim Video dialog box opens. To trim the beginning of the video clip, drag the start point (green marker) to the right until you reach a new starting point. To trim the end of a video clip, drag the end point (red marker) to the left until you reach a new ending point. If you want to precisely choose a new beginning or ending point for the video clip, you can click the up or down arrows on the Start Time and End Time text boxes.

PowerPoint 2013

Inserting Graphics, Media, and Objects

Insert and Trim Audio

Learning
Outcomes
• Insert, edit, and
  play a sound file

PowerPoint allows you to insert sound files in your presentation in the same way you insert digital video. You can add sounds to your presentation from files on a storage device, the Internet, or a network drive. The primary use of sound in a presentation is to provide emphasis to a slide or an element on the slide. For example, if you are creating a presentation about a raft tour on the Colorado River, you might consider inserting a rushing water sound on a slide showing a photograph of people rafting. **CASE** *You insert a recorded sound file of a review from a satisfied customer on Slide 6 of the presentation to enhance the message on the slide.*

STEPS

QUICK TIP
To insert a sound from the Internet, click the Audio button, then click Online Audio.

1. **Click the Slide 6 thumbnail in the Thumbnails pane, click the INSERT tab on the Ribbon, click the Audio button in the Media group, then click Audio on My PC**
   The Insert Audio dialog box opens. Common sound formats you can insert into a presentation include Windows audio files (waveform) (.wav), MP3 audio files (.mp3), and Windows Media Audio files (.wma).

2. **Navigate to the location where you store your Data Files, click PPT G-7.wma, then click Insert**
   A sound icon with an audio control bar appears in the center of the slide as shown FIGURE G-9.

QUICK TIP
You can hide the sound icon during a slide show by clicking the Hide During Show check box in the Audio Options group.

3. **Drag the sound icon 🔊 beneath the slide text, then click the Play/Pause button ▶ in the audio control bar**
   The sound icon moves off the picture and plays one time through. After hearing the audio play, you decide to trim the start point to cut out the beginning of the audio clip.

4. **Click the Trim Audio button in the Editing group on the AUDIO TOOLS PLAYBACK tab**
   The Trim Audio dialog box opens as shown in FIGURE G-10. Notice on the audio timeline there is a start point (green marker) and an end point (red marker), which identify the beginning and end of the audio. The audio is 11.517 seconds long.

5. **Click the Play button ▶ in the Trim Audio dialog box, watch the sound on the audio timeline, then drag the start point ⏸ to the right to about 00:03.000**
   The audio will now start at this point when played. The end of the audio also needs to be adjusted.

QUICK TIP
You can use book-marks to manually start or end an audio or jump to a precise point in the audio.

6. **Click the End Time down arrow until 00:11 appears as shown in FIGURE G-11, click OK, then click ▶ in the audio control bar**
   The audio now plays between the new start and end points. By default, the audio plays when you click the sound icon during a slide show.

7. **Click the Start button in the Audio Options group, then click Automatically**
   The audio will now run automatically as soon as the slide appears in Slide Show view.

8. **Click the Slide Show button 🖵 on the status bar, then listen to the audio**
   Notice that the sound icon appears during the slide show.

9. **Press [Esc], click a blank area of the slide, then save your changes**

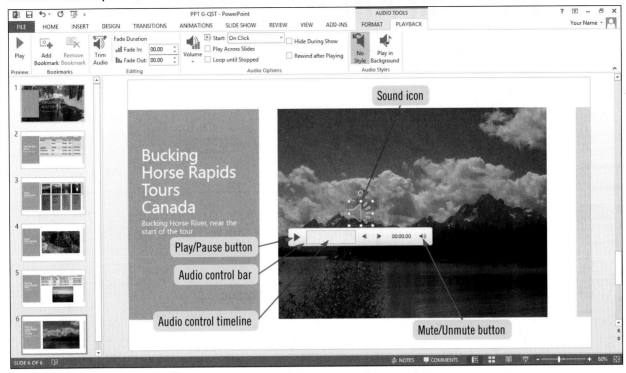

FIGURE G-10: Trim Audio dialog box

FIGURE G-11: Trim Audio dialog box with trimmed audio

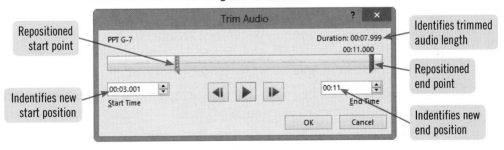

Recording a narration on a slide

If your computer has speakers, a sound card, and a microphone, you can record a voice narration and then play it during a slide show. To record a narration, click the INSERT tab on the Ribbon, click the Audio button in the Media group, then click Record Audio. The Record Sound dialog box opens. To start recording, click the Record button in the dialog box, then click the Stop button when you are finished. A sound icon appears on the slide. Narration recordings and other sounds are embedded in the presentation and will increase the PowerPoint file size. You can preview a narration in Normal view by pointing to the sound icon on the slide, then clicking the Play/Pause button in the audio control bar.

Edit and Adjust a Picture

Learning Outcomes
- Replace a picture
- Remove picture background
- Convert picture to SmartArt graphic

Inserting pictures and other media to your slides can dynamically enhance the message of your presentation. When working with pictures in PowerPoint, you have a number of available design options you can use to format pictures in creative ways, including artistic effects, color saturation, color tone, recoloring, sharpening, brightness, contrast, and background removal. These advanced picture-formatting features can dramatically change how a picture appears, and they can be useful when you are trying to match the picture to other content in the presentation. **CASE** ▶ *On Slide 5 you experiment with PowerPoint's picture tools.*

STEPS

QUICK TIP
To compress a picture, select the picture, click the Compress Pictures button in the Adjust group, choose the options you want, then click OK.

1. **Click the Slide 5 thumbnail in the Thumbnails pane, click the picture, click the PICTURE TOOLS FORMAT tab on the Ribbon, click the Width text box in the Size group, type 5.5, then press [Enter]**

   The picture proportionally increases in size.

2. **Click the Change Picture button in the Adjust group**

   The Insert Pictures dialog box opens. Use this dialog box to search for a replacement picture. The file can be on your computer, available through Office.com, on a Web page on the Internet, or in your SkyDrive folder. The current picture does not convey the scene you want to display on this slide.

3. **Click the From a file Browse button, navigate to the location where you store your Data Files, click PPT G-8.jpg, then click Insert**

   A new picture takes the place of the original picture and uses the same proportions. Eliminating the background of a picture can highlight the subject or remove distracting aspects of the picture.

4. **Click the Remove Background button in the Adjust group**

   The BACKGROUND REMOVAL tab opens on the Ribbon. The background is highlighted in pink. The picture displays a removal marquee box with sizing handles that surrounds the subject of the picture you want to keep, as shown in **FIGURE G-12**.

5. **Drag the removal marquee sizing handles to match FIGURE G-13, then click the Keep Changes button in the Close group**

   The entire sky portion of the picture is removed from the picture.

QUICK TIP
To make one color in a picture transparent, select the picture, click the Color button in the Adjust group, click Set Transparent Color, then click the color on the picture you want to make transparent.

6. **Click the Color button in the Adjust group, click Saturation: 0% in the Color Saturation section, click the Corrections button in the Adjust group, then click Brightness: +40% Contrast: +20% in the Brightness/Contrast section (4th row)**

   The picture color, saturation, brightness, and contrast change. The picture formatting is interesting, but you decide the picture looks better the way it was previous to the formatting changes.

7. **Click the Reset Picture button in the Adjust group, right-click the picture, then click Send to Back in the shortcut menu**

   All of the formatting applied to the picture is removed, and the picture is reset to its original condition. The picture is moved behind the table on the slide.

8. **Click the Picture Layout button in the Picture Styles group, click Bending Picture Semi-Transparent Text (2nd row), click the text box, then type Mt. Robson**

   The picture is converted to a SmartArt graphic with a stylistic text box.

9. **Position ⍾ over the SmartArt graphic border, drag the SmartArt graphic to the area of the slide shown in FIGURE G-14, click a blank area of the slide, then save your work**

FIGURE G-12: Picture with background area to be removed

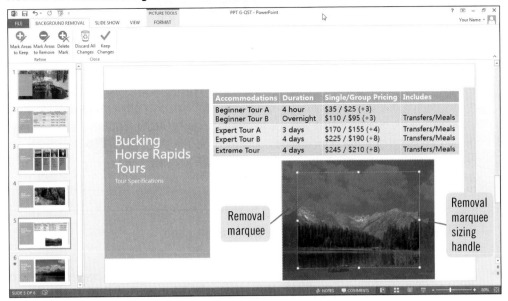

FIGURE G-13: Adjusted removal marquee

FIGURE G-14: Picture converted to SmartArt graphic

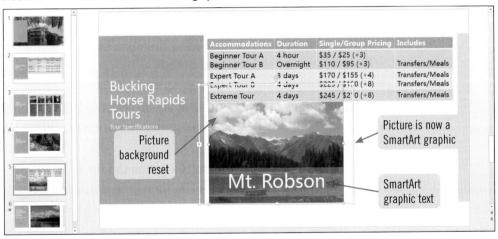

Things to know about picture compression

It's important to know that when you compress a picture you change the amount of detail in the picture, so it might look different than it did before the compression. Compressing a picture changes the amount of color used in the picture with no loss of quality. By default, all inserted pictures in PowerPoint are automatically compressed using the settings in the PowerPoint Options dialog box. To locate the compression settings, click the FILE tab, click Options, then click Advanced in the left pane. In the Image Size and Quality section, you can change picture compression settings or stop the automatic compression of pictures. If you want to apply an effect from the Artistic Effects gallery to a compressed picture, compress the picture first to maintain the best picture quality possible.

Add Action Buttons

Learning
Outcomes
• Create action
 button
• Duplicate action
 buttons

An **action button** is an interactive button that you create from the Shapes gallery to perform a specific task. For example, you can create an action button to play a video or a sound, or to link to another slide in your presentation. Action buttons can also link to a Web page on the Internet, a different presentation, or any file created in another program. You can also run a macro or another program using an action button. A **macro** is a set of actions that you use to automate tasks. Action buttons are commonly used in self-running presentations and presentations published on the Web. **CASE** *You finish working on this presentation by adding action buttons to each slide, which will allow you to move from slide to slide and back to the first slide.*

STEPS

1. **Click the** Slide 1 thumbnail **in the Thumbnails pane**

   Slide 1 appears in the Slide pane.

QUICK TIP

Any shape in the Shapes gallery as well as most objects can be an action button. Click the shape or object, click the INSERT tab, click the Action button in the Links group, then select an action.

2. **Click the** More button ⩒ **in the Drawing group to open the Shapes gallery, click** Action Button: Forward or Next ▷ **in the Action Buttons section, press and hold [Shift], drag to create a button as shown in** FIGURE G-15, **then release [Shift]**

   A small action button appears on the slide, and the Action Settings dialog box opens. Pressing [Shift] while you create a shape maintains the shape's proportions as you change its size.

3. **Make sure** Next Slide **is selected in the Hyperlink to list, then click** OK

   The dialog box closes. The action button now has an action, in this case, linking to the next slide.

4. **Click the** DRAWING TOOLS FORMAT tab **on the Ribbon, click** ⩒ **in the Shape Styles group, point to** Other Theme Fills, **then click** Style 2

   The new theme fill makes the action button easier to see on the slide.

QUICK TIP

Use the arrow keys on your keyboard or press [Alt] while dragging the action button to nudge the action button into place.

5. **Drag the** action button **to the lower-left corner of the rectangle shape, then right-click the** action button

   The shortcut menu opens.

6. **Click** Copy **in the shortcut menu, click the** Slide 2 thumbnail **in the Thumbnails pane, then click the** Paste button **in the Clipboard group**

   An exact copy of the action button, including the associated action, is placed on Slide 2.

7. **Paste a copy of the** action button **on Slides 3, 4, and 5, click the** Slide 6 thumbnail **in the Thumbnails pane, click** ⩒ **in the Drawing group, then click** Action Button: Home 🏠 **in the Action Buttons section**

8. **Use [Shift] to create a similar-sized action button as you did for Slide 1, make sure** First Slide **is selected in the Hyperlink to list, click** OK, **then drag the** action button **to the lower-left corner of the rectangle shape**

   Compare your screen to FIGURE G-16.

9. **Click the** Slide Show button 🖵 **on the status bar, listen to the audio, click the** Home action button, **click the** action buttons **to move from Slide 2 to Slide 6, then press [Esc] to end the slide show**

   The pointer changes to 👆 when you click each action button.

10. **Add your name to the slide footer, save your changes, submit your presentation to your instructor, click the** FILE tab **on the Ribbon, then click** Close **to close the presentation, but do not exit PowerPoint**

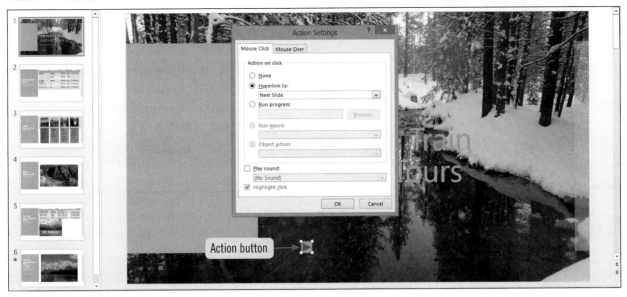

Change the transparency of a picture

Pictures in PowerPoint are commonly used as slide backgrounds, individual objects on a slide, or inserted in another object, such as a SmartArt graphic. To change the transparency of a picture used as a slide background, insert the picture as a slide background using the Format Background button on the DESIGN tab, then adjust the Transparency slider in the Format Background pane. To change the transparency of a picture you want to insert on a slide, first draw a shape from the Shapes gallery, such as a rectangle the size you want the picture to be, then right-click the shape. Click Format Shape on the shortcut menu, click FILL, click the Picture or texture fill option button, click the File button, locate and insert the picture, then move the Transparency slider in the Format Picture pane.

Insert Hyperlinks

While creating a presentation, there might be a circumstance where you want to view a document that either won't fit on the slide or is too detailed for your presentation. In these cases, you can insert a **hyperlink**, a specially formatted word, phrase, graphic, or drawn object that you click during a slide show to "jump to," or display, another slide or PowerPoint presentation in your current presentation; a document from another program, like Word; or a Web page. A hyperlinked object is similar to a linked object because you can modify the object in its source program from within PowerPoint. **CASE** *You add two hyperlinks to the primary presentation you have been working on that provide more detail on the Jasper bicycle tour.*

STEPS

1. **Open the presentation** PPT G-9.pptx **from the location where you store your Data Files, then save the presentation as** PPT G-Final.pptx

2. **Click the** Slide 11 thumbnail **in the Thumbnails pane, select** Route highlights **in the text object, click the** INSERT tab **on the Ribbon, then click the** Hyperlink button **in the Links group**

   The Insert Hyperlink dialog box opens. The Existing File or Web Page button is selected in the Link to: pane, and the Current Folder button is selected in the Look in pane. The location where you store your Data Files should be the open folder.

   QUICK TIP
   Links can also be established between slides of the same presentation, a new presentation, an email address, or any Web page.

3. **Click the file** PPT G-10.docx, **click** OK, **then click in a blank area of the slide**

   Now that you have made the text "Route highlights" a hyperlink to the file PPT G-10.docx, the text is formatted in a tan color and is underlined, which is how a hyperlink is formatted in this theme.

4. **Click the** Slide Show button 🖵 **on the status bar, point to** Route highlights, **notice the pointer change to** 🖑, **then click** Route highlights

   Microsoft Word opens, and the Word document containing a detailed description of the Vancouver-to-Calgary train tour appears, as shown in **FIGURE G-17**.

5. **Click the** down scroll arrow **and read the document, then close the** Word window

   The PowerPoint slide reappears in Slide Show view.

   QUICK TIP
   To edit, open, copy, or remove a hyperlink, right-click the hyperlink, then click the appropriate command on the shortcut menu.

6. **Press** [Esc], **click the** Slide 12 thumbnail **in the Thumbnails pane, right-click the** Information action button, **click** Hyperlink, **click the** Hyperlink to option button, **click the** Hyperlink to list arrow, **then click** Other PowerPoint Presentation

   The Hyperlink to Other PowerPoint Presentation dialog box opens.

7. **Open the file** PPT G-QST.pptx **(that you worked on earlier in this unit) from the location where you store your Data Files, then click** OK

   The Hyperlink to Slide dialog box opens. You can choose which slides you want to link to.

8. **Click** OK **to link to Slide 1, click** OK **to close the Action Settings dialog box, click** 🖵, **click the** Information action button, **click the** action buttons **to view the slides in the presentation, press** [Esc] **to end the slide show, then press** [Esc] **again**

   The slide show ends. The hyperlinks and action buttons all work correctly.

9. **Add your name to the slides footer, save your changes, then click the** Slide Sorter button ⊞ **on the status bar**

   Compare your screen to **FIGURE G-18**.

10. **Submit your presentation to your instructor, close the presentation, then exit PowerPoint**

FIGURE G-17: Linked Word document

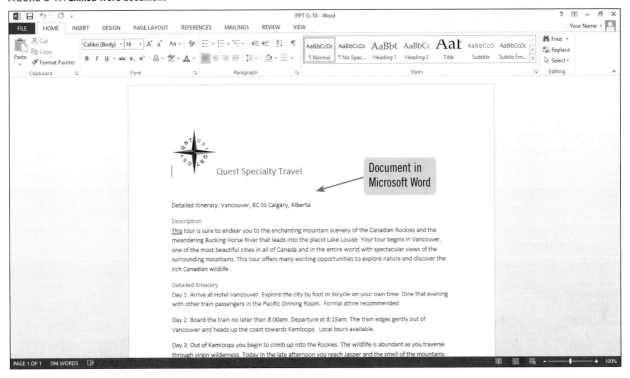

FIGURE G-18: Final presentation in Slide Sorter view

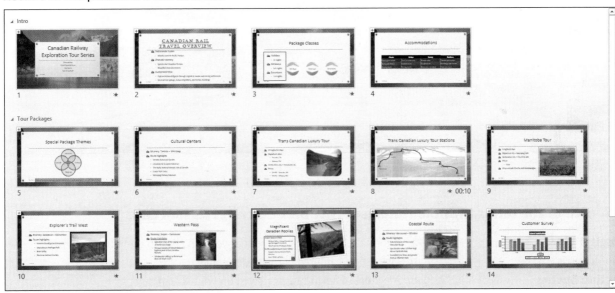

Inserting a screenshot

Using the Screenshot button in the Images group on the INSERT tab, you can insert a picture, or screenshot, of an open program window or a specific part of the window. A screenshot is simply a picture of the window displayed on your screen. For example, you could use the screenshot feature to insert a picture of information you found on a Web page or found in other documents or programs that might not be easily transferable to PowerPoint. Screenshots are static and are not able to be updated if the source information changes. Only open nonminimized windows are available to be captured as a screenshot. When you click the Screenshot button all open program windows appear in the Available Windows gallery. To take a screenshot of part of a window, click the Screenshot button, then click Screen Clipping.

Practice

Concepts Review

Label each element of the PowerPoint window shown in FIGURE G-19.

FIGURE G-19

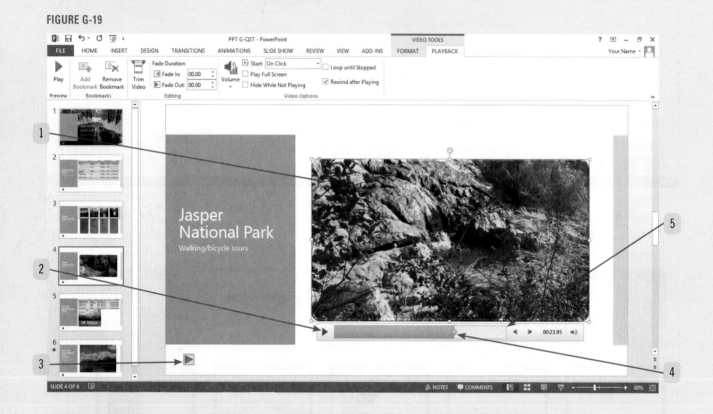

Match each of the terms with the statement that best describes its function.

6. **Digital video**
7. **Bookmark**
8. **Action button**
9. **Hyperlink**
10. **Screenshot**
11. **Animated video**

a. A formatted word or graphic that you can click to jump to a Web page
b. Live action captured with a video camera
c. A picture of a window displayed on your screen
d. An interactive object that performs a specific task
e. Indicates a point of interest in a video
f. Multiple images streamed together that move during a slide show

Select the best answer from the list of choices.

12. Use a _____ to display and organize related information.
    a. Hyperlink
    b. Table
    c. SmartArt graphic
    d. Screenshot

13. Which of the following statements about trimming a video clip is *not* true?
    a. Move the start point and end point to trim out the middle of a video clip.
    b. Move the start point to trim the beginning of a video clip.
    c. Moving the start point creates a new beginning point in the video.
    d. Move the end point to trim the end of a video clip.

14. A(n) _____ file format is a specific file format that "locks" the file from future changes.
    a. Movie
    b. MP4
    c. Protected
    d. Fixed layout

15. In PowerPoint, a hyperlink can be used to:
    a. Start the slide show from a table.
    b. Display an Excel file during a slide show.
    c. Animate text or graphics.
    d. Format text in a picture.

16. Which of the following combines content with an illustrative diagram?
    a. Hyperlink
    b. Table
    c. SmartArt
    d. Action button

Skills Review

1. **Create a custom table.**
   a. Start PowerPoint, open the presentation PPT G-11.pptx from the location where you store your Data Files, then save it as **PPT G-France**.
   b. Go to Slide 4, select the table, click the TABLE TOOLS DESIGN tab, click the More button in the Table Styles group, then click the Dark Style 1 - Accent 4 in the Dark section.
   c. Click the Pen Weight button in the Draw Borders group, select 2¼ pt, click the Pen Color button, then click White, Background 1.
   d. Apply the 2¼-pt line style to the vertical border lines between the cells in the first row, then click the Draw Table button.
   e. Select the whole table, click the TABLE TOOLS LAYOUT tab, click the Cell Margins button in the Alignment group, then click Wide.
   f. Click anywhere in the bottom row, then click the Insert Below button in the Rows & Columns group.
   g. Click the left cell of the new row, type **Tomme de Savoie**, press [Tab], type **Valencay**, then save your changes.

2. **Design a SmartArt graphic.**
   a. Go to Slide 3, click the SmartArt graphic, then click the SMARTART TOOLS DESIGN tab.
   b. Click the More button in the Layouts group, then click Vertical Picture Accent List in the fourth row.
   c. Click the Add Shape list arrow in the Create Graphic group, then click Add Shape After.
   d. Open the Text pane, type **Production**, press [Enter], click the Demote button in the Create Graphic group, type **Cow cheese 1.32 million tons**, press [Enter], type **Goat cheese 0.97 million tons**, press [Enter], type **Blue cheese 0.19 million tons**.
   e. Close the Text pane, click the Change Colors button in the SmartArt Styles group, then click Colorful Range - Accent Colors 4 to 5 in the Colorful section.
   f. Click the Right to Left button in the Create Graphic group, then save your changes.

3. **Enhance a SmartArt graphic.**
   a. Click the SMARTART TOOLS FORMAT tab, click the top picture circle shape in the SmartArt graphic, click the Smaller button in the Shapes group, then decrease the size of the two other circle shapes.

PowerPoint 2013

Skills Review (continued)

   b. Click the Insert picture icon in the bottom picture circle shape, then locate and insert the file PPT G-12.jpg from the location where you store your Data Files.

   c. Follow the above instructions, insert the file PPT G-12.jpg to the other two circle shapes, then save your changes.

4. Insert and edit digital video.

   a. Go to Slide 2, click the INSERT tab on the Ribbon, click the Video button in the Media group, then click Video on My PC.

   b. Locate the file PPT G-13.mp4 from the location where you store your Data Files, click the Insert list arrow, then click Link to File.

   c. Click the number in the Height text box in the Size group, type **3**, press [Enter], then move the video clip to the bottom-left corner of the slide.

   d. Move the pointer over the video control timeline, click at approximately 00:15.16 in the timeline, click the Poster Frame button in the Adjust group then click Current Frame.

   e. On the VIDEO TOOLS PLAYBACK tab, click the Rewind after Playing check box, then add a bookmark at about the 00:05.05 point on the video control timeline.

   f. Preview the video clip in Slide Show view, then save your presentation.

5. Insert and trim audio.

   a. Go to Slide 4.

   b. Click the INSERT tab, click the Audio button in the Media group, then click Audio on My PC.

   c. Locate and insert the sound file PPT G-14.wma from the location where you store your Data Files.

   d. Preview the sound, set the sound to start automatically during a slide show, then drag the sound icon above the table.

   e. Use the Trim Audio dialog box to change the start point of the audio clip to 00:01.300 and the end point to 00:07.100.

   f. Click the Hide During Show check box in the Audio Options group, click the Slide Show button on the status bar, review the slide, press [Esc], then save your presentation.

6. Edit and adjust a picture.

   a. Go to Slide 5, click the Picture, then change the picture with PPT G-15.jpg.

   b. Change the color of the picture to Temperature: 11200 K (Color Tone section), then correct the picture to Brightness: –20% Contrast: +20%.

   c. Change the picture to an Accented Picture layout using the Picture Layout button, then type **St. Elise**.

7. Add action buttons.

   a. Go to Slide 1, click the More button in the Drawing group, then click Action Button: Forward or Next.

   b. Draw a small button, click OK in the Action Settings dialog box, then position the button in the upper-left corner of the slide.

   c. Click the DRAWING TOOLS FORMAT tab on the Ribbon, click the More button in the Shape Styles group, then click Colored Fill - Orange, Accent 2 in the second row.

   d. Copy and paste the action button on Slides 2, 3, and 4.

   e. Go to Slide 5, click the More button in the Drawing group, click Action Button: Beginning, draw a small button, click OK, then drag the button to the upper-left corner of the slide.

   f. Go to Slide 4, click the action button, click the Format Painter button in the Clipboard group, click Slide 5, then click the action button.

   g. Run the slide show from Slide 1, test the action buttons, exit the slide show, then save your work.

8. Insert hyperlinks.

   a. Go to Slide 5, then select the words "Jon Bedat, Cheese Daily" in the text object.

   b. Click the INSERT tab on the Ribbon, click the Hyperlink button, locate the file PPT G-16.docx from the location where you store your Data Files, then click OK.

   c. Click in the Notes pane, then type **The hyperlink opens Jon's review of the Camembert**.

Skills Review (continued)

d. Open Slide Show view, click the hyperlink, read the review, then close the Word window.

e. Press [Esc], then add your name as a footer to the slides.

f. Check the spelling in the presentation, view the presentation in Slide Show view from Slide 1.

g. Make any necessary changes. The completed presentation is shown in FIGURE G-20.

h. Submit your presentation to your instructor, then save and close the presentation.

FIGURE G-20

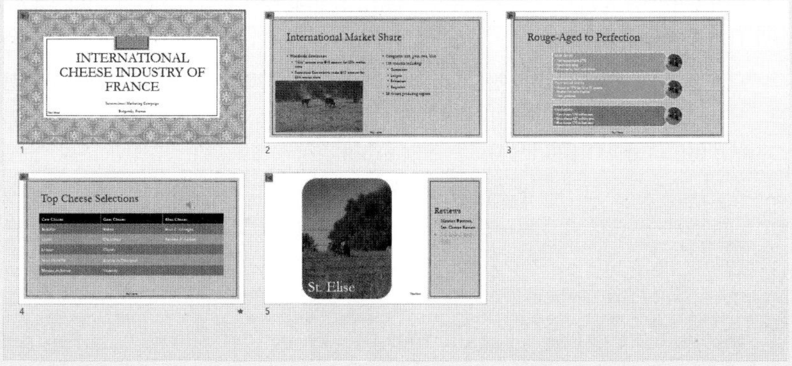

Independent Challenge 1

Fuller Brothers Engineering is a mechanical and industrial design company that specializes in designing manufacturing plants around the world. As a company financial analyst, you need to investigate and report on a possible contract to design and build a large manufacturing plant in India.

a. Open the file PPT G-17.pptx, then save it as **PPT G-India**.

b. On Slide 3, apply the table style Themed Style 1 - Accent 3, then draw a 3-pt dotted line down the column divider of the table using the Pen Style button.

c. Select the top row of the table, insert a row above the top row, type **Line Item** in the left cell, then type **Budget** in the right cell.

d. Click the Overhead/Benefits cell, split the cell into two columns and one row, then move the word "Benefits" to the new cell and delete the slash.

e. Create a new SmartArt graphic on Slide 4 using the Step Up Process layout, then add two new shapes to the graphic.

f. Starting with the bottom-left shape, type the following in the shapes: **Planning & Design**, **Site Acquisition**, **Site Development**, **Construction**, and **Building Final**.

g. Change the colors of the graphic to a colorful theme, then apply a 3D style.

h. Change the shape of the last shape in the SmartArt graphic using the Change Shape button, then use the Smaller button in the Shapes group to make each shape smaller.

i. Add your name as a footer on the slides, then save your changes.

j. Check the presentation spelling, view the presentation in Reading View, submit your presentation to your instructor, then close the presentation and exit PowerPoint.

Independent Challenge 2

You work for The Juric Group, a large investment banking firm in White Plains, New York. Juric is considering buying Sentinel Financial Services, a smaller investment company. As part of the company financial operations team, you need to present some projections regarding the purchase to a special committee formed by Juric to study the proposed deal. *Note: To complete the Independent Challenge, your computer must be connected to the Internet.*

a. Open the file PPT G-18.pptx from the location where you store your Data Files, then save it as **PPT G-Sentinel**.

b. On Slide 3, apply a table style from the Light Style 2 row of the Table Styles gallery, then format the three column divider lines in the first row of the table as 2¼ pt dash dot line.

Independent Challenge 2 (continued)

c. Click the First Column check box in the Table Style Options group.

d. Convert the text on Slide 5 to a SmartArt graphic using one of the List layouts.

e. Format the SmartArt graphic by applying an Accent 2 color theme, then change the SmartArt style to Intense Effect.

f. Create a new slide after Slide 3, enter **Juric Profits** as the slide title, then link a digital or animated video from the Internet using the Video button on the INSERT tab. Use the words **business** or **profits** to search for an appropriate short video that you can link to, or ask your instructor or technical support person for assistance.

g. Add a bookmark to the video, then set a new preview image using the Poster Frame button.

h. Select the word **Sentinel** on Slide 2, then use the Hyperlink button on the INSERT tab, locate the file PPT G-19.pptx from the location where you store your Data Files, then click OK.

i. Add your name as a footer on the slides, check the spelling of the presentation, then save your changes.

j. View the presentation in Slide Show view. Be sure to click the hyperlink on Slide 2 and watch the video on Slide 4.

k. Submit your presentation to your instructor, close the presentation, then exit PowerPoint.

Independent Challenge 3

You have been recently hired at General Services Inc., a U.S. company that exports goods and services to companies in all parts of Asia, including Japan, South Korea, China, and the Philippines. One of your new responsibilities is to prepare short presentations on different subjects for use on the company Web site using data provided to you by others in the company. *Note: To complete the Independent Challenge, your computer must be connected to the Internet.*

a. Open the file PPT G-20.pptx from the location where you store your Data Files, then save it as **PPT G-General**.

b. Add a design theme, background shading, or other objects to make your presentation look professional.

c. Convert the text on Slide 3 to a SmartArt graphic, then format the graphic using any of the formatting commands available.

d. Insert a sound on Slide 2 from the Internet using the Audio button on the INSERT tab. Use the words **harbor** or **ship**, to search for an appropriate short sound clip on the Internet, or ask your instructor or technical support person for assistance.

e. Set the audio clip to play automatically in Slide Show view, click the Rewind after Playing check box on the AUDIO TOOLS PLAYBACK tab, then move the sound icon to the bottom of the slide.

f. Change the layout, and format the charts on Slides 4 and 5.

g. Create, format, and position Forward action buttons on Slides 1–5.

h. Create, format, and position Back action buttons on Slides 2–6, then create, format, and position a Home action button on Slide 6. Slide 6 will have two action buttons.

i. Add your name as a footer to the slides, check the spelling of the presentation, save your changes, then view the presentation in Slide Show view. See FIGURE G-21.

j. Submit your presentation to your instructor, close the presentation, then exit PowerPoint.

FIGURE G-21

Independent Challenge 4: Explore

One of the assignments in your business course at the university is to give a 10-minute presentation on any subject to the class. The goal of the assignment is for you to persuade the class (and your instructor) to make an informed decision about a product, marketing idea, or some other business concept.

To develop the content of this presentation:

- Choose your own subject matter, for example, new electronic device, clothing line, or concept car.
- Use your own media clips (pictures, sounds, or video) or use the Internet to search for appropriate clips.

a. Create a new presentation, then save it as **PPT G-Course**.

b. Add your name and the slide number as the footer on all slides.

c. Decide on a presentation subject, then think about what results you want to see and what information you will need to create the slide presentation.

d. Give each slide a title, add text where appropriate, then apply an appropriate theme.

e. Insert an appropriate audio clip from your computer or the Internet. If you have a microphone, you can record your own sound to insert into the presentation.

f. Insert an appropriate video clip from your computer or the Internet. If you have a video camera, you can record your own video to insert into the presentation.

g. Use the formatting and playback tools to trim the audio and video clips, and then format the clips as necessary.

h. Create a table and a SmartArt graphic with appropriate information, then format the objects. An example of a presentation slide might look like FIGURE G-22.

i. Check the spelling of the presentation, view the final presentation in Slide Show view, save the final version, then submit the presentation to your instructor.

j. Close the presentation, then exit PowerPoint.

FIGURE G-22

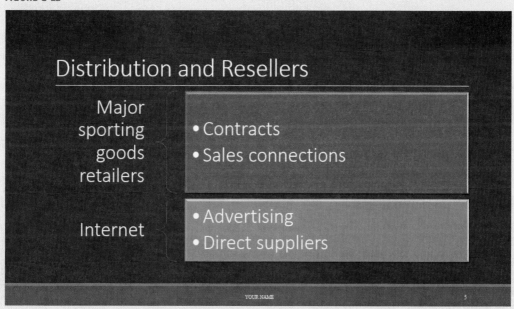

Visual Workshop

Create a new presentation, then save it as **PPT G-Show**. Locate the file PPT G-21.jpg from the location where you store your Data Files, then insert the picture. Change the width of the picture to 6", then remove the background from the picture. On the BACKGROUND REMOVAL tab, click the Mark Areas to Remove button, then click the rose stem as shown in FIGURE G-23. Click the Keep Changes button in the Close group to save the changes to the picture and create a finished slide that looks like the example in FIGURE G-24. Add your name as a footer on the slide, save the presentation, then submit the presentation to your instructor.

FIGURE G-23

FIGURE G-24

Using Advanced Features

CASE Before you distribute the Canadian train tour presentation, you need to have other people in the company review it. Once others have reviewed your presentation, you can incorporate their changes and comments. You will then create a custom slide show, change slide show options, and prepare the presentation for distribution. You end your day by creating a photo album of your last train trip in Canada and make it possible for others to view the photo album on the Internet.

Unit Objectives

After completing this unit, you will be able to:

- Customize handout and notes masters
- Send a presentation for review
- Combine reviewed presentations
- Set up a slide show

- Create a custom show
- Prepare a presentation for distribution
- Create a photo album
- Deliver a presentation online

Files You Will Need

PPT H-1.pptx	PPT H-9.jpg
PPT H-2.pptx	PPT H-10.jpg
PPT H-3.jpg	PPT H-11.jpg
PPT H-4.jpg	PPT H-12.jpg
PPT H-5.jpg	PPT H-13.pptx
PPT H-6.jpg	PPT H-14.pptx
PPT H-7.pptx	PPT H-15.pptx
PPT H-8.pptx	PPT H-16.jpg

Customize Handout and Notes Masters

Learning Outcomes
• Modify the handout master
• Change page orientation

It is often helpful to provide your audience with supplemental materials of the presentation. Creating handouts for your audience provides them a way to follow along and take notes during your presentation. As the presenter, creating notes pages that you can refer to while giving the presentation can be useful, especially when your presentation is complex or detailed. Before you create handouts or notes pages you might want to customize them to fit your specific needs. **CASE** ▶ *You plan to create supplemental materials to hand out when you give the presentation. You customize the handout master by changing the slides per page and the background style. Then you modify the notes master by changing the page setup and the notes page orientation. Finally, you print both handouts and notes pages.*

STEPS

1. **Start PowerPoint, open the presentation PPT H-1.pptx from the location where you store your Data Files, then save the presentation as PPT H-QST**

2. **Click the VIEW tab on the Ribbon, then click the Handout Master button in the Master Views group**

   The presentation's Handout Master view opens. The master has six large empty placeholders that represent where the slides will appear on the printed handouts. The four smaller placeholders in each corner of the page are the header, footer, date, and number placeholders. Notice the date placeholder in the upper-right corner displays today's date.

   QUICK TIP
   To change the orientation of the slides on the handout, click the Handout Orientation button in the Page Setup group.

3. **Click the Background Styles button in the Background group, then click Style 7**

   When you print handouts on a color printer, they will have a blue fill background.

4. **Click the Slides Per Page button in the Page Setup group, then click 3 Slides on the menu**

   Three slide placeholders appear on the left side of the handout as shown in FIGURE H-1.

5. **Click the Header placeholder, drag the Zoom Slider on the status bar to 100%, type Canadian Train Tours, press [Pg Dn], click the Footer placeholder, then type your name**

   Now your handouts are ready to print when you need them.

6. **Click the Fit slide to current window button 🖼 on the status bar, then click the Close Master View button in the Close group**

   Your presentation is in Normal view so you don't see the changes you just made in this view.

   QUICK TIP
   To create custom theme fonts, click the VIEW tab, click the Slide Master button, click the Fonts button, then click Customize Fonts.

7. **Click the VIEW tab on the Ribbon, then click the Notes Master button in the Master Views group**

   Notes Master view opens. It has four corner placeholders—one each for the header, footer, date, and page number—a large notes text box placeholder, and a large slide master image placeholder.

8. **Click the Notes Page Orientation button in the Page Setup group, then click Landscape**

   The page orientation changes to landscape. Notice that all of the text placeholders are now resized to fill the width of the page. Compare your screen to FIGURE H-2.

9. **Click the Close Master View button in the Close group, submit the presentation to your instructor, then save your work**

   If required by your instructor, print the presentation with a handout or notes page setting.

FIGURE H-1: Handout Master view

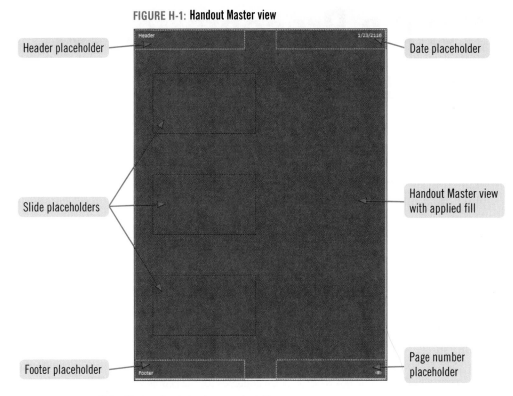

Header placeholder

Date placeholder

Slide placeholders

Handout Master view with applied fill

Footer placeholder

Page number placeholder

FIGURE H-2: Notes Master view in landscape orientation

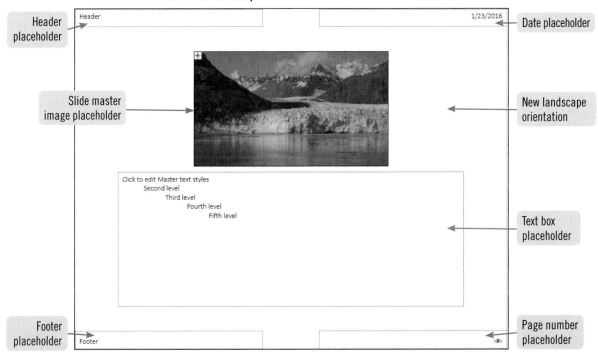

Header placeholder

Date placeholder

Slide master image placeholder

New landscape orientation

Click to edit Master text styles
  Second level
    Third level
      Fourth level
        Fifth level

Text box placeholder

Footer placeholder

Page number placeholder

Creating handouts in Microsoft Word

Sometimes it's helpful to use a word-processing program like Microsoft Word to create detailed handouts or notes pages. You might also want to create a Word document based on the outline of your presentation. To send your presentation to Word, click the FILE tab on the Ribbon, click Export, click Create Handouts, then click the Create Handouts button. The Send to Microsoft Word dialog box opens and provides you with five document layout options. There are two layouts that include notes entered in the Notes pane. Select a layout, then click OK. Word opens and a new document opens with your inserted presentation, using the layout you selected. To send just the text of your presentation to Word, click the Outline only page layout. To link the slides to your Word document, which will reduce the file size of the handout, click the Paste link option button.

Send a Presentation for Review

When you finish creating a presentation, it is often helpful to have others look over the slides for accuracy and clarity. If you are not in the same location as the reviewers, and you have Microsoft Outlook on your computer, you can open Outlook directly from PowerPoint and send a presentation file as an attachment in an email. A reviewer can open the presentation, make changes and comments, and then email it back to you. **CASE** *Use Outlook to send the presentation to your supervisor for her comments and suggestions.*

STEPS

1. **Click the FILE tab on the Ribbon, click Share, click Email in the Share section, then click the Send as Attachment button in the Email section**

   Microsoft Outlook opens with a new message window as shown in FIGURE H-3. The subject text box includes the name of the presentation, and the Attached text box shows the presentation is automatically attached to the email.

2. **Click the To button in the Outlook message window**

   The Select Names: Contacts dialog box opens. If you have added Contacts to the address book in Outlook, you can use this dialog box to select email addresses for the people you want to review the presentation.

3. **Click Cancel, then type your email address in the To text box**

   Your email address appears in the To text box in the Outlook message window.

4. **Click in the message body, then type Please review and get back to me. Thanks.**

   The email is ready to send. Compare your screen to FIGURE H-4.

5. **Click the Send button in the Outlook message window**

   The Outlook message window closes. Outlook sends the email message with the attached presentation file.

6. **Start Outlook, click the SEND/RECEIVE tab on the Ribbon, then click the Send/Receive All Folders button in the Send & Receive group**

   You may have to wait a short time before the email message you sent to yourself arrives in the Inbox with the PowerPoint file attachment. If the email message is selected, it appears in the Reading pane. You see that the message carries the attached presentation.

7. **Click the Outlook Close button** ☒

   Outlook closes, and the PowerPoint window appears on your screen.

FIGURE H-3: Outlook message window

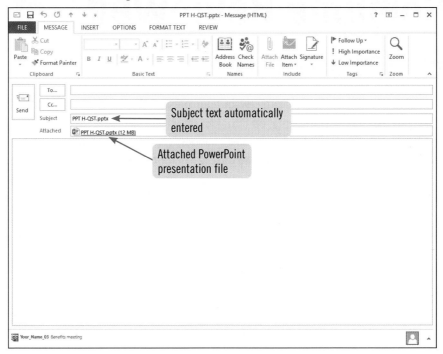

Subject text automatically entered

Attached PowerPoint presentation file

FIGURE H-4: Completed Outlook message window

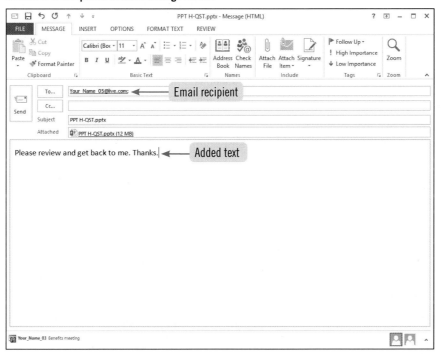

Email recipient

Added text

Packaging a presentation

Before you copy and distribute one or more presentations, you should always inspect the presentations for personal or confidential information. Once you are ready to save the presentations to a CD or folder, open a presentation, click the FILE tab, then click Export. Click Package Presentation for CD, then click the Package for CD button. The Package for CD dialog box opens with the current open presentation shown in the list of files to be copied.

At this point you can add or remove presentations that you want packaged together. All linked and embedded objects are included in the package. In the Package for CD dialog box, click the Copy to Folder button to save the presentations to a folder on your computer or network, or insert a CD into your computer and click the Copy to CD button. Follow the instructions, then click Close when the saving process is completed.

PowerPoint 2013

Combine Reviewed Presentations

After a reviewer completes their review of your presentation and sends it back, you can merge the changes in the reviewer's presentation into your original presentation using the Compare command on the REVIEW tab. You can accept individual changes, changes by slides, changes by reviewer if there is more than one reviewer, or all changes to the presentation. You also have the option of rejecting some or all of the changes and ending the review without making all of the changes. **CASE** ▶ *You sent the QST presentation to your supervisor who has reviewed the presentation and sent it back to you. You are now ready to combine the reviewed presentation with your original one.*

STEPS

1. **Click the REVIEW tab on the Ribbon, then click the Compare button in the Compare group**

   The Choose File to Merge with Current Presentation dialog box opens.

2. **If necessary, navigate to the location where you store your Data Files, click PPT H-2.pptx, then click Merge**

   The reviewed presentation is merged with your original one, and the Revisions pane opens showing the reviewer's changes and comments in the Slide Changes section. Slide 5 is selected because it is the first slide with changes or comments. Reviewer's changes and comments also appear on the slide as shown in **FIGURE H-5**. The reviewer made multiple changes to the text box at the bottom of Slide 5 and left one comment.

3. **Click the All changes to TextBox 2 check box, then review the changes in the text object**

   The text box line style, fill style, text format, and size and position change. The change icon and all five check boxes now have check marks in them indicating that the change has been accepted.

4. **Click the comment icon on the slide, then read the comment in the Comments pane**

   The Comments pane opens to the right of the Revisions pane and displays the reviewer's comment, as shown in **FIGURE H-6**.

5. **Click the Next button twice in the Compare group, then click the Deleted "Luxury" check box on the slide**

   Slide 8 appears in the Slide pane. By clicking the check box next to the change icon you see how the title will look if the word "Luxury" is deleted from the title text object.

6. **Click the Deleted "Luxury" check box to remove the check mark**

   The check mark in the change icon is removed and the word "Luxury" reappears in the title text object indicating the reviewer's change was rejected.

7. **Click the Next button in the Compare group, click the Chart contents check box on the slide, then read the comment in the Comments pane**

   The Food category for the Pacific data series changes to reflect the data change by the reviewer.

8. **Click the Delete button list arrow in the Comments group, click Delete All Comments and Ink in This Presentation, then click Yes in the message dialog box**

   All of the comments in the presentation are now deleted.

9. **Click the End Review button in the Compare group, read the message dialog box, click Yes, close the Comments pane, then save your work**

   The Revisions pane and the Comments pane close. All applied changes are made, and any changes you didn't accept are discarded.

FIGURE H-5: Open Revisions pane showing reviewer's changes

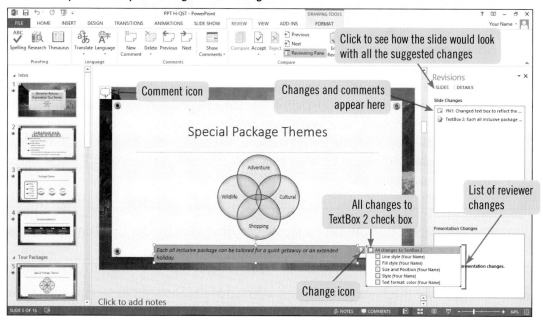

FIGURE H-6: Open Comments pane and accepted reviewer's changes

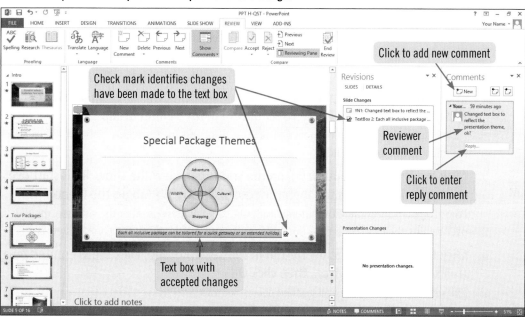

Coauthoring a presentation

By using collaboration software, such as Office 365 SharePoint, or saving a presentation to a SkyDrive location, you have the ability to work with others on a presentation over the Internet at the same time. To set up a presentation to be coauthored with you as the original author, click the FILE tab, click Share, click Invite People, click Save To Cloud, then click your SkyDrive location. Choose a shared location or server to store a primary copy of your presentation, then click the Save button. Open the presentation and begin working, and if someone else is working on the presentation, you will see a Co-authoring icon in the status bar. All changes made to the presentation are recorded, including who is working on the presentation and where in the presentation they are working. When updates to a presentation are available, an Updates Available button appears in the status bar. To use this feature, all authors must have PowerPoint 2010 or later installed on their computers.

Set Up a Slide Show

Learning
Outcomes
• Automate a slide
  show
• Hide a slide

With PowerPoint, you can create a self-running slide show that plays without user intervention. For example, you can set up a presentation so viewers can watch a slide show on a stand-alone computer, in a booth or **kiosk**, at a convention, trade show, shopping mall, or some other public place. You can also create a self-running presentation on a CD, DVD, or Flash drive. You have a number of options when designing a self-running presentation; for example, you can include hyperlinks or action buttons to assist your audience as they move through the presentation. You can also add a synchronized voice that narrates the presentation, and you can set either manual or automatic slide timings. **CASE** ▶ *You prepare the presentation so it can be self-running.*

STEPS

1. **Click the SLIDE SHOW tab on the Ribbon, then click the Set Up Slide Show button in the Set Up group**

   The Set Up Show dialog box has options you use to specify how the show will run.

2. **Make sure the All option button is selected in the Show slides section, then make sure the Using timings, if present option button is selected in the Advance slides section**

   All the slides in the presentation are included in the slide show, and PowerPoint will advance the slides at time intervals you set.

3. **Click the Browsed at a kiosk (full screen) option button in the Show type section of the Set Up Show dialog box**

   This option allows you to have a self-running presentation that can be viewed without a presenter. See **FIGURE H-7**.

4. **Click OK, click the TRANSITIONS tab on the Ribbon, click the On Mouse Click check box in the Timing group to remove the check mark, click the After up arrow until 00:05.00 appears, then click the Apply To All button in the Timing group**

   Each slide in the presentation now will now be displayed for 5 seconds before the slide show advances automatically to the next slide.

5. **Click the Slide Show button 🖥 on the status bar, view the show, let it start over from the beginning, press [Esc], then click the SLIDE SHOW tab on the Ribbon**

   PowerPoint advances the slides automatically at 5-second intervals. After the last slide, the slide show starts over because the kiosk slide show option loops the presentation until someone presses [Esc].

6. **Click the Set Up Slide Show button in the Set Up group, click the Presented by a speaker (full screen) option button, then click OK**

   The slide show options are back to their default settings.

7. **Click the Slide 1 thumbnail in the Thumbnails pane, click the Hide Slide button in the Set Up group, click the From Beginning button in the Start Slide Show group, then press [Esc]**

   The slide show begins with Slide 2. Notice the Slide 1 thumbnail in the Thumbnails pane is dimmed and has a hidden slide icon on its number indicating it is hidden, as shown in **FIGURE H-8**.

8. **Right-click the Slide 1 thumbnail in the Thumbnails pane, click Hide Slide in the shortcut menu, then save your changes**

   Slide 1 is no longer hidden, or dimmed, and the hidden slide icon is removed.

Using Advanced Features

FIGURE H-7: Set Up Show dialog box

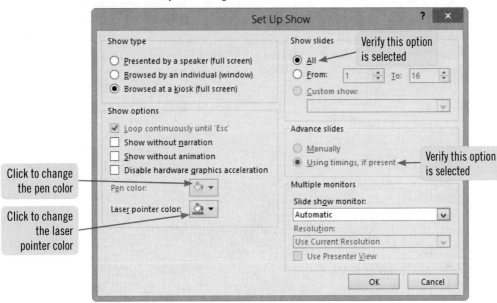

FIGURE H-8: Slide 1 is a hidden slide

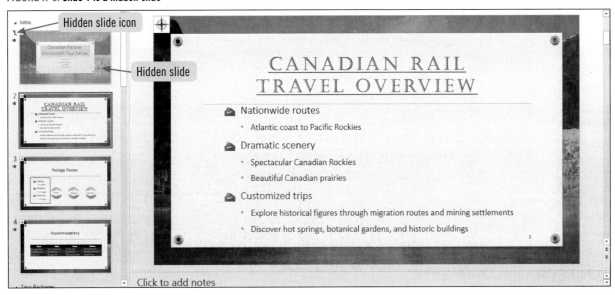

Apps for Office

Mini applications, or **apps**, are now available to download to PowerPoint and your other Office programs for free (or for a small fee) from the Microsoft Office Store on the Internet. Apps can help you speed up and locate information on the Internet and help you be more productive when creating content for your presentation. Typical apps available to download to PowerPoint include navigation and mapping apps, dictionary and word usage apps, as well as news and social media apps. To install an app for the first time, click the Apps for Office button list arrow, click See All, then click Office Store in the message box. Locate an app on the Internet, then add it using your Microsoft account. To use an app already installed, click the INSERT tab on the Ribbon, click the Apps for Office button list arrow, then click the app.

Create a Custom Show

A custom show gives you the ability to adapt a presentation for use in different circumstances or with different audiences. For example, you might have a 25-slide presentation that you show to new customers, but only 12 of those slides are necessary for a presentation for existing customers. PowerPoint provides two types of custom shows: basic and hyperlinked. A basic custom show is a separate presentation or a presentation that includes slides from the original presentation. A hyperlinked custom show is a separate (secondary) presentation that is linked to a primary custom show or presentation. You can also use the laser pointer to help you focus the audience's attention on specific areas of slides. **CASE** *You have been asked to create a version of the Canadian Train Tours presentation for a staff meeting, so you create and view a custom slide show containing only the slides appropriate for that audience. You also learn to use the laser pointer during a slide show.*

STEPS

1. **Click the SLIDE SHOW tab on the Ribbon, click the Custom Slide Show button in the Start Slide Show group, click Custom Shows to open the Custom Shows dialog box, then click New**

   The Define Custom Show dialog box opens. The slides that are in your current presentation are listed in the Slides in presentation list box.

2. **Click the Slide 1 check box, click the check boxes for Slides 7–13, then click Add**

   The eight slides you selected move to the Slides in custom show list box, indicating that they will be included in the custom show. See FIGURE H-9.

3. **Click 8. Coastal Route in the Slides in custom show list, then click the slide order Up button ↑ once**

   The slide moves from eighth place to seventh place in the list. You can arrange the slides in any order in your custom show by clicking the slide order Up or Down arrows.

4. **Click 3. Trans Canadian Luxury Tour Stations in the Slides in custom show list, click the Remove button ☒, drag to select the existing text in the Slide show name text box, type Brief Presentation 1, then click OK**

   The Custom Shows dialog box lists your custom presentation. The custom show is not saved as a separate presentation file even though you assigned it a new name. To view a custom slide show, you must first open the presentation you used to create the custom show in Slide Show view. You then can open the custom show from the Custom Shows dialog box.

5. **Click Show, view the Brief Presentation 1 slide show, then press [Esc] to end the slide show**

   The slides in the custom show appear in the order you set in the Define Custom Show dialog box. At the end of the slide show, you return to the presentation in Normal view.

6. **Click the From Beginning button in the Start Slide Show group, right-click the screen, point to Custom Show, then click Brief Presentation 1**

   The Brief Presentation custom show appears in Slide Show view.

7. **When Slide 1 appears, press and hold [Ctrl], press and hold the left mouse button, move the laser pointer around the slide as shown in FIGURE H-10, release [Ctrl], then release the left mouse button**

   Automatic slide timings are set so your slide show can advance to the next slide even though you use the laser pointer. You can use the laser pointer in any presentation on any slide during a slide show.

8. **Press [Esc] at any point to end the slide show, then save your changes**

FIGURE H-9: Define Custom Show dialog box

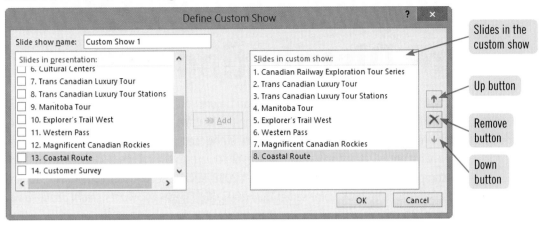

FIGURE H-10: First slide of custom slide show with laser pointer

Link to a custom slide show

You can use action buttons to switch from the "parent" show to the custom show. Click the Shapes button in the Drawing group on the HOME tab, then click an action button. Draw an action button on the slide. Click the Hyperlink to list arrow, click Custom Show, click the custom show you want to link, then click OK.

Now when you run a slide show you can click the action button you created to run the custom show. You can also create an interactive table of contents using custom shows. Create your table of contents entries on a slide, then hyperlink each entry to the section it refers to using a custom show for each section.

Prepare a Presentation for Distribution

Learning
Outcomes
• Protect a
  presentation with
  a password
• Check presentation
  compatibility

Reviewing and preparing your presentation before you share it with others is an essential step, especially with so many security and privacy issues on the Internet. One way to help secure your PowerPoint presentation is to set a security password, so only authorized people can view or modify its content. If you plan to open a presentation in an earlier version of PowerPoint, it is a good idea to determine if the presentation is compatible. Some features in PowerPoint 2013, such as sections and SmartArt graphics, are not compatible in versions of PowerPoint earlier than 2003. **CASE** ➤ *You want to learn about PowerPoint security and compatibility features so you can use them on presentations and other documents.*

STEPS

1. **Click the Slide 1 thumbnail in the Thumbnails pane, click the FILE tab on the Ribbon, click the Protect Presentation button, then click Encrypt with Password on the menu**
   The Encrypt Document dialog box opens.

2. **Type 123abc**
   As you type, solid black symbols appear in the text box, as shown in **FIGURE H-11**, which hides the password and makes it unreadable. This protects the confidentiality of your password if anyone happens to be looking at your screen while you type.

   TROUBLE
   If you mistype the password in the Confirm Password dialog box, an alert dialog box opens.

3. **Click OK to open the Confirm Password dialog box, type 123abc, then click OK**
   A password is now required to open this presentation. Once the presentation is closed, this password must be entered in the Password dialog box to open the presentation. The presentation is now password protected from unauthorized users.

4. **Click Close, click Save to save changes, click the FILE tab, then click PPT H-QST.pptx in the Recent Presentations list**
   The Password dialog box opens.

   QUICK TIP
   To set other password options, open the Save As dialog box, click Tools, then click General Options.

5. **Type 123abc, then click OK to open the presentation**
   The presentation opens. Be aware that if you don't remember your password, there is no way to open or view the presentation.

6. **Click the FILE tab on the Ribbon, click the Protect Presentation button, click Encrypt with Password, select the password, press [Delete], click OK, then click Save**
   The password is removed and is no longer needed to open the presentation.

   QUICK TIP
   Click the FILE tab, click the Check for Issues button, then click Check Accessibility to check for potential issues for people with reading disabilities.

7. **Click the FILE tab on the Ribbon, click the Check for Issues button, then click Check Compatibility**
   The Compatibility Checker analyzes the presentation, and the Microsoft PowerPoint Compatibility Checker dialog box opens, as shown in **FIGURE H-12**. Each item in the dialog box represents a feature that is not supported in earlier versions of PowerPoint. This means that if you try to run this presentation using an earlier version of PowerPoint, the items listed will function in a limited capacity or not at all.

8. **Click the down scroll arrow, read all of the items in the dialog box, click OK, add your name to the notes and handouts footer, then click the Slide Sorter button ⊞ on the status bar**
   The dialog box closes. Compare your screen to **FIGURE H-13**.

9. **Save your work, submit your presentation to your instructor, then close the presentation but do not exit PowerPoint**

FIGURE H-11: Encrypt Document dialog box

Hidden password

FIGURE H-12: Compatibility Checker dialog box

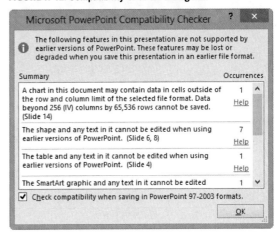

FIGURE H-13: Final presentation in Slide Sorter view

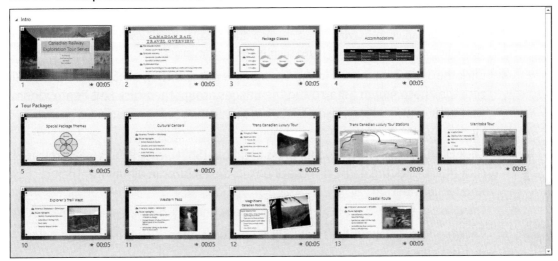

Recording a slide show

With the Record Slide Show feature you have the ability to record and save audio narrations, slide and animation timings, and laser pointer gestures for each slide during a slide show. This feature is great to use if you want to record audience comments so that people who were unable to attend the presentation live can view and listen to it later. To record a slide show, click the SLIDE SHOW tab, click the Record Slide Show button list arrow in the Set Up group, then start recording from the beginning or the current slide. You then have to choose which elements you want to record during the slide show. If you choose to record audio narrations, you must have a microphone, a sound card, and speakers. A sound icon appears on every narrated slide.

Create a Photo Album

Learning Outcomes
• Create a photo album
• Customize a photo album

A PowerPoint photo album is a presentation designed specifically to display photographs. You can add pictures to a photo album from any storage device such as a hard drive, flash drive, digital camera, scanner, or Web camera. As with any presentation, you can customize the layout of a photo album presentation by adding title text to slides, applying frames around the pictures, and applying a theme. You can also format the pictures of the photo album by adding a caption, converting the pictures to black and white, rotating them, applying artistic effects, and changing their brightness and contrast. **CASE** ▶ *On a break from work, you decide to create a personal photo album showing some of the slides you took on your last train trip in Canada.*

STEPS

1. **Click the INSERT tab on the Ribbon, click the Photo Album list arrow in the Images group, then click New Photo Album**
   The Photo Album dialog box opens.

2. **Click File/Disk, select the file PPT H-3.jpg from the location where you store your Data Files, then click Insert**
   The picture appears in the Preview box and is listed in the Pictures in album list, as shown in FIGURE H-14.

3. **Click Create, save the presentation as PPT H-Train Album to the location where you store your Data Files, then change the presentation title from "Photo Album" to My Photos**
   A new presentation opens. PowerPoint creates a title slide along with a slide for the picture you inserted. The computer user name appears in the subtitle text box by default.

4. **Click the Slide 2 thumbnail in the Thumbnails pane, click the INSERT tab on the Ribbon, click the Photo Album list arrow in the Images group, then click Edit Photo Album**
   The Edit Photo Album dialog box opens. You can use this dialog box to add and format pictures and modify the slide layout in the photo album presentation.

5. **Click File/Disk, click PPT H-4.jpg, press and hold [Shift], click PPT H-6.jpg, release [Shift], click Insert, click the 4 PPT H-6 check box in the Pictures in album list, then click the Rotate Right button** 🔄
   Three more pictures are added to the presentation, and picture PPT H-6.jpg is rotated to the right 90 degrees.

6. **Click the Picture layout list arrow, click 2 pictures, then click the Captions below ALL pictures check box**

7. **Click the Frame shape list arrow, click Soft Edge Rectangle, click Update, then click the Slide 2 thumbnail in the Thumbnails pane**
   Two pictures with a caption below each picture (currently the picture filename) appear on each slide, and each picture is formatted with a soft edge.

8. **Click the Slide Sorter view button** ⊞**, then drag the Zoom Slider** ▯ **on the status bar until your screen looks similar to FIGURE H-15**

9. **Add your name to the slides footer, save your changes, then submit your presentation to your instructor**

FIGURE H-14: Photo Album dialog box

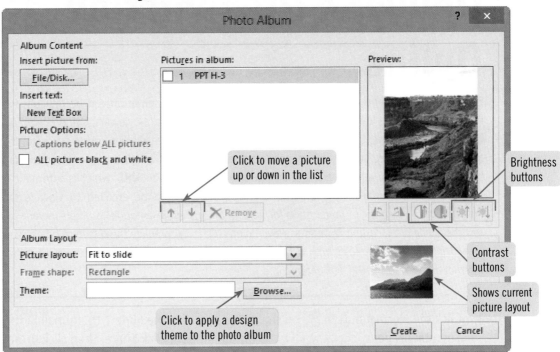

FIGURE H-15: Completed photo album

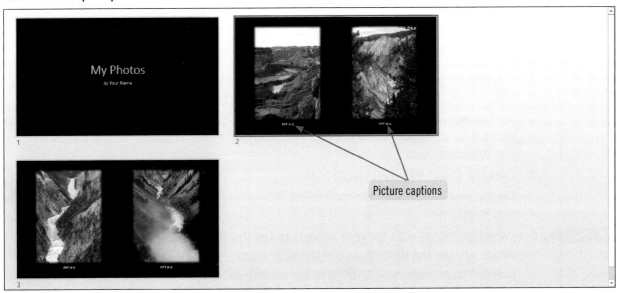

Publish slides to a Slide Library

If your computer is connected to a network server running Office SharePoint Server 2007 or Microsoft SharePoint Server 2010 software, you can store slides in a folder called a **Slide Library** for others to access, modify, and use. Using a Slide Library, others can make changes to your slides, and you in turn can track and review all changes and have access to the latest version of your slides. To publish slides from PowerPoint to a Slide Library (after a Slide Library is created on a server), click the FILE tab, click Share, click Publish Slides, then click the Publish Slides button. The Publish Slides dialog box opens. Use Browse in the dialog box to select the Slide Library location you are going to use. To add slides to a Slide Library, click the check box next to each slide, then click Publish.

Deliver a Presentation Online

Being able to assemble everyone in the same room for a presentation can be difficult, which is why PowerPoint provides a way to share your presentation with remote viewers. Using PowerPoint, you can host an online presentation in real time over the Internet to viewers using Microsoft's free Office Presentation Service. Viewers of an online presentation need to have a computer connected to the Internet, a Web browser, and a link to an Internet address, called a **URL**, which is automatically supplied by PowerPoint. The URL link for your online broadcast can be emailed to viewers directly from PowerPoint. **CASE** ▶ *In preparation for hosting an online presentation to others in your company, you test the online broadcasting features in PowerPoint. NOTE: To complete this lesson as a host, you need to be logged into PowerPoint 2013 with a Microsoft account and have Internet access. As a viewer, you need Internet access and the URL link entered into a Web browser.*

STEPS

1. **Click the** Normal button ▣ **on the status bar, click the** Slide 1 thumbnail **in the Thumbnails pane, click the** FILE tab **on the Ribbon, click** Share, **then click** Present Online
   Read the information on the screen. If you don't have a Microsoft account, you need to acquire one from the Microsoft Website before you proceed.

   > **TROUBLE**
   > If you get a service error message, try to connect again. See your instructor or technical support person for additional help.

2. **Click the** Present Online button
   The Present Online dialog box opens, and PowerPoint connects to the Office Presentation Service online. Once connected, PowerPoint prepares your presentation to be viewed online, which may take a couple of minutes. The Present Online dialog box eventually displays a URL link, as shown in FIGURE H-16. Your presentation is broadcasting right now.

3. **If approved by your instructor, click the** Send in Email link **to open the Outlook window, type an** email address **in the To text box, then click** Send
   The Microsoft Outlook window opens with the URL link in the message box and is then sent to the person you want to view the online presentation. Anyone you provide the URL link to can enter the link into their Web browser and watch the broadcast.

4. **Click the** START PRESENTATION button
   The first slide of the presentation opens in Slide Show view. Make sure viewers can see the presentation in their Web browser.

   > **QUICK TIP**
   > Until you end the broadcast or close the presentation, you are continuously broadcasting the presentation.

5. **Press [Spacebar], wait for your viewers to see the slide, press [Spacebar], wait for your viewers to see the slide, then end the slide show**
   Each slide in the presentation is viewed by you and your online viewers. A new tab appears on the Ribbon, as shown in FIGURE H-17. Use this tab to start the slide show from different slides, share meeting notes using OneNote, invite others to view the broadcast, and end the broadcast.

6. **When you are finished broadcasting click the** End Online Presentation button **in the Present Online group**
   A message box opens asking if you want to end the online presentation.

7. **Click** End Online Presentation, **close the presentation, then exit PowerPoint**
   The online presentation stops, and the presentation closes.

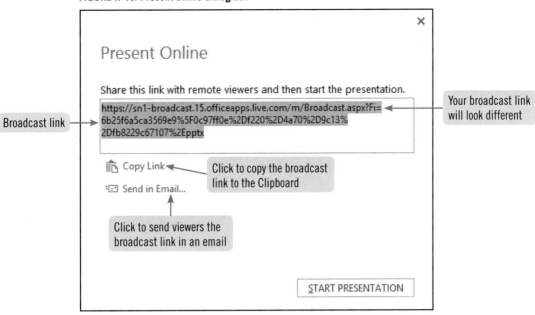

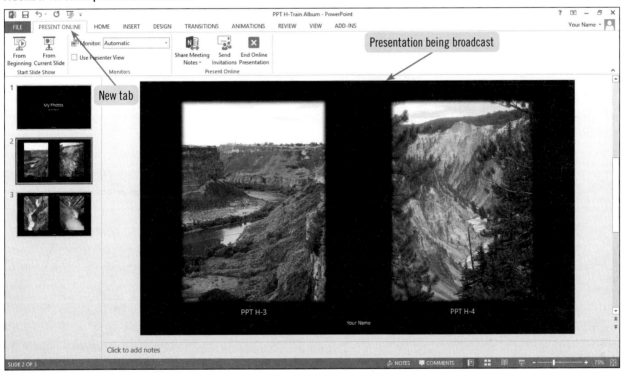

Supported PowerPoint features and online presentations

Not all PowerPoint features are supported for broadcasting, and some features are altered altogether. For example, slide transitions in your presentation are converted to Fade and sounds, including narrations, or videos are not transmitted. Also, you can-not annotate or markup slides during an online presentation, and hyperlinks are not shown to your audience. Keep in mind too that if you have a large presentation you might have file size limitations imposed on your presentation file when trying to broadcast.

Practice

Put your skills into practice with **SAM Projects**! SAM Projects for this unit can be found online. If you have a SAM account, go to www.cengage.com/sam2013 to download the most recent Project Instruction and Start Files.

Concepts Review

Label each element of the PowerPoint window shown in FIGURE H-18.

FIGURE H-18

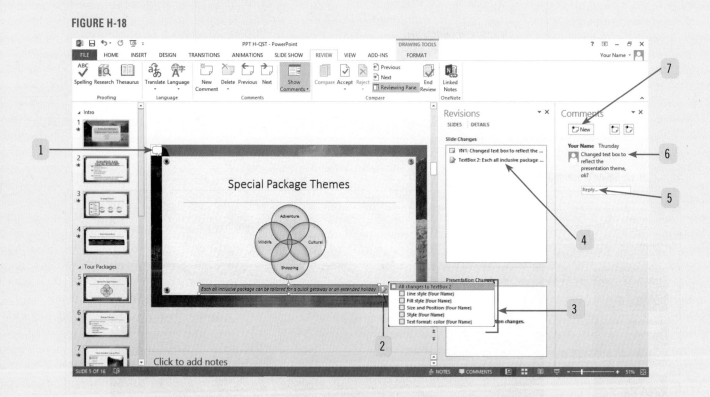

Match each term with the statement that best describes its function.

8. Kiosk
9. Basic custom show
10. URL
11. Slide Library
12. Hyperlinked custom show

a. A slide show created from selected slides in a presentation
b. A small booth for a stand-alone computer that can run a slide show without user intervention
c. A folder on a network server that stores slides for others to access and modify
d. A separate presentation that is connected to a custom show
e. An Internet Web address

Select the best answer from the list of choices.

13. Which of the following statements is *not* true about a presentation set to run at a stand-alone computer?
    a. The presentation can loop continuously.
    b. The presentation works best with manual slide timings.
    c. You can use action buttons to progress through the slides.
    d. You don't have to be present to run the slide show.

14. When you combine two presentations together, you are _____ all the changes from one presentation into your original presentation.
    a. Linking   c. Removing
    b. Hyperlinking   d. Merging

15. Which of the following actions is *not* possible with PowerPoint?
    a. Distribute a presentation on a CD.   c. Coauthor a presentation using a SkyDrive location.
    b. Markup slides during an online presentation.   d. Publish slides to a Slide Library.

16. Creating a _____ helps keep your presentation secure.
    a. Slide Library   c. Password
    b. Shared server   d. Hyperlink

17. Use the _____ feature to send invitations to others to watch a presentation live using a browser over the Internet.
    a. Broadcast   c. Review
    b. Package   d. Publish

18. What do you create when you want to show selected slides in a presentation tailored to a specific audience?
    a. Custom show   c. Packaged presentation
    b. URL file   d. Broadcast

19. Which of the following identifies features that might not work in earlier versions of PowerPoint?
    a. Document Inspector   c. Compatibility Checker
    b. SkyDrive Server   d. Kiosk

20. A _____ is a presentation designed specifically to display pictures.
    a. Slide Library   c. Picture template
    b. Broadcast   d. Photo album

Skills Review

1. **Customize handout and notes masters.**
    a. Start PowerPoint, open the file PPT H-7.pptx from the drive and folder where you store your Data Files, then save it as **PPT H-Java**. *Note: You need to have access to Outlook and the Internet to complete all the steps in this Skills Review.*
    b. Switch to Handout Master view, then change the slides per page to 4 slides.
    c. Change the handout orientation to Landscape, then type **Old Java House** in the header text placeholder.
    d. Type your name in the footer text placeholder, then switch to Notes Master view.
    e. Change the background style to Style 6, type **Product Report** in the header text placeholder, then type your name in the footer text placeholder.
    f. Close Notes Master view, then save your work.

2. **Send a presentation for review.**
    a. Click the FILE tab, click Share, click Email, then click the Send as Attachment button.
    b. Type a brief message in the email message, then send the presentation to yourself.
    c. Open Microsoft Outlook, open the message you sent to yourself, then close Outlook.

Skills Review (continued)

3. **Combine reviewed presentations.**
   a. Click the REVIEW tab, then click the Compare button in the Compare group.
   b. Navigate to the location where you store your Data Files, click PPT H-8.pptx, then click Merge.
   c. Accept the changes to the text box on Slide 1, then click the Next button in the Compare group.
   d. Accept the changes to the text object, read the comment on the slide, then click the Next button in the Comments group.
   e. Read the comment, delete all comments in the presentation, then close the Comments pane.
   f. End the review, click Yes to save the review changes, go to Slide 1, then save your work.

4. **Set up a slide show.**
   a. Click the SLIDE SHOW tab, click the Set Up Slide Show button, use automatic slide timings, set up a slide show so it will be browsed at a kiosk, then click the TRANSITIONS tab.
   b. Remove the check mark from the On Mouse Click check box, set a slide timing of 3 seconds to all the slides, run the slide show all the way through to Slide 1, then end the slide show.
   c. Change the slide show options to be presented by a speaker, then change the slide timings to manual in the Set Up Show dialog box.
   d. Run through the slide show from Slide 1 using the action buttons at the bottom of the slides. Move forward and backward through the presentation, watching the animation effects as they appear, then press [Esc] when you are finished.
   e. Hide Slide 5, then run through the slide show.
   f. When you have finished viewing the slide show, reset the slide timings to automatic, then save your work.

5. **Create a custom show.**
   a. Create a custom show called **Goals** that includes Slides 2, 3, 4, and 5.
   b. Move Slide 3 Performance Series above Slide 2 Lecture Series.
   c. View the show from within the Custom Shows dialog box, then press [Esc] to end the slide show.
   d. Go to Slide 1, begin the slide show, then, when Slide 1 appears, go to the Goals custom show.
   e. View the custom slide show, return to Normal view, then save your work.

6. **Prepare a presentation for distribution.**
   a. Click the FILE tab, click Protect Presentation, then click Encrypt with Password.
   b. Type **12345**, then type the same password in the Confirm Password dialog box.
   c. Close the presentation, save your changes, open the presentation, then type **12345** in the Password dialog box.
   d. Open the Encrypt Document dialog box again, then delete the password.
   e. Click the FILE tab, click Check for Issues, click Check Compatibility, read the information, then close the dialog box.
   f. Save your work, add your name to the slides footer, then check the spelling in the presentation. The completed presentation is shown in FIGURE H-19.

   FIGURE H-19

   g. Submit your presentation to your instructor, then close the presentation.

7. **Create a photo album.**
   a. Create a new photo album presentation, navigate to the location where you store your Data Files, then insert the files PPT H-9.jpg, PPT H-10.jpg, PPT H-11.jpg, and PPT H-12.jpg.

Skills Review (continued)

b. Rotate picture PPT H-11.jpg to the left, move the picture so it is fourth in the list, create the photo album, then save it as **PPT H-Three Lakes** to the location where you store your Data Files.

c. Change the title on the title slide to **Three Lakes Trip**, then type your name in the subtitle text box.

d. Open the Edit Photo Album dialog box, change the picture layout to 1 picture, then change the frame shape to Rounded Rectangle.

FIGURE H-20

e. Make all pictures black and white, add captions to all pictures, update the presentation, add your name to the slide footers, then save your changes.

f. Submit your presentation to your instructor. The completed photo album is shown in **FIGURE H-20**.

8. Deliver a presentation online.

a. Click the FILE tab, click Share, click Present Online, then click the Present Online button.

b. Send invitations to people you want to view the broadcast using the Send in Email link in the Present Online dialog box.

c. Start the online presentation, then move through each slide in the presentation.

d. When you are finished broadcasting, end the online presentation, save your work, close the presentation, then exit PowerPoint.

Independent Challenge 1

You work for Enchanted Islands Inc., an international tour company that provides specialty tours to destinations throughout Asia and the Pacific. You have to develop presentations that the sales force can use to highlight different tours at conferences and meetings. To complete the presentation, you need to create at least two of your own slides. Assume that Enchanted Islands is currently running Internet specials: 20% off regular price on tours to Fiji and the Cook Islands. Also assume that Enchanted Islands offers tour packages to the Philippines, Japan, Australia, and New Zealand.

a. Start PowerPoint, open the presentation PPT H-13.pptx, then save it as **PPT H-Pacific** to the location where you store your Data Files.

b. Open the REVIEW tab on the Ribbon, merge the file PPT H-14.pptx, then apply all changes to the presentation.

c. Read all comments in the presentation, then delete the comment on the Departing Cities slide.

d. Use the Previous button in the Comments group to move back to slides that have comments, then write a reply comment to each of the original comments.

e. Use the Compatibility Checker on the presentation.

f. Use the information provided in the introduction of this Independent Challenge to help you develop additional content for two new slides.

g. Insert and format at least three different media clips (pictures, videos, clip art, or sounds). Use approved media clips from legal sources.

h. Apply slide transitions, timings, and animations to all the slides in the presentation.

i. Convert the text on Slide 2 to a SmartArt diagram, then format the diagram using the techniques you learned in this book.

Independent Challenge 1 (continued)

j. Use the Compatibility Checker again on the presentation. Note any differences, then view the presentation in Slide Show view and use the laser pointer.

k. Add your name as a footer on all notes and handouts, then check the spelling in the presentation.

l. Submit your presentation to your instructor, close the presentation, then exit PowerPoint.

Independent Challenge 2

You work in Sacramento, California, at the State Agricultural Statistics Agency. Part of your job is to compile agricultural information gathered from the counties of California and create presentations that display the data for public viewing. You are currently working on a summary presentation that will be made public on the agency Web site.

a. Start PowerPoint, open the presentation PPT H-15.pptx, then save it as **PPT H-CA Ag** to the location where you store your Data Files.

b. Convert the information on Slide 5 to a SmartArt diagram using one of the Picture list layouts, then increase the size of the picture placeholders.

c. Insert the file PPT H-16.jpg from the location where you store your Data Files for all of the pictures in the SmartArt graphic.

d. Format the SmartArt diagram using the commands on the SMARTART TOOLS DESIGN and FORMAT tabs.

e. Change the table layout on Slide 4 so the table displays the information properly, split the Cattle and Calves cell into two cells, then format the table.

f. Create a custom slide show that displays any four slides from the presentation, then save it as **Top Ag Counties**.

g. Insert and format at least two media clips (pictures, videos, clip art, or sounds). Use approved media clips from legal sources.

h. Change the handout master to nine slides per page, then apply the Style 10 background style.

i. Save the presentation, add your name as the footer on all notes and handouts, check the spelling of the presentation, then view the presentation in Slide Show view.

j. Submit your presentation to your instructor, close the presentation, then exit PowerPoint.

Independent Challenge 3

You are the assistant director of operations at EastWest Container, Inc., an international marine shipping company based in San Diego, California. EastWest handles 35 percent of all the trade between Asia, the Middle East, and the West Coast of the United States. You need to give a quarterly presentation to the company's operations committee outlining the type and amount of trade EastWest handled during the previous quarter.

Plan a presentation with at least six slides that details the type of goods EastWest carries. Create your own content, but assume the following:

- EastWest hauls automobiles from Tokyo to San Diego. EastWest can usually haul between 2,800 and 3,500 automobiles in a quarter.
- EastWest hauls large equipment made by Caterpillar Tractor and John Deere Tractor from the United States.
- EastWest hauls common household goods that include electronic equipment, appliances, toys, and furniture.
- EastWest owns 10 cargo ships that can operate simultaneously. All 10 ships were in operation during the last quarter.

Note: To complete the Independent Challenge, your computer must be connected to the Internet.

a. Start PowerPoint, create a new presentation, save it as **PPT H-EastWest**, then apply a design theme to the presentation.

b. Use the information provided to help develop the content for your presentation. If you have Internet access, use the Internet to research the shipping business.

Independent Challenge 3 (continued)

c. Insert and format at least two media clips (pictures, videos, clip art, or sounds). Use approved media clips from legal sources.

d. Set transitions and animations, rehearse slide timings, then view the presentation in Slide Show view.

e. Change the handout master to 4 slides per page, change the background style to Style 7, then change the orientation to Landscape.

f. Send the presentation to a friend as an email attachment.

g. Check the spelling of the presentation, add your name as a footer on all notes and handouts, then save your work.

h. Submit your presentation to your instructor, close the presentation, then exit PowerPoint.

Independent Challenge 4: Explore

Your assignment for your American history class is to create a photo album based on your personal family history. You must use your own pictures of past family members, homes, businesses, vacations, and other pictures that help tell your personal family life story and history.

a. Start PowerPoint, create a photo album presentation, insert your pictures, then save the presentation as **PPT H-My Family History** to the location where you store your Data Files.

b. Enter a title in the title text placeholder, add your name to the subtitle text placeholder and as the footer on the notes and handouts, than apply a design.

c. Use the Edit Photo Album dialog box to format the pictures as needed. An example of a family photo album is shown in FIGURE H-21.

d. Send the presentation for review to at least one friend, and ask them to provide changes and comments. Use the Compare feature to merge your original presentation with the reviewed presentation.

e. Accept or reject reviewer changes, then leave any comments made by the reviewer in your presentation.

f. Check the spelling of the presentation, save your changes, then broadcast this presentation to two friends using the Present Online feature.

g. Click the FILE tab, click Export, click Create Handouts, then click the Create Handouts button.

h. Click the Blank lines next to slides option button, click OK, then save the Word document as **PPT H-History Handout** to the location where you store your Data Files.

i. Submit your presentation and your handout to your instructor. Close the Word document, exit Word, close the presentation, then exit PowerPoint.

FIGURE H-21

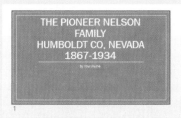

Visual Workshop

Create a presentation and save it as **PPT H-Project Final**. Use an instructor-approved topic and the following task list to help you complete this Visual Workshop:

- Create and save a new presentation, then enter and format slide text.
- Create and format new slides, then create slide sections.
- Apply a design theme and variation or template.
- Insert and format at least one picture, video, and audio.
- Insert, format, and merge shapes, then insert and format a SmartArt graphic.
- Insert, format, and animate a chart, then apply animations, transitions, and timings to objects and slides.
- Modify slide, handout and notes masters, then create a custom show.
- Insert action buttons and hyperlinks, then deliver an online presentation.

Add your name as a footer on the slide, save the presentation, then submit the presentation to your instructor. FIGURE H-22 shows an example of a presentation you can create.

FIGURE H-22

Working in the Cloud

CASE ▶ In your job for the Vancouver branch of Quest Specialty Travel, you travel frequently, you often work from home, and you also collaborate online with colleagues and clients. You want to learn how you can use SkyDrive with Office 2013 to work in the Cloud so that you can access and work on your files anytime and anywhere. (*Note*: SkyDrive and Office Web Apps are dynamic Web pages, and might change over time, including the way they are organized and how commands are performed. The steps and figures in this appendix reflect these pages at the time this book was published.)

Unit Objectives

After completing this unit, you will be able to:

- Understand Office 2013 in the Cloud
- Work Online
- Explore SkyDrive
- Manage Files on SkyDrive
- Share Files
- Explore Office Web Apps
- Complete a Team Project

Files You Will Need

WEB-1.pptx
WEB-2.docx

Understand Office 2013 in the Cloud

Learning
Outcomes
• Describe Office
  2013 Cloud
  Computing
  features
• Define SkyDrive
• Define Office
  Web Apps

The term **cloud computing** refers to the process of working with files and apps online. You may already be familiar with Web-based e-mail accounts such as Gmail and outlook.com. These applications are **cloud-based**, which means that you do not need a program installed on your computer to run them. Office 2013 has also been designed as a cloud-based application. When you work in Office 2013, you can choose to store your files "in the cloud" so that you can access them on any device connected to the Internet. **CASE** ▶ *You review the concepts related to working online with Office 2013.*

DETAILS

- **How does Office 2013 work in the Cloud?**

  When you launch an Office application such as Word or Excel, you might see your name and maybe even your picture in the top right corner of your screen. This information tells you that you have signed in to Office 2013, either with your personal account or with an account you are given as part of an organization such as a company or school. When you are signed in to Office and click the FILE tab in any Office 2013 application such as Word or Excel, you see a list of the files that you have used recently on your current computer and on any other connected device such as a laptop, a tablet or even a Windows phone. The file path appears beneath each filename so that you can quickly identify its location as shown in FIGURE WEB-1. Office 2013 also remembers your personalized settings so that they are available on all the devices you use.

- **What are roaming settings?**

  A **roaming setting** is a setting that travels with you on every connected device. Examples of roaming settings include your personal settings such as your name and picture, the files you've used most recently, your list of connected services such as Facebook and Twitter, and any custom dictionaries you've created. Two particularly useful roaming settings are the Word Resume Reading Position setting and the PowerPoint Last Viewed Slide setting. For example, when you open a PowerPoint presentation that you've worked on previously, you will see a message similar to the one shown in FIGURE WEB-2.

- **What is SkyDrive?**

  SkyDrive is an online storage and file sharing service. When you are signed in to your computer with your Microsoft account, you receive access to your own SkyDrive, which is your personal storage area on the Internet. On your SkyDrive, you are given space to store up to 7 GB of data online. A SkyDrive location is already created on your computer as shown in FIGURE WEB-3. Every file you save to SkyDrive is synced among your computers and your personal storage area on SkyDrive.com. The term **synced** (which stands for synchronized) means that when you add, change or delete files on one computer, the same files on your other devices are also updated.

- **What are Office Web Apps?**

  Office Web Apps are versions of Microsoft Word, Excel, PowerPoint, and OneNote that you can access online from your SkyDrive. An Office Web App does not include all of the features and functions included with the full Office version of its associated application. However, you can use the Office Web App from any computer that is connected to the Internet, even if Microsoft Office 2013 is not installed on that computer.

- **How do SkyDrive and Office Web Apps work together?**

  You can create a file in Office 2013 using Word, Excel, PowerPoint, or OneNote and then save it to your SkyDrive. You can then open the Office file saved to SkyDrive and edit it using your Office 2013 apps. If you do not have Office 2013 installed on the computer you are using, you can edit the file using your Web browser and the corresponding Office Web App. You can also use an Office Web App to create a new file, which is saved automatically to SkyDrive while you work and you can download a file created with an Office Web App and work with the file in the full version of the corresponding Office application.

FIGURE WEB-1: FILE tab in Microsoft Excel

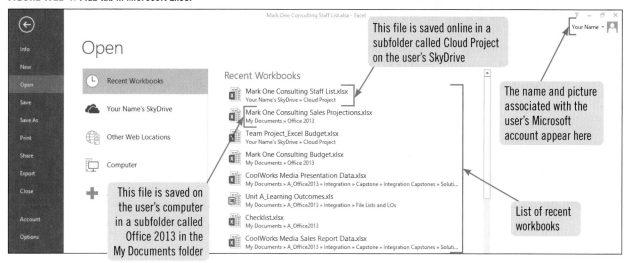

FIGURE WEB-2: PowerPoint Last Viewed Slide setting

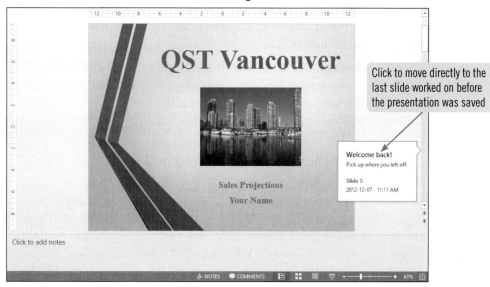

FIGURE WEB-3: Saving a Word file on SkyDrive

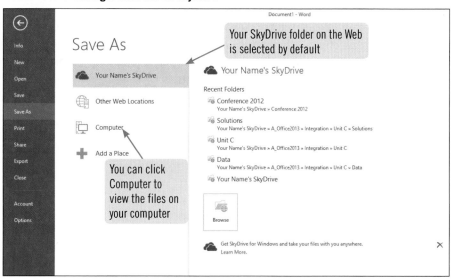

Work Online

When you work on your own computer, you are usually signed in to your Microsoft account automatically. When you use another person's computer or a public computer, you will be required to enter the password associated with your Microsoft account to access files you have saved on Windows SkyDrive. You know you are signed in to Windows when you see your name and possibly your picture in the top right corner of your screen. *Note*: To complete the steps below, you need to be signed in to your Microsoft account. If you do not have a Microsoft account, see "Getting a Microsoft account" in the yellow box. **CASE** ▶ *You explore the settings associated with your account, learn how to switch accounts, and sign out of an account.*

STEPS

1. **Sign in to Windows, if necessary, launch Word, click** Blank document, **then verify that your name appears in the top right corner of your screen**

2. **Click the** list arrow **to the right of your name, as shown in** FIGURE WEB-4, **then click** About me **and sign in if prompted**

   Internet Explorer opens and your Profile page appears. Here, you can add or edit your contact information and information about your workplace. You can also change the name and picture that appear in the top right corner of your window.

3. **Click the** list arrow **next to Profile in the top left corner of your screen, above the picture**

   The tiles representing the services your Windows account is connected to appear as shown in FIGURE WEB-5. Note that if you have connected your Microsoft account to accounts in other services such as Facebook, LinkedIn, or outlook.com, you will see these connections in the appropriate app. For example, your connections to Facebook and LinkedIn appear in the People app.

4. **Click a blank area below the apps tiles, click** Your Name **in the top right corner, then click** Account settings

   Either you are taken directly to the Microsoft account screen or, depending on your security settings, a Sign in screen appears. To make changes to your account, you might need to enter the password associated with your account. You can also choose to sign in with a different Microsoft account. Once you sign in, you can change the information associated with your account such as your name, email address, birth date, and password. You can also choose to close your Microsoft account, which deletes all the data associated with it.

5. **Click the** Close button [×] **in the upper right corner of the window to remove the Sign-in window, click** Close all tabs **to return to Word, then click the** list arrow [▼] **next to Your Name in the top right corner of the Word window**

   To sign out of your account, you can click Sign Out at the top of the Accounts dialog box that appears when you click Account Settings. When you are working on your own computers, you will rarely need to sign out of your account. However, if you are working on a public computer, you may want to sign out of your account to avoid having your files accessible to other users.

6. **Click** Switch account

   You can choose to sign into another Microsoft account or to an account with an organization.

7. **Click the** Close button [×]

   You are returned to a blank document in Word.

8. **Exit Word**

FIGURE WEB-4: Viewing Windows account options in Word

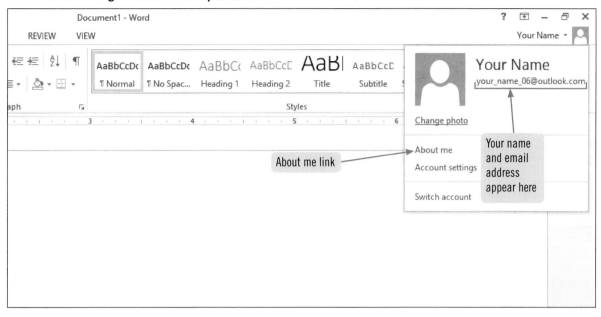

FIGURE WEB-5: Connected services associated with a Profile

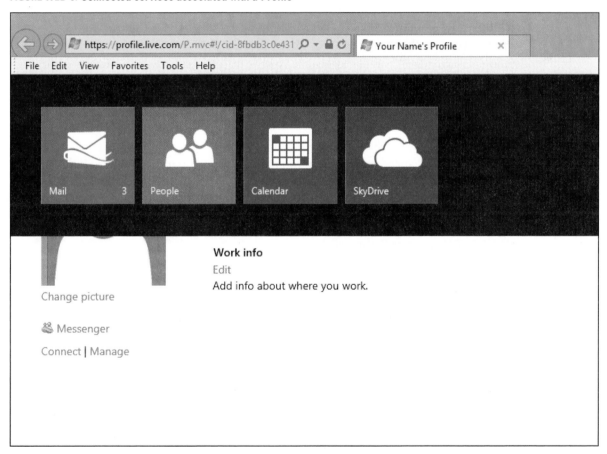

Getting a Microsoft account

If you have been working with Windows and Office 2013, you might already have a Microsoft account, which was previously referred to as a Windows Live ID. You also have an account if you use outlook.com (formerly Hotmail), SkyDrive, Xbox LIVE, or have a Windows Phone. A Microsoft account consists of an email address and a password. If you wish to create a new Microsoft account, go to https://signup.live.com/ and follow the directions provided.

Explore SkyDrive

Learning Outcomes
• Save a file to SkyDrive
• Create a folder on SkyDrive

SkyDrive works like the hard drive on your computer. You can save and open files from SkyDrive, create folders, and manage your files. You can access the files you save on SkyDrive from any of your connected devices and from anywhere you have a computer connection. **CASE** *You open a PowerPoint presentation, save the file to your SkyDrive, then create a folder.*

STEPS

1. **Start PowerPoint, then open the file** WEB-1.pptx **from the location where you store your Data Files**

2. **Click the** FILE **tab, click** Save As, **then click** Your Name's SkyDrive **(top selection) if it is not already selected**

3. **Click the** Browse button

   The Save As dialog box opens, showing the folders stored on your SkyDrive. You may have several folders already stored there or you may have none.

4. **Click** New folder, **type** Cengage, **then press** [Enter]

5. **Double-click** Cengage, **select** WEB-1.pptx **in the File name text box, type** WEB-QST Vancouver 1 **as shown in** FIGURE WEB-6, **then click** Save

   The file is saved to the Cengage folder on the SkyDrive that is associated with your Microsoft account. The PowerPoint window reappears.

6. **Click the** FILE **tab, click** Close, **click the** FILE **tab, then click** Open

   WEB-QST Vancouver 1.pptx appears as the first file listed in the Recent Presentations list, and the path to your Cengage folder on your SkyDrive appears beneath it.

7. **Click** WEB-QST Vancouver 1.pptx **to open it, then type your name where indicated on the title slide**

8. **Click** Slide 2 **in the Navigation pane, select** 20% **in the third bullet, type** 30%, **click the** FILE **tab, click** Save As, **click** Cengage **under Current Folder, change the file name to** WEB-QST Vancouver 2, **then click** Save

9. **Exit PowerPoint**

   A new version of the presentation is saved to the Cengage folder that you created on SkyDrive.

How to disable default saving to Skydrive

You can specify how you want to save files from Office 2013 applications. By default, files are saved to locations you specify on your SkyDrive. You can change the default to be a different location. In Word, PowerPoint, or Excel, click the FILE tab, then click Options. Click Save in the left sidebar, then in the Save section, click the Save to Computer by default check box, as shown in FIGURE WEB-7. Click OK to close the PowerPoint Options dialog box. The Save options you've selected will be active in Word, PowerPoint, and Excel, regardless of which application you were using when you changed the option.

FIGURE WEB-6: Saving a presentation to SkyDrive

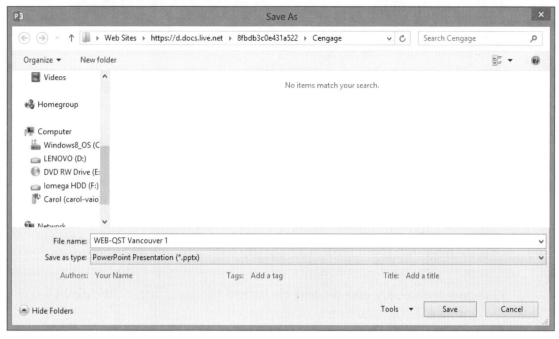

FIGURE WEB-7: Changing the default Save location in PowerPoint

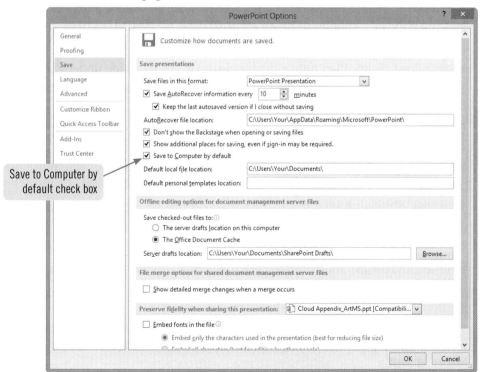

Manage Files on SkyDrive

You are automatically connected to SkyDrive when you sign into your Microsoft account and launch an Office 2013 application. You can also access SkyDrive through your Web browser or from the SkyDrive App in Windows 8. When you start the SkyDrive App, you can upload and download files, create folders, and delete files. You can also download the SkyDrive app to your tablet or other mobile device so you can access files wherever you have an Internet connection. When you access SkyDrive from Internet Explorer, you can do more file management tasks, including renaming and moving files. **CASE** ▶ *You explore how to work with SkyDrive from your Web browser and from the SkyDrive App.*

STEPS

1. **Launch Internet Explorer or another Web browser, type** skydrive.com **in the Address box, then press** [Enter]

   If you are signed in to your Microsoft account, your SkyDrive opens. If you are not signed in, the login page appears where you can enter the email address and password associated with your Microsoft account.

2. **Sign in if necessary, click the blue tile labeled** Cengage, **then right-click** WEB-QST Vancouver 1.pptx **as shown in** FIGURE WEB-8

   You can open the file in the PowerPoint Web App or in PowerPoint, download the file to your computer, share it, embed it, and perform other actions such as renaming and deleting.

3. **Click** Download, **click** Open **in the bar at the bottom of the screen, then click** Enable Editing

   The presentation opens in PowerPoint where you can save it to your computer hard drive or back to SkyDrive.

4. **Click the** DESIGN **tab, click the** More button ▼ **in the Themes group, select the** Wisp **theme, click the** FILE **tab, click** Save As, **click** Computer, **click** Browse, **navigate to a location on your computer or on an external drive such as a USB flash drive, click** Save, **then exit PowerPoint**

5. **Launch PowerPoint, then notice the files listed in the left pane under Recent**

   The file you just saved to your computer or external drive appears first and the file saved to the Cengage folder on SkyDrive appears second.

6. **Click the second listing, notice that the file is not updated with the Wisp design, then exit PowerPoint**

   When you download a file from SkyDrive, changes you make are not saved to the version on SkyDrive. You can also access SkyDrive from your Windows 8 screen by using the SkyDrive app.

7. **Show the Windows 8 Start screen, click the** SkyDrive **tile, open the Cengage folder, right-click** WEB-QST Vancouver 1, **view the buttons on the taskbar as shown in** FIGURE WEB-9, **click the** Delete **button on the taskbar, then click** Delete

8. **Right-click** WEB-QST Vancouver 2, **click the** New Folder **button on the taskbar, type** Illustrated, **then click** Create folder

   You can rename and move files in SkyDrive through Internet Explorer.

9. **Move the mouse pointer to the top of the screen until it becomes the hand pointer, drag to the bottom of the screen to close the SkyDrive App, click the** Internet Explorer **tile on the Start screen, go to** skydrive.com, **right-click** WEB-QST Vancouver 2 **on the SkyDrive site, click** Move to, **click the** ▶ **next to Cengage, click** Illustrated, **then click** Move

FIGURE WEB-8: **File management options on SkyDrive**

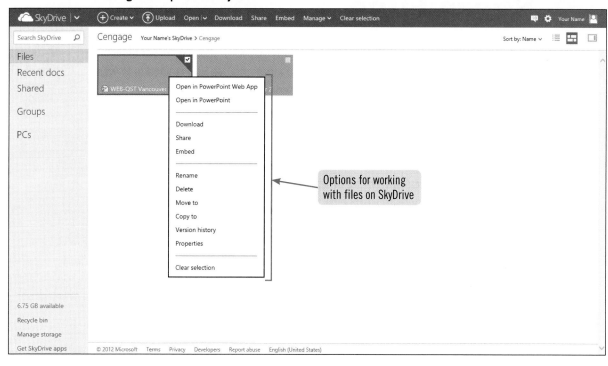

FIGURE WEB-9: **File management options on SkyDrive App**

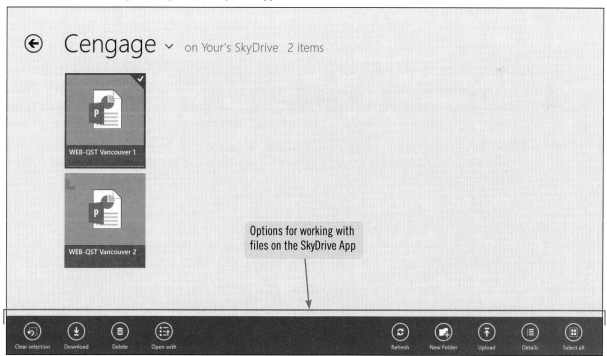

Share Files

One of the great advantages of working with SkyDrive is that you can share your files with others. Suppose, for example, that you want a colleague to review a presentation you created in PowerPoint and then add a new slide. You can, of course, e-mail the presentation directly to your colleague who can then make changes and e-mail the presentation back. Alternatively, you can share the PowerPoint file directly from SkyDrive. Your colleague can edit the file using the PowerPoint Web App or the full version of PowerPoint, and then you can check the updated file on SkyDrive. In this way, you and your colleague are working with just one version of the presentation that you both can update. **CASE** ▶ *You have decided to share files in the Illustrated folder that you created in the previous lesson with another individual. You start by sharing files with your partner and your partner can share files with you.*

STEPS

TROUBLE
If you cannot find a partner, you can email the file to yourself.

1. **Identify a partner with whom you can work, and obtain his or her e-mail address; you can choose someone in your class or someone on your e-mail list, but it should be someone who will be completing these steps when you are**

2. **Right-click the Illustrated folder, then click Sharing as shown in** FIGURE WEB-10

3. **Type the e-mail address of your partner**

4. **Click in the Include a personal message box, then type Here's the presentation we're working on together as shown in** FIGURE WEB-11

5. **Verify that the Recipients can edit check box is selected, then click Share**
   Your partner will receive a message advising him or her that you have shared the WEB-QST Vancouver 2.pptx file. If your partner is completing the steps at the same time, you will receive an e-mail from your partner.

TROUBLE
If you do not receive a message, your partner has not yet completed the steps to share the folder.

6. **Check your e-mail for a message advising you that your partner has shared a folder with you**
   The subject of the e-mail message will be "[Name] has shared documents with you."

7. **If you have received the e-mail, click the Show content link that appears in the warning box, if necesary, then click WEB-QST Vancouver 2.pptx in the body of the e-mail message**
   The PowerPoint presentation opens in the Microsoft PowerPoint Web App. You will work in the Web App in the next lesson.

Co-authoring documents

You can work on a document, presentation, or workbook simultaneously with a partner. First, save the file to your SkyDrive. Click the FILE tab, click Share, then click Invite People. Enter the email addresses of the people you want to work on the file with you and then click Share. Once your partner has received, opened, and started editing the document, you can start working together. You will see a notification in the status bar that someone is editing the document with you. When you click the notification, you can see the name of the other user and their picture if they have one attached to their Windows account. When your partner saves, you'll see his or changes in green shading which goes away the next time you save. You'll have an opportunity to co-author documents when you complete the Team Project at the end of this appendix.

FIGURE WEB-10: Sharing a file from SkyDrive

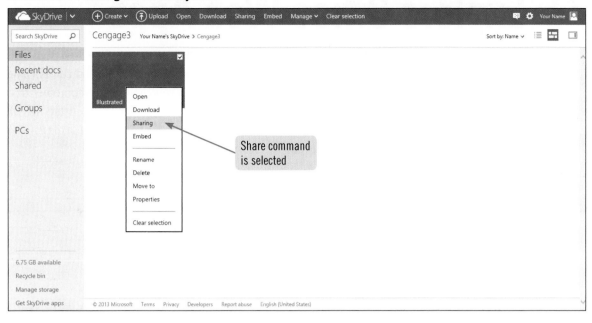

FIGURE WEB-11: Sharing a file with another person

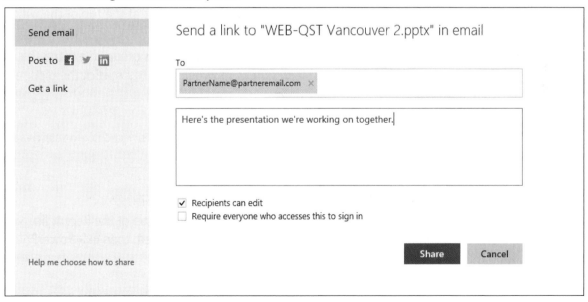

Explore Office Web Apps

As you have learned, a Web App is a scaled-down version of an Office program. Office Web Apps include Word, Excel, PowerPoint, and OneNote. You can use the Office Web Apps to create and edit documents even if you don't have Office 2013 installed on your computer and you can use them on other devices such as tablets and smartphones. From SkyDrive, you can also open the document in the full Office application if the application is installed on the computer you are using. **CASE** ▶ *You use the PowerPoint Web App and the full version of PowerPoint to edit the presentation.*

STEPS

1. **Click EDIT PRESENTATION, then click Edit in PowerPoint Web App**

   Presentations opened using the PowerPoint Web App have the same look and feel as presentations opened using the full version of PowerPoint. However, like all of the Office Web Apps, the PowerPoint Web App has fewer features available than the full version of PowerPoint.

2. **Review the Ribbon and its tabs to familiarize yourself with the commands you can access from the PowerPoint Web App**

   TABLE WEB-1 summarizes the commands that are available.

3. **Click Slide 3, click the text Hornby Island, click it again and select it, then type Tofino so the bullet item reads Tofino Sea Kayaking**

4. **Click outside the text box, click the DESIGN tab, then click the More Themes list arrow ⏷ to show the selection of designs available**

   A limited number of designs are available on the PowerPoint Web App. When you want to use a design or a command that is not available on the PowerPoint Web App, you open the file in the full version of PowerPoint.

5. **Click on a blank area of the slide, click OPEN IN POWERPOINT at the top of the window, then click Yes in response to the message**

6. **Click the DESIGN tab, click the More button ⏷ in the Themes group to expand the Themes gallery, select the Quotable design as shown in FIGURE WEB-12, click the picture on Slide 1, then press [Delete]**

7. **Click the Save button 🖫 on the Quick Access toolbar**

   The Save button includes a small icon indicating you are saving to SkyDrive and not to your computer's hard drive or an external drive.

8. **Click the Close button ✖ to exit PowerPoint**

   You open the document again to verify that your partner made the same changes.

9. **Launch PowerPoint, click WEB-QST Vancouver 2.pptx at the top of the Recent list, verify that the Quotable design is applied and the picture is removed, then exit PowerPoint**

Exploring other Office Web Apps

Three other Office Web Apps are Word, Excel, and OneNote. You can share files on SkyDrive directly from any of these applications using the same method you used to share files from PowerPoint. To familiarize yourself with the commands available in an Office Web App, open the file and then review the commands on each tab on the Ribbon. If you want to perform a task that is not available in the Web App, open the file in the full version of the application.

FIGURE WEB-12: Selecting the Quotable design

Quotable slide design selected

TABLE WEB-1: Commands on the PowerPoint Web App

tab	category/group	options
FILE	Info	• Open in PowerPoint (also available on the toolbar above the document window)
		• Previous Versions
	Save As	• Where's the Save Button?: In PowerPoint Web App, the presentation is being saved automatically so there is no Save button
		• Download: use to download a copy of the presentation to your computer
	Print	• Create a printable PDF of the presentation that you can then open and print
	Share	• Share with people - you can invite others to view and edit your presentation
		• Embed - include the presentation in a blog on Web site
	About	• Try Microsoft Office, Terms of Use, and Privacy and Cookies
	Help	• Help with PowerPoint questions, Give Feedback to Microsoft, and modify how you can view the presentation (for example, text only)
	Exit	• Close the presentation and exit to view SkyDrive folders
HOME	Clipboard	• Cut, Copy, Paste, Format Painter
	Delete	• Delete a slide
	Slides	• Add a new slide, duplicate a slide, hide a slide
	Font	• Change the font, size, style, and color of selected text
	Paragraph	• Add bullets and numbering, indent text, align text, and change text direction
	Drawing	• Add text boxes and shapes, arrange them on the slide, apply Quick Styles, modify shape fill and outline, and duplicate a shape
INSERT	Slides	• Add new slides with selected layout
	Images	• Add pictures from your computer, online pictures, or screen shots
	Illustrations	• Add shapes, SmartArt, or charts
	Links	• Add links or actions to objects
	Text	• Add comments, text boxes, headers and footers, and other text elements
	Comments	• Add comments
DESIGN	Themes	• Apply a limited number of themes to a presentation and apply variants to a selected theme
		• Apply variants to a selected theme
ANIMATIONS	Animation	• Apply a limited number of animation effects to a slide element and modify existing timings
TRANSITIONS	Transitions to This Slide	• Apply a limited number of transition effects to slides and chose to apply the effect to all slides
VIEW	Presentation Views	• You can view the slide in Editing View, Reading View, Slide Show View, and Notes View and you can show any comments made by users who worked on PowerPoint using the full version

Team Project

Introduction

From SkyDrive, you can easily collaborate with others to produce documents, presentations, and spreadsheets that include each user's input. Instead of emailing a document to colleagues and then waiting for changes, you can both work on the document at the same time online. To further explore how you can work with SkyDrive and Office 2013, you will work with two other people to complete a team project. The subject of the team project is the planning of a special event of your choice, such as a class party, a lecture, or a concert. The special event should be limited to a single afternoon or evening.

Follow the guidelines provided below to create the files required for the team project. When you have completed the project, the team will submit a Word document containing information about your project, as well as three files related to the project: a Word document, a PowerPoint presentation, and an Excel workbook.

Project Setup

As a team, work together to complete the following tasks.

a. Share email addresses among all three team members.

b. Set up a time (either via email, an online chat session, Internet Messaging, or face to face) when you will get together to choose your topic and assign roles.

c. At your meeting, complete the table below with information about your team and your special event.

Team Name (last name of one team member or another name that describes the project.)
Team Members
Event type (for example, party, lecture, concert, etc.)
Event purpose (for example, fundraiser for a specific cause, celebrate the end of term, feature a special guest, etc.)
Event location, date, and time
Team Roles indicate who is responsible for each of the following three files (one file per team member)
Word document:
Excel workbook:
PowerPoint presentation:

Document Development

Individually, complete the tasks listed below for the file you are responsible for. You need to develop appropriate content, format the file attractively, and then be prepared to share the file with the other team members.

Word Document

The Word document contains a description of your special event and includes a table listing responsibilities and a time line. Create the Word document as follows:

1. Create a Cloud Project folder on your SkyDrive, then create a new Word document and save it as **Cloud Project_ Word Description** to the Cloud Project folder.

Document Development (continued)

2. Include a title with the name of your project and a subtitle with the names of your team members. Format the title with the Title style and the subtitle with the Subtitle style.

3. Write a paragraph describing the special event—its topics, purpose, the people involved, etc. You can paraphrase some of the information your team discussed in your meeting.

4. Create a table similar to the table shown below and then complete it with the required information. Include up to ten rows. A task could be "Contact the caterers" or "Pick up the speaker." Visualize the sequence of tasks required to put on the event.

Task	Person Responsible	Deadline

5. Format the table using the table style of your choice.

6. Save the document to your SkyDrive. You will share the document with your team members and receive feedback in the next section.

Excel Workbook

The Excel workbook contains a budget for the special event. Create the Excel workbook as follows:

1. Create a new Excel workbook and save it as **Cloud Project_Excel Budget** to the Cloud Project folder on your SkyDrive.

2. Create a budget that includes both the revenues you expect from the event (for example, ticket sales, donations, etc.) and the expenses. Expense items include advertising costs (posters, ads, etc.), food costs if the event is catered, transportation costs, etc. The revenues and expenses you choose will depend upon the nature of the project.

3. Make the required calculations to total all the revenue items and all the expense items.

4. Calculate the net profit (or loss) as the revenue minus the expenses.

5. Format the budget attractively using fill colors, border lines, and other enhancements to make the data easy to read.

6. Save the workbook to your SkyDrive. You will share the workbook with your team members and receive feedback in the next section.

PowerPoint Presentation

The PowerPoint presentation contains a presentation that describes the special event to an audience who may be interested in attending. Create the PowerPoint presentation as follows:

1. Create a new PowerPoint presentation and save it as **Cloud Project_PowerPoint Presentation** to the Cloud Project folder on your SkyDrive.

2. Create a presentation that consists of five slides including the title slide as follows:

   a. Slide 1: Title slide includes the name of the event and your team members

   b. Slide 2: Purpose of the party or event

   c. Slide 3: Location, time, and cost

   d. Slide 4: Chart showing a breakdown of costs (to be supplied when you co-author in the next section)

   e. Slide 5: Motivational closing slide designed to encourage the audience to attend; include appropriate pictures

3. Format the presentation attractively using the theme of your choice.

4. Save the presentation to your SkyDrive. You will share the presentation with your team members and receive feedback.

Co-Authoring on Skydrive

You need to share your file, add feedback to the other two files, then create a final version of your file. When you read the file created by the other two team members, you need to add additional data or suggestions. For example, if you created the Excel budget, you can provide the person who created the PowerPoint presentation with information about the cost breakdown. If you created the Word document, you can add information about the total revenue and expenses contained in the Excel budget to your description. You decide what information to add to each of the two files you work with.

1. Open the file you created.
2. Click the **FILE tab**, click **Share**, then click **Invite People**.
3. Enter the email addresses of the other two team members, then enter the following message: **Here's the file I created for our team project. Please make any changes, provide suggestions, and then save it. Thanks!** See FIGURE WEB-13.

FIGURE WEB-13

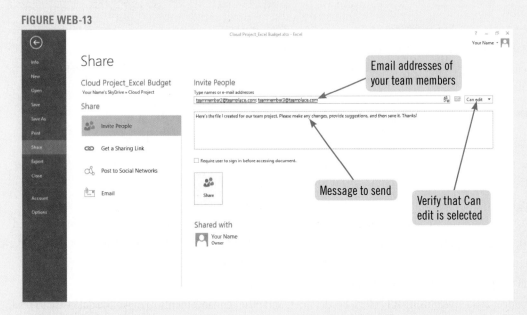

4. Click the **Share button**.
5. Allow team members time to add information and comments to your file. Team members should save frequently. When the file is saved, it is saved directly to your SkyDrive. Note that you can work together on the document or you can work separately. You can also choose to make changes with the full version of the Office 2013 applications or with the Office Web Apps. When someone is working on your file, you will see their user name on the status bar.
6. Decide which changes you want to keep, make any further changes you think are needed to make the document as clear as possible, then save a final version.

Project Summary

When you are pleased with the contents of your file and have provided feedback to your team members, assign a team member to complete the following tasks and then complete your portion as required.

1. Open **WEB-2.docx** from the location where you save your Data Files, then save it to your Cloud Project folder on your SkyDrive as **Cloud Project_Summary**.
2. Read the directions in the document, then enter your name as Team Member 1 and write a short description of your experience working with SkyDrive and Office 2013 to complete the team project.
3. Share the file with your team members and request that they add their own names and descriptions.
4. When all team members have finished working on the document, save all the changes.
5. Make sure you store all four files completed for the project in the Cloud Project appendix on your SkyDrive, then submit them to your instructor on behalf of your team.

Glossary

Action button An interactive button created from the Shapes gallery that you click in Slide Show view to perform an activity, such as advancing to the next slide.

Active cell The selected cell in a worksheet.

Adjustment handle A small yellow handle that changes the appearance of an object's most prominent feature.

Align To place objects' edges or centers on the same plane.

Animated video A video that contains multiple images that stream together to give the illusion of motion.

Animation tag Identifies the order an object is animated on a slide during a slide show.

Annotate A freehand drawing on the screen made by using the pen or highlighter tool. You can annotate only in Slide Show view.

Apps Mini applications available for download to PowerPoint from the Microsoft Office Store on the Internet. Apps can be used for mapping, word usage, and other productivity applications.

Axis label Text in the first row and column of a worksheet that identifies data in a chart.

Background The area behind the text and graphics on a slide.

Background graphic An object placed on the slide master.

Bookmark A point in a video that can be used to jump to a specific point in the video; identified with a yellow circle in the video control timeline.

Broadcast Present a slide show to an audience over the Internet in real time using a Web browser.

Bullet A small graphic symbol, usually a round or square dot, that is placed at the left of a new line; used to identify the beginning of a new item in a list.

Category axis The axis in a chart that contains the categories or labels defining the data series.

Category axis title A title entered on the category axis of a chart that contains the categories or labels defining the data series.

Cell The intersection of a column and row in a worksheet, or table.

Chart A graphical representation of numerical data from a worksheet. Chart types include 2-D and 3-D column, bar, pie, area, and line charts.

Cloud computing When data, applications, and resources are stored on servers accessed over the Internet or a company's internal network rather than on user's computers.

Column heading The box containing the column letter on top of the columns in the worksheet.

Comments button A button on the PowerPoint status bar in Normal view allows you to open the Comments pane where you can create, edit, select, and delete comments.

Compatibility Checker Finds potential compatibility issues between a PowerPoint 2013 presentation and earlier versions of PowerPoint.

Connection site An anchor point to attach a line or an arrow on a shape.

Content placeholder A placeholder that is used to enter text or objects such as clip art, charts, or pictures.

Crop To hide part of an object, such as using the Cropping tool to delete a part of a picture.

Data series A column or row in a worksheet.

Data series label Text in the first row and column of a worksheet that identifies data in a chart.

Data series marker A graphical representation of a data series, such as a bar or column.

Destination file The file an object is embedded into, such as a presentation.

Destination presentation The presentation you insert slides to when you reuse slides from another presentation.

Digital signature A way to authenticate a presentation file using computer cryptography. A digital signature is not visible in a presentation.

Digital video Live action captured in digital format by a video camera.

Distribute To evenly divide the space horizontally or vertically between objects relative to each other or the slide edges.

Document Inspector A PowerPoint feature that examines a presentation for hidden data or personal information.

Embedded object An object that is created in one application and inserted to another; can be edited using the original program file in which they were created.

Error bars Used in a chart to identify potential error amounts relative to each data marker in a data series.

Exception A change you make directly to text on the slide, which does not match the theme fonts on the slide master.

Fixed layout format A specific file format, such as .pdf or .xps, that locks the file so no changes can be made but allows viewing and printing of the file.

Gallery A visual collection of choices you can browse through to make a selection. Often available with Live Preview.

Gridlines Evenly spaced horizontal and vertical lines on the slide that help you align objects.

Group A PowerPoint feature in which you combine multiple objects into one object.

Groups Areas of the Ribbon that arrange commands based on their function, for example, text formatting commands such as Bold, Underline, and Italic are located on the HOME tab, in the Font group.

Handout Master view The master view used to specify the header and footer placeholders, the page orientation, and specify the number of slides to print for printed handouts.

Hanging indent The first line of a paragraph begins to the left of all subsequent lines of text.

Hyperlink An object (a filename, word, phrase, or graphic) that, when clicked, "jumps to" another location in the current file or opens another PowerPoint presentation, a Word, Excel, or Access file, or an address on the Web. *See also* Link.

Indent levels Text levels in the master text placeholder. Each level is indented a specified amount from the left margin, and you control their placement by dragging indent markers on the ruler.

Indent markers Small markers (two triangles and one square) on the horizontal ruler that indicate the indent settings for the selected text.

Insertion point A blinking vertical line that indicates where the next character will appear when text is entered in a text placeholder in PowerPoint.

Kiosk A freestanding booth usually placed in a public area that can contain a computer used to display information.

Landscape A slide orientation that displays slides horizontally (wider than taller).

Laser pointer A virtual pointer that moves as you move the mouse used in Slide Show view to highlight parts of the slide.

Leading The spacing between lines of text in a text object within the same paragraph.

Legend Text box feature in a chart that provides an explanation about the data presented in a chart.

Link A connection between a source file and a destination file, which when the source file is updated, the destination file can also be updated. *See also* Hyperlink.

Live Preview A feature that shows you the result of an action such as a theme change before you apply the change.

Macro A set actions that are used to automate tasks.

Major gridlines Identify major units on a chart axis.

Margins The distance between the edge of the text and all four edges of the text box.

Master Thumbnails pane On the left side of Slide Master view, used to navigate through the master slide layouts.

Master view A specific view in a presentation that stores information about font styles, text placeholders, and color themes. There are three master views: Slide Master view, Handout Master view, and Notes Master view.

Masters One of three views that stores information about the presentation theme, fonts, placeholders, and other background objects. The three master views are Slide Master view, Handout Master view, and Notes Master view.

Merge A feature in PowerPoint used to combine multiple shapes together; provides you a way to create a variety of unique geometric shapes that are not available in the Shapes gallery.

Metadata Another name for document properties that includes the author name, the document subject, the document title, and other personal information.

Mini toolbar A small toolbar that appears next to selected text that contains basic text-formatting commands.

Minor gridlines Identify minor units on a chart axis.

Narration A voice recording you make using a microphone on one or more slides. Narrations can be heard through speakers or a headset during a slide show.

Normal view The primary view that you use to write, edit, and design your presentation. Normal view is divided into three panes: Thumbnails, Slide, and Notes.

Notes button A button on the status bar in PowerPoint that opens the Notes pane.

Notes Master view The master view for Notes Pages view.

Notes Page view A presentation view that displays a reduced image of the current slide above a large text box where you can type notes.

Notes pane The area in Normal view that shows speaker notes for the current slide; also in Notes Page view, the area below the slide image that contains speaker notes.

Object An item you place or draw on a slide that can be modified. Examples of objects include drawn lines and shapes, text, and imported pictures.

Office Web App Versions of the Microsoft Office applications with limited functionality that are available online from Windows Live SkyDrive. Users can view documents online and then edit them in the browser using a selection of functions.

Online collaboration The ability to incorporate feedback or share information across the Internet or a company network or intranet.

Outline view A view in PowerPoint where you can enter text on slides in outline form.

Pane A section of the PowerPoint window, such as the Slide or Thumbnails pane.

Paragraph spacing The space before and after paragraph text.

Paste Special A method that is used to paste text or objects using special formats, such as plain text without formatting or an object as a picture.

Photo album A type of presentation designed specifically to display photographs.

Picture A digital photograph, piece of line art, or other graphic that is created in another program and is inserted into PowerPoint.

Portrait A slide orientation that displays slides vertically (taller than wider).

Poster frame The image that appears on an inserted digital video, also known as the preview image.

PowerPoint window A window that contains the running PowerPoint application. The PowerPoint window includes the Ribbon, panes, and Presentation window.

Presentation software A software program used to organize and present information typically as part of an electronic slide show.

Presenter view A PowerPoint view you access while in Slide Show view. Typically you use this view when showing a presentation through two monitors, one that you see as the presenter and one that the audience sees.

Preview image *See* Poster frame.

Previewing Prior to printing, seeing onscreen exactly how the printed document will look.

Quick Access toolbar A small toolbar on the left side of a Microsoft application program window's title bar, containing buttons that you click to quickly perform common actions, such as saving a file.

Quick Style Determines how fonts, colors, and effects of the theme are combined and which color, font, and effect is dominant. A Quick Style can be applied to shapes or text.

Reading view A view you use to review your presentation or present a slide show to someone on a computer monitor.

Read-only A file that can't be edited or modified.

Removal marquee box The box that surrounds the part of a picture that you want to retain when the background or other areas of the picture are being deleted.

Removal marquee sizing handle The sizing handles around a removal marquee box that are dragged to change how much of the background or sections of a picture are to be deleted.

Ribbon A wide band of buttons spanning the top of the PowerPoint window that organizes all of PowerPoint's primary commands.

Rotate handle A small round arrow at the top of a selected object that you can drag to rotate the selected object.

Row heading The box containing the row number to the left of the row in a worksheet.

Screen capture An electronic snapshot of your screen, as if you took a picture of it with a camera, which you can paste into a document.

Screenshot A static picture you take of an open program window; can be inserted on a slide.

Selection box A dashed border that appears around a text object or placeholder, indicating that it is ready to accept text.

Sizing handles The small squares that appear around a selected object. Dragging a sizing handle resizes the object.

SkyDrive An online storage and file sharing service. Access to SkyDrive is through a Windows Live account.

Slide layout This determines how all of the elements on a slide are arranged, including text and content placeholders.

Slide Library A folder where you store presentation slides for others to access, modify, or use.

Slide pane The main section of Normal view that displays the current slide.

Slide Show view A view that shows a presentation as an electronic slide show; each slide fills the screen.

Slide Sorter view A view that displays a thumbnail of all slides in the order in which they appear in your presentation; used to rearrange slides and slide transitions.

Slide thumbnail *See* Thumbnail.

Slide timing The amount of time each slide is visible on the screen during a slide show.

Slide transition The special effect that moves one slide off the screen and the next slide on the screen during a slide show. Each slide can have its own transition effect.

Smart Guides A feature in PowerPoint used to help position objects relative to each other and determine equal distances between objects.

SmartArt A professional quality graphic diagram that visually illustrates text.

SmartArt Style A pre-set combination of formatting options that follows the design theme that you can apply to a SmartArt graphic.

Source file Where an object you create with the source program is saved.

Source presentation The presentation you insert slides from when you reuse slides from another presentation.

Source program The program in which a file was created.

Status bar The bar at the bottom of the PowerPoint window that contains messages about what you are doing and seeing in PowerPoint, such as the current slide number or the current theme.

Subtitle text placeholder A box on the title slide reserved for subpoint text.

Tab A section of the Ribbon that identifies groups of commands like the HOME tab.

Tab selector Tab icon on the horizontal ruler that, when clicked, cycles through four tab alignment options.

Template A type of presentation that contains custom design information made to the slide master, slide layouts, and theme.

Text placeholder A box with a dotted border and text that you replace with your own text.

Theme A set of colors, fonts, and effects that you apply to a presentation from the Themes Gallery.

Theme colors The set of 12 coordinated colors that make up a PowerPoint presentation; a theme assigns colors for text, lines, fills, accents, hyperlinks, and background.

Theme effects The set of effects for lines and fills.

Theme fonts The set of fonts for titles and other text.

Thumbnail A small image of a slide. Thumbnails are visible on the Thumbnails pane and in Slide Sorter view.

Thumbnails pane On the left side of the Normal view, used to quickly navigate through the slides in your presentation by clicking the thumbnails on this pane.

Tick mark A small line of measurement that intersects an axis and identifies the categories, values, or series of a chart.

Title placeholder A box on a slide reserved for the title of a presentation or slide.

Title slide The first slide in a presentation.

Trendline A graphical representation of an upward or downward movement in a data series, used to predict future tendencies.

URL Abbreviation for uniform resource locator, which is an address of a Web page on the Internet.

Value axis The axis in a chart that contains the values or numbers defining the data series.

Value axis title A title entered on the value axis of a chart that contains values or numbers defining the data series.

Variant A custom variation of the applied theme that uses different colors, fonts, and effects.

Video frame A single photographic image, or picture, in a video.

View A way of displaying a presentation, such as Normal view, Reading view, Notes Page view, Slide Sorter view, and Slide Show view.

View Shortcuts The buttons at the bottom of the PowerPoint window on the status bar that you click to switch among views.

Windows Live A collection of services and Web applications that people can access through a login. Windows Live services include access to email and instant messaging, storage of files on SkyDrive, sharing and storage of photos, networking with people, downloading software, and interfacing with a mobile device.

WordArt A set of decorative styles or text effects that is applied to text.

Worksheet The grid of rows and columns that stores the numerical data for a chart.

XML Acronym that stands for eXtensible Markup Language, which is a language used to structure, store, and send information.

Zoom slider A feature on the status bar that allows you to change the zoom percentage of a slide.

Index

A

About command, PowerPoint Web App, CL 13
Accent colors, PPT 77
Access, OFF 2, OFF 3
  filename and file extension, OFF 8
accessibility, reading disabilities, PPT 180
action buttons, PPT 158–159
  custom shows, PPT 179
  nudging, PPT 158
  shapes, PPT 158
active cell, PPT 56
Add Animation feature, PPT 102
Add or Remove Columns button, PPT 101
advancing slides, PPT 14
Align command, PPT 38, PPT 104
Align Text button, PPT 110
aligning cells, PPT 62
aligning objects, PPT 38, PPT 39
animated video, PPT 152
animation(s), PPT 82–83
  attaching sound, PPT 83
  categories, PPT 82
  charts, PPT 130–131
  deleting animation effects, PPT 102
  parts of grouped objects, PPT 82
  starting timing operations, PPT 103
Animation command, PowerPoint Web App, CL 13
Animation gallery, PPT 102
Animation Painter, PPT 102
animation pane, PPT 130
animation tags, PPT 82, PPT 102
animation timings, PPT 102, PPT 103
ANIMATIONS tab, PPT 83, PPT 102
  PowerPoint Web App, CL 13
annotating slides, PPT 78, PPT 79
app(s), PPT 177
  launching, OFF 4–5
  Office Web Apps. *See* Office Web Apps
applications, cloud-based, CL 2
artistic effects, PPT 52, PPT 76
audience, identifying, PPT 4
audio
  animations, PPT 83
  bookmarks, PPT 154

  inserting, PPT 154, PPT 155
  recording narration on slides, PPT 155
  slide transitions, PPT 80
  trimming, PPT 154, PPT 155
Audio button, PPT 154, PPT 155
AUDIO TOOLS PLAYBACK tab, Trim Audio
  button, PPT 154
AutoFit options, PPT 8
AutoFit Options button, PPT 125
automatic spell checking, PPT 85
Available Windows gallery, PPT 161
axes, charts, PPT 58

B

background
  customizing, PPT 76, PPT 77
  inserting pictures as, PPT 131
background graphics, PPT 76
Backstage view, OFF 6, OFF 7
backward compatibility, OFF 11
black and white presentations, PPT 7
  changing photo album pictures to black and
    white, PPT 182
Black and White tab, VIEW tab, PPT 7
BMP (Device Independent Bitmap) format,
  PPT 53
bookmarks, audio, PPT 154
broadcasting, PPT 184–185
  supported PowerPoint features, PPT 185
bullets
  increasing and decreasing level in SmartArt
    graphics, PPT 148
  picture, PPT 106
  resetting to default, PPT 106
  slides, PPT 10
  SmartArt, PPT 30
Bullets and Numbering dialog box, PPT 106

C

category axis, PPT 58
cells, charts, PPT 56, PPT 57
  active, PPT 56
  color, PPT 62
  formatting, PPT 126

cells, tables changing height and width, PPT 146
  merging, PPT 146
Change Colors button, PPT 124
Change Entrance Effect dialog box, PPT 102
Change File Type button, PPT 151
Change Shape button, PPT 150
chart(s)
  animating, PPT 130–131
  area, PPT 57
  cells. *See* cells, charts
  colors, PPT 124
  column, PPT 57
  combo, PPT 57
  copying and pasting, PPT 132
  creating, PPT 122
  customizing, PPT 126–127
  editing data, PPT 58, PPT 59
  embedding, PPT 122, PPT 123, PPT 132–133
  entering data, PPT 58, PPT 59
  filtering data, PPT 126
  formatting, PPT 122, PPT 123
  formatting elements, PPT 128–129
  hyperlinks, PPT 59
  inserting, PPT 56–57
  line, PPT 57
  linking, PPT 122, PPT 123
  modifying, PPT 122, PPT 124–125
  pasting from one presentation to another,
    PPT 132
  pie, PPT 57
  radar, PPT 57
  stock, PPT 57
  surface, PPT 57
  text, dividing and fitting, PPT 125
  types, PPT 57
  worksheets, PPT 56
  X Y (scatter), PPT 57
Chart button, PPT 56, PPT 122
Chart Elements button, PPT 122
Chart Filters button, PPT 122, PPT 126
chart styles, PPT 58
Chart Styles button, PPT 122
CHART TOOLS DESIGN tab, PPT 56, PPT 57,
  PPT 58, PPT 59
CHART TOOLS FORMAT tab, PPT 128

Check Compatibility feature, PPT 86
Choose Files to Merge with Current Presentation dialog box, PPT 174–175
Clipboard (Office), OFF 5
Clipboard (Windows), OFF 13
Clipboard command, PowerPoint Web App, CL 13
cloud computing, OFF 9, PPT 17
  definition, CL 2
  SkyDrive. *See* SkyDrive
cloud-based applications, CL 2
  Office Web Apps. *See* Office Web Apps
coauthoring presentations, PPT 175
collaborating, PPT 2
  combine presentation, PPT 174
  compare presentations, PPT 174
  send presentations for review, PPT 172
colors
  charts, changing, PPT 124
  laser pointer use, PPT 178
  making transparent, PPT 156
  matching using Eyedropper, PPT 33
  table cells, PPT 62
  themes, PPT 12, PPT 77, PPT 134
Colors button, PPT 134
column(s), text boxes, PPT 101
column headings, PPT 56, PPT 57
combining reviewed presentations, PPT 174–175
comments, PPT 112, PPT 113
  deleting, PPT 174
  replying to, PPT 112
  review, PPT 174
Comments button, PPT 6, PPT 7
Comments command, PowerPoint Web App, CL 13
Comments pane, opening, PPT 112
compatibility, OFF 2
Compatibility Checker, PPT 180, PPT 181
Compatibility Mode, OFF 11
Compress Pictures button, PPT 156
Compress Pictures dialog box, PPT 52
compressing pictures, PPT 156, PPT 157
Confirm Password dialog box, PPT 180
connectors, PPT 98–99
  drawing, PPT 98, PPT 99
  formatting, PPT 98, PPT 99
  rerouting, PPT 98, PPT 99
content placeholders, PPT 10
Convert button, PPT 148
coordinates, PPT 33
copying
  hyperlinks, PPT 160
  noncontiguous slides, PPT 60

Office Clipboard, OFF 5
  shapes, PPT 36, PPT 37
copying and pasting Excel charts, PPT 122, PPT 132
copyright, PPT 5
Create a PDF/XPS button, PPT 151
Create Handouts button, PPT 171
cropping, PPT 52, PPT 53
Custom Shows dialog box, PPT 178
custom slide layouts, PPT 75, PPT 104–105
custom slide shows, PPT 178–179
  linking to, PPT 179
  printing, PPT 178
custom tables, PPT 146–147
custom themes, PPT 76, PPT 77
  fonts, PPT 170
Customize Quick Access Toolbar button, OFF 12, PPT 3
customizing
  charts, PPT 126–127
  handouts, PPT 170, PPT 171
  notes masters, PPT 170, PPT 171
  PowerPoint installation, PPT 129
  slide size and orientation, PPT 99
  themes, PPT 13
cutting items, Office Clipboard, OFF 5

D

data markers, animating, PPT 130
data series, PPT 56
data series labels, PPT 56, PPT 57
data series markers, PPT 56, PPT 57
date and time, add to slide footer, PPT 40
Define Custom Show dialog box, PPT 178, PPT 179
Delete command, PowerPoint Web App, CL 13
deleting. *See also* removing
  animation effects, PPT 102
  comments, PPT 174
  slides, PPT 60
Demote button, PPT 148
design, determining, PPT 4
DESIGN tab, PPT 76
  Format Background button, PPT 131, PPT 159
  Format Background command, PPT 107
  PowerPoint Web App, CL 13
  Slide Size command, PPT 99
design themes, PPT 12
Desktop, saving files to, OFF 8
destination file, PPT 132
  linking worksheets, PPT 134
  updating linked worksheets, PPT 136

destination presentation, PPT 60
Device Independent Bitmap (BMP) format, PPT 53
dialog box launcher, OFF 6, OFF 7
dictionary, PPT 127
digital signatures, PPT 87
digital video, PPT 152–153
  animated, PPT 152
  editing, PPT 152
  inserting, PPT 152, PPT 153
  trimming, PPT 153
  volume, PPT 152
displaying slide masters, PPT 74
Distribute command, PPT 38, PPT 104
distributing objects, PPT 39
document(s), OFF 12. *See also* file(s)
  co-authoring, CL 10
Document Inspector, PPT 86, PPT 87
Document Properties panel, PPT 86, PPT 87
Document Recovery task pane, OFF 15
document window, OFF 6, OFF 7
.docx (Microsoft Word Document) format, PPT 50
drawing
  connectors, PPT 98, PPT 99
  on slides in slide show view, PPT 78, PPT 79
  tables, PPT 63
Drawing command, PowerPoint Web App, CL 13
DRAWING TOOLS FORMAT tab, PPT 35, PPT 37, PPT 38, PPT 64

E

editing
  chart data, PPT 58, PPT 59
  digital video, PPT 152
  links, PPT 137, PPT 160
  pictures, PPT 156, PPT 157
  points of shapes, PPT 37
  shapes, PPT 36, PPT 37
  slide text, PPT 8
email, sending presentations, PPT 51
  for review, PPT 172–173
embedded objects, PPT 56
embedding
  charts, PPT 122, PPT 123, PPT 132–133
  linking compared, PPT 135
  worksheets, PPT 133
Encrypt Document dialog box, PPT 180, PPT 181
Equation button, PPT 149
EQUATION TOOLS DESIGN tab, PPT 149
error bars, PPT 122
evaluating presentations, PPT 88–89

Excel, OFF 2, OFF 3
  copying and pasting charts, PPT 122, PPT 132
  filename and file extension, OFF 8
  linking worksheets, PPT 134–135
  Office Web App, CL 12
  worksheets. *See* worksheets
exit animation effects, PPT 130
Exit command, PowerPoint Web App, CL 13
Eyedropper, matching colors, PPT 33

F

fade effects, digital video, PPT 152
fair use, PPT 5
file(s), OFF 10, OFF 11. *See also* document(s);
  presentation(s)
  blank, creating, OFF 8
  creating, OFF 8, OFF 9
  definition, OFF 8
  integrating, OFF 2
  names, OFF 8
  opening, OFF 10, OFF 11
  read-only, PPT 86
  recovering, OFF 15
  saving. *See* saving files
  sharing, SkyDrive, CL 10–11
file extensions, OFF 8
file formats
  fixed, PPT 151
  supported in PowerPoint 2013, PPT 151
file management, SkyDrive, CL 8–9
FILE tab, CL 2, CL 3, OFF 7, PPT 11, PPT 65,
  PPT 85, PPT 129
  Change File Type button, PPT 151
  compression settings, PPT 157
  Create Handouts button, PPT 171
  Package Presentation for CD button, PPT 173
  PowerPoint Web App, CL 13
  Publish Slides button, PPT 183
filtering data in charts, PPT 126
fixed layout format, PPT 151
Followed hyperlink color, PPT 77
font(s)
  replacing, PPT 29
  saving with presentation, PPT 9
Font Color gallery, PPT 28
Font command, PowerPoint Web App, CL 13
font themes, PPT 106
footers. *See* slide footers
Format Axis pane, PPT 126
Format Background button, PPT 107, PPT 131
Format Painter, PPT 100
  locking, PPT 100

Format Picture pane, PPT 100
  Transparency slider, PPT 159
Format Shape pane, PPT 110
formatting
  chart cells, PPT 126
  chart elements, PPT 128–129
  connectors, PPT 98, PPT 99
  digital video, removing, PPT 152
  master text, PPT 106–107
  shapes, setting default, PPT 38
  tables, PPT 62
  text, PPT 28–29
  text boxes, PPT 55

G

GIF (Graphics Interchange Format), PPT 53
grammar checking, PPT 85
  in language other than English, PPT 27
graphics. *See also* picture(s)
  background, PPT 76
  saving slides as, PPT 53
  Smart Art. *See* SmartArt
Graphics Interchange Format (GIF), PPT 53
gray scale, viewing presentations, PPT 7
Grayscale tab, VIEW tab, PPT 7
gridlines, PPT 126, PPT 127
group(s), OFF 6, PPT 6, PPT 7
Group command, PPT 38
grouping objects, PPT 38, PPT 39

H

handout(s)
  creating in Word, PPT 171
  customizing, PPT 170, PPT 171
  printed, PPT 3
Handout Master view, PPT 170, PPT 171
hanging indents, PPT 108
header(s), inserting on notes and handouts,
  PPT 40
Header and Footer dialog box, PPT 40,
  PPT 41
Height command, PPT 35
Help button, OFF 14
Help command, PowerPoint Web App, CL 13
Help window, OFF 14, OFF 15
hidden slides, viewing in Slide Show view,
  PPT 176
Hide During Show check box, PPT 154
hiding
  slides, temporarily, PPT 78
  sound icon, PPT 154

HOME tab
  Add or Remove Columns button, PPT 101
  New Slide list arrow, PPT 132
  PowerPoint Web App, CL 13
.htm (HTML) format, PPT 50
hyperlink(s), PPT 160–161
  charts, PPT 59
  copying, PPT 160
  custom shows, PPT 178
  editing, PPT 160
  opening, PPT 160
  removing, PPT 160
Hyperlink color, PPT 77

I

Illustrations command, PowerPoint Web App,
  CL 13
Images command, PowerPoint Web App, CL 13
indent(s)
  hanging, PPT 108
  markers, PPT 109
  master text, PPT 108–109
indent levels, PPT 108
indent markers, PPT 108
Info command, PowerPoint Web App, CL 13
Insert Audio dialog box, PPT 154, PPT 155
Insert Chart dialog box, PPT 56, PPT 57
Insert Chart icon, PPT 122
Insert Object dialog box, PPT 133
Insert Outline dialog box, PPT 50
Insert Picture dialog box, PPT 52, PPT 74,
  PPT 150
Insert Slide Master button, PPT 104
INSERT tab, PPT 54, PPT 59
  Audio button, PPT 155
  Chart button, PPT 122
  Equation button, PPT 149
  Object button, PPT 122, PPT 133
  PowerPoint Web App, CL 13
  Screenshot button, PPT 161
insertion point, OFF 8, PPT 8
integrating files, OFF 2
interface, OFF 2

J

Joint Photographic Experts Group (JPEG)
  format, PPT 53

K

kiosks, PPT 176

L

language pack, PPT 27
laser pointer, changing colors, PPT 178
launching apps, OFF 4–5
layouts, slide, custom, PPT 75, PPT 104–105
leading, PPT 110
legends, PPT 56, PPT 57
link(s). *See also* hyperlink(s)
   editing, PPT 137
   updating, PPT 136
linking
   charts, PPT 122, PPT 123
   to custom slide shows, PPT 179
   embedding compared, PPT 135
   Excel worksheets, PPT 134–135
Links command, PowerPoint Web App, CL 13
Links dialog box, PPT 137
Live Preview, OFF 6, OFF 7, PPT 12
locking Format Painter, PPT 100

M

macros, PPT 158
major gridlines, PPT 126
margins, PPT 110
marking presentations as final, PPT 86, PPT 87
marquees, editing pictures, PPT 156
master(s), PPT 75
   displaying, PPT 74
   exceptions, PPT 107
   inserting, PPT 104
   modifying, PPT 74–75
   overriding, PPT 107
   restore, PPT 105
Master Layout dialog box, PPT 105
master text
   changing indents, PPT 108–109
   formatting, PPT 106–107
Master Thumbnails pane, PPT 104
mathematical equations, PPT 149
merging
   cells in a table, PPT 146
   presentations, PPT 174
   shapes, PPT 34, PPT 35
message, determining, PPT 4
metadata, PPT 86
Microsoft Access. *See* Access
Microsoft accounts, OFF 9
   new, creating, CL 5
   signing in to, CL 4
   signing out of, CL 4

Microsoft Excel. *See* Excel
Microsoft Office. *See also* Access; Excel;
   PowerPoint; Word
   benefits, OFF 2
   launching apps, OFF 4–5
   moving between programs, OFF 4
   user interface, OFF 6
Microsoft Office 365, OFF 3
Microsoft Office 365 Home Premium
   edition, OFF 3
Microsoft Office 365 SharePoint, PPT 175
Microsoft Office Web Apps, PPT 17
Microsoft Outlook. *See* Outlook
Microsoft PowerPoint. *See* PowerPoint
Microsoft PowerPoint Compatibility Checker
   dialog box, PPT 180, PPT 181
Microsoft Translator, PPT 84, PPT 85
Microsoft Windows. *See* Windows *entries*
Microsoft Word. *See* Word
Microsoft Word Document (.docx)
   format, PPT 50
Mini toolbar, PPT 28, PPT 29
minor gridlines, PPT 126, PPT 127
moving
   connectors, PPT 98, PPT 99
   objects to top of stack, PPT 34
   slides, PPT 50
multiple presentations, working on
   simultaneously, PPT 60
multiple windows, PPT 61

N

narration, recording on slides, PPT 155
new slide(s), adding, PPT 10
New Slide list arrow, PPT 132
noncontiguous slides, copying, PPT 60
Normal view, PPT 6, PPT 14, PPT 15
notes, entering and printing, PPT 11
Notes button, PPT 6, PPT 7
Notes Master view, PPT 170, PPT 171
notes masters, customizing, PPT 170, PPT 171
Notes Page, PPT 3
Notes Page view, PPT 14, PPT 15
Notes pane, PPT 11
nudging action buttons, PPT 158

O

object(s). *See also specific objects*
   aligning, PPT 38, PPT 39
   distributing, PPT 39
   embedded, PPT 56

   grouping, PPT 38, PPT 39
   moving to top of stack, PPT 34
Object button, PPT 122, PPT 133
.odp (Open Document Presentation)
   file format, PPT 151
Office. *See* Access; Excel; Microsoft Office;
   PowerPoint; Word
Office Clipboard, OFF 5
Office Web Apps, CL 2, CL 12–13
OneNote, Office Web App, CL 12
online collaboration, OFF 2, OFF 9
online presentations, PPT 184–185
   supported PowerPoint features, PPT 185
Open as Copy option, Open dialog box, OFF 10
Open dialog box, OFF 10, OFF 11
Open Document Presentation (.odp) file
   format, PPT 151
opening
   Comments pane, PPT 112
   files, OFF 10, OFF 11
   hyperlinks, PPT 160
   PowerPoint 97-2007 presentations in
      PowerPoint 2013, PPT 26
   text pane, PPT 148
Open-Read-Only option, Open dialog box,
   OFF 10
Outline view, PPT 14, PPT 15
   text entry, PPT 26–27
Outlook, sending presentations, PPT 51
   for review, PPT 172–173
output, determining type, PPT 4
overriding slide masters, PPT 107

P

Package for CD dialog box, PPT 173
Package Presentation for CD button, PPT 173
packaging presentations, PPT 173
page setup, PPT 99
panes, PPT 6
Paragraph command, PowerPoint Web App, CL 13
Paragraph dialog box, PPT 110
paragraph spacing, PPT 110
password(s), PPT 180
Password dialog box, PPT 180
Paste button, options, PPT 147
Paste Special command, PPT 123
pasting items. *See also* copying and pasting
   Excel charts
   Office Clipboard, OFF 5
Pen annotation tool, PPT 78
permissions, setting, PPT 89
photo album(s), PPT 182–183

Photo Album dialog box, PPT 182, PPT 183
Photo Album template, PPT 112
picture(s). *See also* graphics
    adjusting, PPT 156, PPT 157
    compressing, PPT 156, PPT 157
    converting to SmartArt graphics, PPT 150
    editing, PPT 156, PPT 157
    inserting, PPT 52, PPT 53
    photo albums, PPT 182–183
    as slide backgrounds, PPT 131
    styling, PPT 52, PPT 53
picture bullets, PPT 106
Picture Layout button, PPT 150
picture placeholders, PPT 104
PICTURE TOOLS FORMAT tab, PPT 52
    Picture Layout button, PPT 150
placeholders
    picture, PPT 104
    positioning, PPT 104
    reapplying, PPT 105
    subtitle text, PPT 8
    title, PPT 8
    text, PPT 8
plain text (.txt) format, PPT 50
planning presentations, PPT 4–5
Portable Network Graphic (PNG)
    format, PPT 53
positioning shapes, PPT 35
.potx (PowerPoint Template) file format,
    PPT 112, PPT 151
PowerPoint, OFF 2, OFF 3
    customizing installation, PPT 129
    file formats supported, PPT 151
    filename and file extension, OFF 8
    Office Web App, CL 12–13
    opening PowerPoint 97-2007 presentations
        in PowerPoint 2013, PPT 26
    overview, PPT 2–3
    saving presentations to run in earlier
        version, PPT 86
    supported features for broadcasting, PPT 185
PowerPoint Last Viewed Slide setting, CL 2
PowerPoint Options dialog box, PPT 9, PPT 85,
    PPT 129
PowerPoint Picture Presentation (.pptx) file
    format, PPT 151
PowerPoint Show (.ppsx) file format, PPT 151
PowerPoint Template (.potx) file format,
    PPT 112, PPT 151
PowerPoint window, PPT 6–7
.ppsx (PowerPoint Show) file format, PPT 151
.pptx (PowerPoint Picture Presentation)
    file format, PPT 151

Present Online dialog box, PPT 184, PPT 185
presentation(s)
    black and white. *See* black and white
        presentations
    coauthoring, PPT 175
    delivering online, PPT 184–185
    digital signatures, PPT 87
    evaluating, PPT 88–89
    gray scale, PPT 7
    marking as final, PPT 86, PPT 87
    merging, PPT 174
    packaging, PPT 173
    planning, PPT 4–5
    preparing for distribution, PPT 180–181
    printing, PPT 16–17
    reviewed, combining, PPT 174–175
    saving as videos, PPT 65
    saving to run in earlier version
        of PowerPoint, PPT 86
    sending for review, PPT 172–173
presentation graphics software. *See*
    PowerPoint; presentation software
presentation software. *See also* PowerPoint
    definition, PPT 2–3
Presentation Views command, PowerPoint
    Web App, CL 13
Presenter view, PPT 78, PPT 79
previewing documents, OFF 12
Print command, PowerPoint Web App, CL 13
Print Layout gallery, PPT 16
Print layout view, OFF 12
printing
    notes, PPT 11
    presentations, PPT 16–17
    slide shows, PPT 178
Promote button, PPT 148
Properties dialog box, PPT 86
Protect Presentation button, PPT 89
Publish as PDF or XPS dialog box, PPT 151
publishing slides to Slide Libraries, PPT 183

Q

Quick Access toolbar, OFF 6, OFF 7, PPT 6,
    PPT 7
    customizing, OFF 12
Quick Styles, PPT 32

R

reading disabilities, accessibility, PPT 180
Reading view, PPT 14, PPT 15
read-only files, PPT 86

reapplying placeholders, PPT 105
Record Slide Show button, PPT 181
Record Sound dialog box, PPT 155
recording slide shows, PPT 181
Rehearse Timings button, PPT 81
rehearsing slide timings, PPT 81
Remove button, PPT 178
removing. *See also* deleting
    formatting from digital video, PPT 152
    hyperlinks, PPT 160
    links to charts, PPT 59
    marquee tool, PPT 156
Replace dialog box, PPT 29
Research button, PPT 127
Research task pane, PPT 127
Reset Design button, PPT 152
resizing shapes, PPT 35
Reuse Slides pane, PPT 60
REVIEW tab, PPT 84
    Research button, PPT 127
reviewed presentations, combining,
    PPT 174–175
Ribbon, OFF 6, OFF 7, PPT 6, PPT 7
Rich Text Format (.rtf) format, PPT 50
roaming settings, CL 2
rotate handle, PPT 32
row(s), new, creating in tables, PPT 62
row headings, PPT 56, PPT 57
.rtf (Rich Text Format) format, PPT 50
ruler, changing master indents, PPT 108–109

S

Save As command, PowerPoint Web App, CL 13
Save As dialog box, OFF 8, OFF 9, OFF 10,
    OFF 11, PPT 112
saving
    files. *See* saving files; saving files to SkyDrive
    fonts, with presentation, PPT 9
    slides as graphics, PPT 53
saving files, OFF 8, OFF 9, OFF 10, OFF 11
    fixed file formats, PPT 151
    presentations as videos, PPT 65
    presentations to run in earlier version of
        PowerPoint, PPT 86
    SkyDrive. *See* saving files to SkyDrive
    as templates, PPT 112
saving files to SkyDrive, OFF 9
    default, disabling, CL 6, CL 7
    presentations, PPT 175
scatter charts, PPT 57
screen captures, OFF 13

Screen Clipping button, PPT 161
screenshot(s), inserting, PPT 161
Screenshot button, PPT 161
ScreenTips, PPT 28
security, passwords, PPT 180
selecting unselected objects, PPT 28
selection boxes, PPT 8
Send to Microsoft Word dialog box, PPT 171
sending presentations for review, PPT 172–173
Set Transparent Color button, PPT 156
Set Up Show dialog box, PPT 176, PPT 177
shape(s)
    action buttons, PPT 158
    duplicating, PPT 36, PPT 37
    editing, PPT 36, PPT 37
    editing points, PPT 37
    filling with pictures, PPT 100
    increasing and decreasing level in SmartArt
        graphics, PPT 148
    inserting, PPT 32–33
    merging, PPT 34, PPT 35
    modifying, PPT 32–33
    positioning, PPT 35
    rearranging, PPT 34, PPT 35
    resizing, PPT 35
    transparency, PPT 32
Shape Fill button, PPT 33
Shape Outline button, PPT 33
Shape, Fill with picture, PPT 100
Share command, PowerPoint Web App, CL 13
sharing files, SkyDrive, CL 10–11
shortcut keys, OFF 4
sizing handles, PPT 8, PPT 35
    SmartArt, PPT 150
SkyDrive, CL 2, CL 6–7
    accessing, CL 8
    file management, CL 8–9
    saving files to. See saving files to SkyDrive
    saving presentations to, PPT 175
    sharing files, CL 10–11
slide(s)
    advancing, PPT 14
    copying and pasting Excel charts to, PPT 122
    customizing size and orientation, PPT 99
    deleting, PPT 60
    editing text, PPT 8
    hidden, viewing in Slide Show view, PPT 176
    hiding temporarily, PPT 78
    moving, PPT 50
    new, adding, PPT 10–11
    noncontiguous, copying, PPT 60
    orientation on handout, PPT 170
    from other presentations, inserting, PPT 60–61

pictures as backgrounds, PPT 131
publishing to Slide Libraries, PPT 183
recording narration on, PPT 155
saving as graphics, PPT 53
slide footers, PPT 40–41
slide layouts, PPT 10, PPT 11
    custom, PPT 75, PPT 104–105
    shortcut menu of commands, opening, PPT 74
Slide Libraries, PPT 60
    publishing slides to, PPT 183
slide master(s). See master(s)
Slide Master button, PPT 134, PPT 170
Slide Master view, PPT 74, PPT 75, PPT 104,
    PPT 106, PPT 131
Slide pane, PPT 6, PPT 7, PPT 60
slide show(s)
    advancing slides, PPT 14
    commands, basic PPT 79
    custom, creating, PPT 178–179
    printing, PPT 178
    recording, PPT 181
    setting up, PPT 176–177
SLIDE SHOW tab, PPT 81
    Record Slide Show button, PPT 181
Slide Show toolbar buttons, PPT 78
Slide Show view, PPT 14, PPT 15
    annotating slides, PPT 78, PPT 79
    drawing on slides, PPT 78, PPT 79
    keyboard commands, PPT 79
Slide Size command, PPT 99
Slide Sorter view, PPT 14, PPT 15
slide thumbnails, PPT 6
slide timings, PPT 80, PPT 81
    rehearsing, PPT 81
slide transitions, PPT 80, PPT 81
    sounds, PPT 80
Slides command, PowerPoint Web App, CL 13
Smart Guides, PPT 34
SmartArt
    choosing graphics, PPT 31
    converting pictures to, PPT 150
    converting text to, PPT 30–31
    converting WordArt objects to, PPT 64
    designing graphics, PPT 148–149
    enhancing graphics, PPT 150–151
SmartArt Styles, PPT 30
SMARTART TOOLS DESIGN tab, Convert
    button, PPT 148
SMARTART TOOLS FORMAT tab, Change
    Shape button, PPT 150
Snipping Tool, OFF 13
sound. See audio
sound icon, hiding, PPT 154

source file, PPT 132
    linking worksheets, PPT 134
    updating linked worksheets, PPT 136
source presentation, PPT 60
source program, PPT 132
Spell Checker feature, PPT 84, PPT 85
spell checking, PPT 84, PPT 85
    automatic, PPT 85
    in language other than English, PPT 27
Split Cells dialog box, PPT 146
start screen, OFF 4, OFF 5
Start timing options for animations, PPT 103
status bar, PPT 6, PPT 7
style, charts, changing, PPT 124, PPT 125
subscript text, PPT 41
subscriptions, Microsoft Office 365, OFF 3
subtitle text placeholders, PPT 8, PPT 9
suites, OFF 2
superscript text, PPT 41
Symbol dialog box, PPT 106, PPT 107
syncing, CL 2

T

tab(s), OFF 6, OFF 7, PPT 6, PPT 7
    markers, PPT 109
    setting, PPT 108, PPT 109
tab selector, PPT 108
table(s)
    cells. See cells, table
    custom, PPT 146–147
    drawing, PPT 63
    formatting, PPT 62
    inserting, PPT 62–63
    merging, PPT 146
TABLE TOOLS DESIGN tab, PPT 62, PPT 63
TABLE TOOLS LAYOUT tab, PPT 62
Tagged Image File Format (TIFF), PPT 53
templates, OFF 4, PPT 112, PPT 113
    themes compared, PPT 113
text
    adjusting, PPT 110–111
    changing direction, PPT 111, PPT 146
    charts, dividing and fitting, PPT 125
    converting to SmartArt, PPT 30–31
    editing, PPT 8
    entering in Outline view, PPT 26–27
    formatting, PPT 28–29
    master. See master text
    replacing, PPT 29
    slides, PPT 8–9
    subscript, PPT 41
    superscript, PPT 41

transparency, PPT 32
  from Word, inserting, PPT 50–51
  WordArt, PPT 64–65
text boxes
  adjusting text, PPT 110–111
  changing formatting defaults, PPT 55
  columns, PPT 101
  creating, PPT 54
  inserting, PPT 54–55
  photo albums, PPT 182
Text command, PowerPoint Web App, CL 13
Text Direction button, PPT 111, PPT 146
text labels, creating, PPT 54
Text Pane, opening and closing, PPT 148
Text Pane button, PPT 148
Text Pane control button, PPT 148
text placeholders, PPT 8, PPT 9
Text/Background colors, PPT 77
theme(s), OFF 2, PPT 12–13
  customizing, PPT 13, PPT 76, PPT 77
  multiple, applying to single presentation, PPT 12
  templates compared, PPT 113
  variants, PPT 76, PPT 77
theme colors, PPT 12, PPT 77
  custom, PPT 134
theme effects, PPT 12
theme fonts, PPT 12
  custom, PPT 170
Themes command, PowerPoint Web App, CL 13
Themes gallery, PPT 12
thesaurus, PPT 127
thumbnails, slides, PPT 6
Thumbnails pane, PPT 6, PPT 7, PPT 60
tick marks, PPT 126
TIFF (Tagged Image File Format), PPT 53
timings, animation, PPT 102, PPT 103
title bar, OFF 6, OFF 7
Title Only layout, PPT 132
title placeholders, PPT 8, PPT 9
touch mode, enabling, OFF 15
Touch Mode button, OFF 15, PPT 3

touch screens, PPT 3
transitions, slides, PPT 80, PPT 81
TRANSITIONS tab, PPT 80
  PowerPoint Web App, CL 13
Transitions to This Slide command, PowerPoint Web App, CL 13
Translator, PPT 84, PPT 85
transparency
  colors, PPT 156
  pictures, PPT 159
  shapes and text, PPT 32
trendlines, PPT 122
Trim Audio button, PPT 154
Trim Audio dialog box, PPT 154, PPT 155
Trim Video button, PPT 153
trimming
  audio, PPT 154, PPT 155
  digital video, PPT 153
.txt (plain text) format, PPT 50

U

updating linked worksheets, PPT 136
URLs (Universal Resource Locators), PPT 184
user interface, OFF 2

V

value axis, PPT 58
variants, themes, PPT 76, PPT 77
video(s)
  digital. *See* digital video
  saving presentations as, PPT 65
VIDEO TOOLS PLAYBACK tab, Trim Video button, PPT 153
view(s), OFF 12–13, PPT 6, PPT 14–15. *See also* specific views
View buttons, OFF 12
View Shortcuts, PPT 6, PPT 7
VIEW tab, OFF 12, PPT 61, PPT 74
  Colors button, PPT 134
  PowerPoint Web App, CL 13
  Slide Master button, PPT 170

viewing, OFF 12, OFF 13
  hidden slides, in Slide Show view, PPT 176
volume, digital video, PPT 152

W

Width command, PPT 35
windows, multiple, PPT 61
Windows Live ID, CL 5. *See also* Microsoft accounts
Windows 7, starting apps, OFF 4, OFF 5
Word, OFF 2, OFF 3
  creating handouts, PPT 171
  file format, PPT 50
  filename and file extension, OFF 8
  inserting text from, PPT 50–51
  Office Web App, CL 12
word and phrase translator, PPT 127
Word Resume Reading Position setting, CL 2
WordArt, PPT 64–65
  converting WordArt to SmartArt, PPT 64
working online, CL 4–5
worksheets, PPT 56
  embedding, PPT 133
  linked, updating, PPT 136–137
  linking, PPT 134–135

X

x-axis, PPT 58

Y

y-axis, PPT 58
Your Profile page, CL 4

Z

Zoom button, OFF 6
Zoom slider, PPT 6, PPT 7
zooming in, OFF 6
zooming out, OFF 6